Alibis and Corroborators

Joshua D. Behl • Megan R. Kienzle
Editors

Alibis and Corroborators

Psychological, Criminological, and Legal Perspectives

Springer

Editors
Joshua D. Behl
Department of Behavioral Sciences
Flagler College
Saint Augustine, FL, USA

Megan R. Kienzle
Department of Criminal Justice
Austin Peay State University
Clarksville, TN, USA

ISBN 978-3-030-95662-2 ISBN 978-3-030-95663-9 (eBook)
https://doi.org/10.1007/978-3-030-95663-9

This Springer imprint is published by the registered company Springer Nature Switzerland AG
The registered company address is: Gewerbestrasse 11, 6330 Cham, Switzerland

Joshua D. Behl:
To my wife, Taylor
Megan R. Kienzle:
To my family
Joshua D. Behl and Megan R. Kienzle:
Together, we would like to also dedicate this book to our advisor, mentor, and friend – Dr. Lora Levett

Preface

Consider this: the police come to your door and ask you where you were on a Monday evening approximately 6 months ago. Without much thought, you reply "I was sitting at home with my family eating dinner." You have just offered the police an alibi. These statements are seemingly innocuous enough. After all, people are accused of crimes all the time. Those that are innocent should have an alibi – or a claim that they were elsewhere at the time of the crime. However, that claim is a lot easier to generate than it is to support. And still easier to support than it is to be believed in court.

This book is the first of its kind to be published on the nascent topic of alibis and corroborators. At the time of this publication, there are roughly 200 articles and book chapters dedicated to the topic of alibis in some capacity. However, the field has yet to be organized in any kind of consistent, coherent manner. Therefore, this book should be viewed as a state of the science on the topic. Each chapter is a complete overview of specific research focus within the larger topic of alibis and corroborators, and each could be viewed as stand-alone chapters. However, we believe that the book is best read in its entirety, as some topics (e.g., generation and believability) go hand in hand.

As you read through this book, you will quickly notice that each chapter has at least one case of wrongful conviction that will be profiled. This case is used as a reference case around which the chapter is structured. What readers will also notice is that there is a lot more work that still needs to be done. To that end, each author developed a series of research questions that the editors compiled into a fairly comprehensive appendix at the back of the book. From graduate students looking for research ideas to seasoned scholars who are interested in such topics as eyewitnesses, social influence, power structures, race, investigator bias, tunnel vision, and lie detection, there is so much that we do not yet know that could be answered by our collective efforts. That is the humble goal of this book – to provide an overview of what we do know so that we can all work together to answer the questions that we do not know.

St. Augustine, FL, USA — Joshua D. Behl
Clarksville, TN, USA — Megan R. Kienzle
November 2021

Acknowledgments

Together, we would like to thank the various faculty and staff at Flagler College and Austin Peay State University who made this project a reality. We also would like to acknowledge Dr. Lora Levett and Dr. Kelsey Henderson who have been a constant support throughout our academic careers. We would not be where we are today without the continuous support and encouragement we have received from all of you. We would also like to recognize and thank our tremendous contributing authors who made our job as editors easy and interesting. This book could not have been possible without them. We would also like to thank the editorial team at Springer for taking a chance and trusting two junior scholars with a first-of-its-kind book of this magnitude.

Acknowledgments by Joshua D. Behl

It is my great pleasure to publicly thank my family for their constant outpouring of love and support. Specifically, to my wife, Taylor, and dog, Ruby; parents, Helen Carnegie and Chuck and Nicole Behl; my siblings, Bryan and Marissa Behl, Amanda and Jared Chute, Jessica and Dan Moose, and Jacob Vondran; and my in-laws, Ruth and Daryl Reimer, and Mark and Julie Allegood as well as a host of siblings-in-law, uncles, aunts, cousins, and many more. To have you all in my corner every day is the greatest blessing. I would also like to acknowledge the support of my Flagler College colleagues who have made working at Flagler College a tremendous pleasure. Worth mentioning again are the debts I owe to my wife, Taylor, for always being there for me through the long nights of editing and Zoom calls; to love you is to know you, to be loved by you is greater than anything in this life. And to my parents, Helen and Chuck, your unconditional love and support throughout my life have made everything I have ever done possible. This book is more a reflection of you than it could ever be of me. Finally, I want to thank my co-editor, Megan, for everything you have done to help throughout my academic career, from being my lab supervisor when I was in undergrad to being my most consistent collaborator, co-author, and friend.

Acknowledgments by Megan R. Kienzle

First and foremost, I want to thank my parents, Carol and Doug, for their never-ending support and encouragement of all I do, both personally and professionally. I am thankful for my sister, Emily, and brother-in-law, Jeremy, and all my aunts, uncles, cousins, and beyond who have been my constant champions since day one. I am blessed with incredible friends from all stages of my life who are now scattered throughout the country (and world). I want to thank them all for being there for me in good times and bad, always ready with a supportive ear to listen, and a laugh to make sure I do not take things too seriously – you know who you are, and I miss you all! I am especially appreciative of my colleagues here at Austin Peay, in the department and elsewhere around campus, for creating a supportive environment in which to thrive. To my favorite fuzzy companion, my dog Nessie, for sleeping at my side while reading, writing, and editing drafts of this book. Finally, I want to thank my incredible co-editor, co-author, colleague, and friend, Josh, for going on this journey together. Without each and every one of you, I would not be who I am, and I am eternally grateful for you every day.

Contents

Editors and Contributors

Editors

Joshua D. Behl Department of Behavioral Sciences, Flagler College, St. Augustine, FL, USA

Megan R. Kienzle Department of Criminal Justice, Austin Peay State University, Clarksville, TN, USA

Contributors

Meredith Allison Elon University, Elon, NC, USA

Stephanie A. Cardenas Williams College, Wachenheim Science Center, Williamstown, MA, USA

Steve D. Charman Florida International University, Miami, FL, USA

Mary Cops University of North Dakota, Grand Forks, ND, USA

William E. Crozier Wilson Center for Science and Justice, Duke Law School, Durham, NC, USA

Scott E. Culhane Department of Criminal Justice, Austin Peay State University, Clarksville, TN, USA

Madison B. Harvey Simon Fraser University, Burnaby, BC, Canada

Andre Kehn University of North Dakota, Grand Forks, ND, USA

Nikola Klassen Simon Frasier University, Burnaby, BC, Canada

Kay L. Levine Emory University School of Law, Atlanta, GA, USA

Lore Mergaerts KU Leuven, Leuven Institute of Criminology, Leuven, Belgium

Colin Miller University of South Carolina School of Law, Columbia, SC, USA

Carolyn Morgan University of Wisconsin-Whitewater, Whitewater, WI, USA

Ricardo Nieuwkamp Expert Research Data Management Competence Centre (RDM-CC), KU Leuven, Leuven, Belgium

Elizabeth A. Olson University of Wisconsin-Whitewater, Whitewater, WI, USA

Heather L. Price Thompson Rivers University, Kamloops, BC, Canada

Laura Shambaugh Florida International University, Miami, FL, USA

Mariah Sorby University of North Dakota, Grand Forks, ND, USA

Deryn Strange John Jay College of Criminal Justice, New York, NY, USA

Chapter 1
Alibis and Corroborators: Psychological, Criminological, and Legal Perspectives

Megan R. Kienzle and Joshua D. Behl

Imagine you are accused of crime. You know you did not do it and are confident others will believe you when you state you were attending your own spouse's funeral at the alleged time of the crime. In fact, you have five alibis attesting to these whereabouts during your later trial. Or perhaps you are a 19-year-old scholarship student-athlete eating dinner with your family, which your parents and sister confirm; however police claim you committed a murder, and your attorney will not even bring up your alibi claim at your capital trial. One would think these examples could not possibly happen; however these were the case for two Innocence Project clients. Mallory Nicholson was convicted of a burglary and sexual assault that took place while he was at his wife's funeral and ultimately spent 21 years in prison before being released on parole in 2003 (Innocence Project, 2021a). Julius Jones has spent 19 years on death row for murder, with his current execution date scheduled for November 18, 2021 (Innocence Project, 2021b). As of November 1, the Oklahoma Pardon and Parole Board recommended clemency, and Julius must now wait to see if the Governor accepts the recommendation (Andone et al., 2021).

A person's claim they were elsewhere during the time of the crime is not a new phenomenon; however the field of alibi research is still somewhat young. While researchers have established an understanding of some basic concepts related to alibi use, there are a host of other factors that we do not yet have a solid understanding of. We hope for this book to spur a new generation of researchers focusing on alibis and corroborating evidence to push the field to build on this foundation and expand the reach and understanding of the topic. To that end, we structured the text

M. R. Kienzle (✉)
Department of Criminal Justice, Austin Peay State University, Clarksville, TN, USA
e-mail: kienzlem@apsu.edu

J. D. Behl
Department of Behavioral Sciences, Flagler College, St. Augustine, FL, USA
e-mail: jbehl@flagler.edu

J. D. Behl, M. R. Kienzle (eds.), *Alibis and Corroborators*,
https://doi.org/10.1007/978-3-030-95663-9_1

to work from broader topics to more specific from beginning to end. Beyond that, we requested that each chapter discuss at least one real-world case to illustrate the ideas and problems they identify in their writing and research.

At its core, an alibi is a claim containing just two pieces of information: a location and a timeframe (Olson & Wells, 2004). As each chapter addresses in the coming pages, these two details provide a wealth of situational differences to expand on that most basic premise. One could back up their alibi statement by considering supporting evidence of different kinds to corroborate the claim. One could consider how the claim itself, and/or the supporting evidence, might be viewed by a host of different evaluators (investigators, attorneys, triers of fact, etc.). An alibi used in one country with an adversarial system could be utilized and viewed quite differently in an inquisitorial system (even when the content of the alibi claim is the same). As researchers and practitioners in the system, we must contend with the idea that not all alibi statements (nor corroborating evidence) is accurate – some even intentionally deceptive.

There are well-known contributing causes to wrongful convictions (Wells et al., 1998; Gould & Leo, 2010), and each chapter points out how these factors (often mistaken eyewitnesses, faulty forensic sciences, prosecutorial misconduct, etc.) can lead to investigators focusing on the wrong suspect. Once this focus has narrowed in on an innocent person, tunnel vision (Dror et al., 2005; Salet & Terpstra, 2014; Rassin, 2018)), confirmation bias (Kassin et al., 2013), or other social-psychological human errors can persist throughout the rest of the criminal justice system process. Evidence can be misinterpreted to be inculpatory; potentially exculpatory can be overlooked or intentionally discarded. However, this is assuming these forms of evidence are there at all. It is possible there was no eyewitness to the crime, or there are not usable fingerprints or DNA evidence left at the scene. Wells et al. (1998) suggest that 28% of the first 40 DNA exonerations listed "no" or "weak" alibi evidence as a factor contributing to the wrongful conviction (a statistic referenced often throughout this text); however we believe this is likely just the tip of the iceberg. Alibis are arguably one of the greatest failures of evidence – there is always an alibi: a location and a time. The concern is whether (1) the suspect remembers it, (2) they can generate (any) evidence to corroborate it, and (3) others (investigators, attorneys, judges, jurors alike) believe it. These problems can lead to further erosion of exculpatory evidence in the investigatory stages, the potential for contamination of other forms of evidence (such as both high- and low-quality independent evidence), and a spiraling process leading to a wrongful conviction. In some cases, when not handled correctly from the start, evidence can be forever damaged (particularly when the evidence is a person's memory for a specific timeframe, as a corroborator is). Cascading effects from a single memory error in an alibi can lead to snowball-like impacts throughout the investigation and subsequent stages, resulting in wrongful convictions and a criminal justice system focus on the wrong person. Even beyond an innocent person targeted for investigation/conviction, this mistaken focus on a person other than the truly guilty party means the actual perpetrator may remain at large, able to continue committing crimes while someone else pays for their offense.

We intend for this book as a whole, and each individual chapter, to serve as a state of the science on alibis and their use/effects. That is, each chapter can stand on its own to give readers complete coverage of the relevant details for that specific topic. There is natural overlap between sections, and we have built in several references to other chapters throughout each writing to ensure those who are interested know where to go next to gain needed contextual information relevant to the originally sought out information. However, for scholars new to the field of alibis and their corroborating evidence, the book as a whole serves as near complete coverage of the approximately 200 articles to date published in the field of alibis. In addition, many of the authors in the following chapters are prominent scholars with well-established lines of research in their topic area. By reading a single book, new alibi scholars can get an overview of dozens of articles summarized by experts in the field. Further, each chapter provides a litany of recommendations for future research, so scholars can best understand where the field, both specifically and generally, is headed.

Before we provide an overview of the text, we do want to address one definitional issue that we have noticed in the literature – namely, that of the term "alibi provider" (for a partial list of examples, see Olson & Wells, 2004; Dahl et al., 2009; Olson & Charman, 2012; Olson & Wells, 2012; Leins & Charman, 2016). While this term is generally used to mean suspects who provide an alibi, the term can be a bit misleading. After all, if an alibi is a claim that one was elsewhere at the time of a crime, both the suspect and the corroborator are alibi providers. While we recognize the need to differentiate between suspects who provide an alibi and suspects who do not provide an alibi, for this text's purposes, and until another term is developed, we requested the authors simply use the term "suspect" and "corroborator" to assist with clarity for the reader. Areas where the differentiation between those suspects who are providing an alibi and those who are not is important, the authors clarified which type they meant for each specific example discussed (see Chap 5).

We start next with an update to Olson and Wells' landmark 2004 taxonomy of alibis – arguably the paper that started it all. In Chap. 2, Olson and Morgan discuss the development of the original taxonomy. They outline the need for a way to categorize the different forms alibi evidence can take and how to consider their belief of the most essential aspect to alibi evidence: the corroboration given with the alibi statement. They discuss how they originally identified the two main types of corroborating evidence (person evidence providing the corroboration through the verbal testimony of another person and physical evidence providing such corroboration through tangible items that demonstrate a location and time). Crucially, the authors identify how perceived ease of fabrication of the person or physical corroborating evidence is likely to elicit varying degrees of strength associated with the evidence by evaluators *and* how this has likely only increased in complexity given the wealth of new and advancing technologies available today that could make fabricating evidence easier to do. Olson and Morgan summarize the testing of the taxonomy that has occurred in the last several years and suggest modifications that may help to make the taxonomy more applicable to current discussions of alibis. Finally they finish their chapter with a number of future directions to further advance the study of the alibi taxonomy in years to come.

After understanding the original taxonomy, we move next to a discussion of how a suspect might put forward an alibi and corroboration known as alibi generation. In Chap. 3, Culhane describes the memory test that is asked of all suspects when pinpointing their alibi by trying to recall their whereabouts for the timeframe in question. He discusses the two-part process by illustrating first the story phase (where the suspect claims their location during the time of the crime is away from the crime location) and second the validation phase (where the suspect must provide supporting evidence of their story claim, typically in the form of person or physical corroborating evidence). He further examines the literature to date on motivational differences for person-based corroboration and ease of fabrication for physical evidence (both part of the original taxonomy). Beyond the original taxonomy, he mentions the technological advancements that may make the physical corroborating evidence more complicated and specifically mentions the potential generation and corroboration of false alibi statements. The legal requirements to disclose alibi statements to the court in different levels and systems are also considered. Culhane ends with a call for additional research on alibis in the context of generating the statement and corroborating evidence to support it.

Once an alibi is generated, the logical next step is to consider how different evaluators might believe it (or not). Allison discusses the believability of alibis by discussing several contextual factors that might impact how different evaluators (police officers, investigators, jurors, attorneys, etc.) might consider the truthfulness and credibility of the alibi itself (and the corroborating evidence to support it). First, Allison summarizes the literature on the relationship effect in person corroboration (such that strangers tend to be more believable than friends or family) as well as the number of corroborators a suspect may have. Other defendant and corroborator characteristics can affect the way that evaluators of different types might weigh the evidence against other pieces of evidence. Similarly, physical evidence of varying types can also influence the evaluator's perceptions of the alibi claim and corroboration, and, while arguably more trusted, its actual use in real cases is less common. Allison also discusses how the consistency of the story matters to evaluators, and the salaciousness of the story can actually serve to bolster the believability of a somewhat scandalous activity. Evaluators' willingness to accept mistakes in memory seems limited, and, when taken in the context of an entire case/trial, evaluators view alibi evidence in light of all other evidence in the case and the timing of collection of the evidence and may be able to heighten sensitivity to concerns in other evidence through the alibi's presence. Finally, Allison ends with a discussion about methodological concerns in alibi research and calls for additional research to be done, ideally using representative, community-based samples, in realistic situations to ensure the validity of the information gained through the studies.

A theoretical perspective could help provide context for how to understand and further the research on alibis and corroborators. In Chap. 5, Charman and Shambaugh posit a tripartite classification system of suspect's alibis. In this perspective, the authors seek to create a structure for how to improve the overall quality of alibi evidence by classifying suspects as (1) deceptive (meaning they are truly guilty perpetrators who are generating an alibi to avoid apprehension and conviction), (2) honest-accurate (meaning truly innocent suspects who are generating truthful alibi information), and (3) honest-mistaken (meaning truly innocent suspects who generate, at least temporarily, incorrect alibi information). From this classification system, the authors develop three strategies that may help increase the quality and diagnosticity of alibi evidence. First, investigative strategies put in place before seeking alibi statements may help reduce honest-mistaken suspects from putting forward (unknowingly) incorrect information in the first place. Second, providing better opportunities throughout the investigative stages to source corroborating evidence could help bolster the believability of honest-accurate suspects. Finally, they discuss the need for procedures to improve evaluators' ability to differentiate between those suspects telling known incorrect information (deceptive) and those who provide honest statements. Research to date that fits the above strategies is summarized, and Charman and Shambaugh end with discussion of the need to empirically test the proposed theory in more direct ways.

While the bulk of the alibi research to date has been in our American adversarial system, Chap. 6 requests a deeper consideration of the way in which our system structures might impact the handling and use of alibi evidence. Nieuwkamp and Mergaerts bring an international perspective to the text by discussing the inquisitorial system's outlook on a suspect's alibi. They begin by briefly outlining the basic differences between the systems and then delve into the similarities and differences in how alibis are sought and handed (in the generation and validation literature) and ultimately interpreted to be truthful or not (in the believability and discrimination literature). The discussion of who in each system is responsible for the various stages where alibi evidence comes in highlights the authors critique about the lack of diversity of perspectives in considering multiple legal systems and structures when researching alibi evidence. The authors also point out the possibility that these differences in research results to date may be a consequence of the samples we utilize. Student samples differ in substantial ways from practitioners working in the fields (in both systems across many countries) and might provide a useful explanation for some of the more prominent differences. Asking students to act as mock investigators or jurors is quite different than asking real-world detectives or attorneys how they consider and handle the gathering and use of alibi evidence.

There is a small but substantial amount of studies examining suspect and corroborator characteristics such as age that are also useful to consider in alibi corroboration discussions. Price, Kehn, Sorby, Harvey, Cops, and Klassen discuss children serving as alibi corroborators in Chap. 7 of the text. The research suggests that there are divergent perspectives in considering children's memories – some believe children to be forthright and honest in their discussions, and others believe children to be more susceptible to suggestion and malleable in their memories. These perspectives make the research discussed in this chapter all the more important. If we understand adult memory and its flaws, can the same be said for youthful memory questioning? Price and her colleagues discuss that children are capable of recalling time, place, and duration of events when questioned; however when considered in the context of child alibi corroboration, the circumstances might make the request more difficult. Further, the authors discuss challenges in motivation, the potential that children, just as adults, can intentionally provide incorrect information. Beyond the truthfulness of the statement itself, we also need to consider how the believability of child-based alibi corroboration will occur. Pre-existing ideas about how credible children can be in a legal context is likely to impact adult evaluator's perceptions as well. As is clear in each chapter, the authors end with a discussion about the numerous ways this topic could be further studied and expanded to broaden our understanding of children's potential role in our legal system's use of alibi corroboration.

Another perspective worth considering is that of attorneys. In Chap. 8, Levine and Miller (both attorneys themselves) discuss the way defense attorneys specifically utilize alibi information in preparing for and presenting evidence in court. Throughout the chapter, the authors present their original data collection from a small sample of practicing defense attorneys to give depth and validity to their discussion. The chapter provides a complete list and history of alibi notice rules for every state in the USA, providing needed context to the legal requirements attorneys, and therefore defendants, must abide by in considering their trial strategy. Particularly enlightening is a discussion of the timing of when alibi evidence is presented (within notice rules conditions) to ensure it is most effective without opening up potential for prosecutorial influence to weaken the corroboration. Finally, the authors discuss concerns illustrating two sides of the coin; first, defense attorneys worry about putting forward an alibi that is later determined to be incorrect and yet also worry about failing to utilize an alibi when it is present and has at least some corroboration. Case law and academic articles are used to illustrate this uniquely non-affirmative defense, claiming the prosecution's case is not sound because they could not have committed the crime due to being somewhere else entirely.

As alluded to in previous chapters, it is possible suspects may (at least initially) put forward an alibi that is not correct. In Chap. 9, Cardenas, Crozier, and Strange discuss the potential for erroneous alibis and how the effect of an incorrect statement can be long-lasting. The authors explain how erroneous alibis can include both those intentionally and unintentionally incorrect alibi statements and how defining what constitutes an erroneous alibi may be more difficult than seems at first glance. For example, if a statement contains only a minor inaccuracy (thinking you came home 15 minutes before your doorbell camera actually shows you did), does that make the entire statement incorrect? How does that inaccurate statement (even if corrected once corroborating evidence is sought) impact evaluator's perceptions of the overall alibi claim? The authors summarize the research suggesting evaluators to be relatively critical of any changes in alibi statements and draw an important distinction between accuracy and believability in erroneous alibi discussions. Further, exculpatory evidence such as an alibi has little research to suggest a base rate for incorrectness (in part or in whole). This topic is particularly relevant in alibi generation discussions and spends a good deal of time discussing memory and its flaws, as did Chap. 3. Additionally, there are social factors such as interrogation tactics and the belief that one's innocence will eventually demonstrate itself that could lead to a suspect's lack of concern over the correctness of their alibi statement. The authors discuss absent alibis and how problems with alibi evidence can transcend throughout the investigation and trial stages, and beyond, and as usual end with a call for more research on erroneous alibis.

Finally, in the last chapter, we wrap up our discussion in highlighting the numerous ways the field could move forward in the coming years. We put forward three possible reasons why research on alibis is perhaps lacking, to date, and argue against such views. While the parallels to eyewitnesses are clear, alibi corroborators have their own set of factors that contribute to the generation and believability of the evidence they provide and, as such, warrant their own line of studies. Not every case has eyewitnesses; however every innocent suspect has an alibi, so it is a wonder why more research and an attempt at deeper understanding for how this unique evidence works (and does not work) are missing. There are chapters we had originally intended to include in this text that simply do not yet have the bulk of research to support a full chapter's worth of writing, many of which are identified in the final chapter for future scholars to take up.

To that end, we wanted to draw particular attention to the myriad questions about alibis and corroboration that remain unanswered and let this book serve not just as a summation, but a starting point for the future of alibi research. While the chapters each discuss some future directions in their own text, we pulled basic research questions (and others added by the authors) in an appendix to delineate the boundaries around alibi research to date and illustrate the range of possibilities left to discover. For scholars new to the field of alibis, any of these ideas could serve as inspiration for a project of your own, or perhaps thesis or dissertation work. For seasoned scholars that are interested in innocence issues, there are intersections with several other topic areas, such as eyewitnesses, interrogations, lie detection, investigator bias, and many more. Regardless of your classification, be it graduate student or professor, psychologist or criminologist, attorney or legal scholar, the importance of this work and the need for more research will be apparent with each new chapter you read.

References

Andone, D., Vera, A., Simonson, A., & Dominguez, C. (2021, November 1). Oklahoma parole board recommends clemency for Julius Jones, who is scheduled to be executed for murder he says he didn't commit. *CNN*. https://www.cnn.com/2021/11/01/us/julius-jones-oklahoma-clemency-hearing/index.html

Dahl, L. C., Brimacombe, C. A., & Lindsay, D. S. (2009). Investigating investigators: How presentation order influences participant–investigators' interpretations of eyewitness identification and alibi evidence. *Law and Human Behavior, 33*(5), 368–380.

Dror, I. E., Peron, A. E., Hind, S. L., & Charlton, D. (2005). When emotions get the better of us: The effect of contextual top-down processing on matching fingerprints. *Applied Cognitive Psychology, 19*(6), 799–809.

Gould, J. B., & Leo, R. A. (2010). One hundred years later: Wrongful convictions after a century of research. *The Journal of Criminal Law and Criminology, 100*(3), 825–868.

Innocence Project. (2021a, May 25). Texas court recommends vacating Mallory Nicholson's 1982 wrongful conviction [Press release]. https://innocenceproject.org/texas-court-recommends-vacating-mallory-nicholsons-1982-wrongful-conviction/

Innocence Project. (2021b, November 1). 8 Facts about Julius Jones, innocent on death row in Oklahoma [Press release]. https://innocenceproject.org/julius-jones-death-row-oklahoma-what-to-know/

Kassin, S., Dror, I., & Kukucka, J. (2013). The forensic confirmation bias: Problems, perspectives, and proposed solutions. *Journal of Applied Research in Memory and Cognition, 2*(1), 42–52.

Leins, D. A., & Charman, S. D. (2016). Schema reliance and innocent alibi generation. *Legal and Criminological Psychology, 21*(1), 111–126.

Olson, E. A., & Charman, S. D. (2012). 'But can you prove it?'–Examining the quality of innocent suspects' alibis. *Psychology, Crime & Law, 18*(5), 453–471.

Olson, E. A., & Wells, G. L. (2004). What makes a good alibi? A proposed taxonomy. *Law and Human Behavior, 28*(2), 157–176.

Olson, E. A., & Wells, G. L. (2012). The alibi-generation effect: Alibi-generation experience influences alibi evaluation. *Legal and Criminological Psychology, 17*(1), 151–164.

Rassin, E. (2018). Reducing tunnel vision with a pen-and-paper tool for the weighting of criminal evidence. *Journal of Investigative Psychology and Offender Profiling, 15*(2), 227–233.

Salet, R., & Terpstra, J. (2014). Critical review in criminal investigation: Evaluation of a measure to prevent tunnel vision. *Policing: A Journal of Policy and Practice, 8*(1), 43–50.

Wells, G. L., Small, M., Penrod, S., Malpass, R. S., Fulero, S. M., & Brimacombe, C. E. (1998). Eyewitness identification procedures: Recommendations for lineups and photospreads. *Law and Human Behavior, 22*(6), 603–647.

Chapter 2
We Have to Start Somewhere: Classifying Alibis to Launch a Literature

Elizabeth A. Olson and Carolyn Morgan

Introduction

In the late 1990s, DNA analysis technology reached a point where it became reliable enough to be used in court, and a number of post-conviction DNA analyses resulted in evidence of wrongful conviction. An analysis of the first 40 post-conviction DNA exoneration cases revealed that a startling percentage of these wrongful convictions – 80% – were the result of mistaken eyewitness identification (Wells et al., 1998), which contributed to the development of national guidelines on collecting eyewitness evidence (Wells et al., 2000). However, 20% of those cases also listed "weak alibi" or "no alibi" as incriminating evidence. For Olson and Wells (2004), this was particularly counterintuitive – alibis should be exculpatory evidence. Given that a bedrock philosophical principle of the criminal justice system is "innocent until proven guilty," how does an absence of innocence-proving evidence indicate guilt? Further, and perhaps more important, how could a poor alibi – or no alibi – be actively incriminating? It does not logically follow that if a suspect does not have an alibi for a particular time, they therefore must have committed a crime during that time.

Perhaps equally concerning, all the wrongfully convicted likely *had* alibis – they were innocent of the crimes for which they had been convicted. Those alibis, however, were not enough to keep them from prison. For example, in 2003, Steven Avery was the 137th American man exonerated by post-conviction DNA testing nearly 18 years after he was convicted of sexual assault and attempted murder (The Innocence Project, n.d., www.innocenceproject.org). In 1985, Penny Beernsten was running along the Lake Michigan shoreline when she was accosted, taken to a wooded area, and assaulted. Based on her description of her attacker, police included

E. A. Olson (✉) · C. Morgan
University of Wisconsin-Whitewater, Whitewater, WI, USA
e-mail: olsone@uww.edu; morganc@uww.edu

J. D. Behl, M. R. Kienzle (eds.), *Alibis and Corroborators*, https://doi.org/10.1007/978-3-030-95663-9_2

Avery in the photospread and later in a live lineup, and Beernsten identified Avery in both. During the investigation, Avery had maintained his innocence, and at trial, Avery presented 16 alibi corroborators who, together, established his whereabouts for the entire day (Ferak, 2016). Some of these corroborators were family and friends; others were strangers – store clerks who presented receipts and testimony that they remembered him because they thought it was unusual that he was shopping with his wife and five children, including 6-day-old twins. This striking alibi, however, was not enough to prevent Avery's conviction, largely on the basis of the eyewitness identification. Later DNA testing linked hair evidence to Gregory Allen, who was at the time serving a sentence for a sexual assault that occurred after the attack on Ms. Beernsten. While Avery was later convicted of the murder of Theresa Halbach in 2005 (and this case was the subject of a Netflix documentary in 2015), his high-profile exoneration in 2003 was notable to Olson and Wells especially because of the number and variety of alibi witnesses Avery brought to the stand.

Upon further investigation of the literature, Olson and Wells found very little psycholegal research into alibis as a phenomenon (2004; see also Sommers & Douglass, 2007; Wells & Olson, 2001). Instead, what little was found pitted alibi corroborators directly against incriminating eyewitnesses (i.e., their focus was from an eyewitness psychology perspective testing how powerful eyewitness evidence could be), rather than any in-depth analysis of alibis as a phenomenon. Thus, an alibi taxonomy and a whole new field of research was formed.

The Need for a Taxonomy

With the dearth of literature into alibis, Olson and Wells (2004) realized that building a literature required some very basic outlining of both terminology and their perception of the scope of the issue. They were able to find some guidance in terms of how the legal system approached alibis: In the criminal justice system, an alibi is "a defense that places the defendant at the relevant time of the crime in a different place than the scene involved and so removed therefrom as to render it impossible for one to be the guilty party" (Nolan, 1990, p. 71). During a police interview or investigation, alibis may be generated and evaluated unsystematically, with little regulation or guidance as to how they should be collected and used. In the context of a trial, alibis may be brought as a formal defense (Burke et al., 2007; Sommers & Douglass, 2007), and it is in this context that the legal system has codified how defendants may use an alibi defense in the form of a prior notice rule. Many US jurisdictions include a prior notice rule, requiring that defendants give pretrial notice that they intend to present an alibi defense, ostensibly to prevent manufacturing an alibi at the last possible moment and thus precluding thorough investigation (see Epstein, 1964; also see Chap. 8 for a more detailed discussion). This context similarly dictates how judges may instruct jurors that the defendant is not required to *prove* an alibi but the burden of *negating* an alibi is on the prosecution (Friedman, 1998). Olson and Wells (2004) argued that legal literature's focus on technicalities of the alibi defense was insufficient to address psychological questions and applied, practical considerations regarding alibi generation and corroboration, investigator decision-making, and juror evaluations – an empirical literature was necessary.

Olson and Wells (2004) realized that increasing understanding of how alibis are generated and evaluated within the criminal justice system required them to develop an initial taxonomy, including conceptual and initial operational definitions to describe alibis for research purposes. At a most basic level, a key baseline to establish is: What makes an alibi a "good" one, or a "bad" one? One key characteristic of an alibi is its function of establishing truth for the suspect. Thus, they used believability as a basis for evaluating and comparing alibis: A "good" alibi is one that is more believable, that investigators and others believe establishes the truth of the suspect's whereabouts, whereas a "bad" alibi is one in which triers of fact (be it law enforcement, attorneys, or juries) are unlikely to believe, or find to be less truthful. Olson and Wells (2004) argued that it would be impossible to create a classification system that could take into account how alibis interact with other elements of a case, such as characteristics of suspects and evaluators, crime type and severity, and incriminating evidence, to produce a final judgment of how absolutely believable an alibi might be. Steven Avery's case, for example, included a number of alibi corroborators and physical evidence in support of his alibi, but these likely interacted with the crime itself, juror impressions of Avery and his corroborators, and juror judgments of detective testimony and Ms. Beernsten's identification to produce the ultimately wrongful guilty verdict. This kind of interaction would be impossible to predict, as case details vary widely. Rather, Olson and Wells chose to base their taxonomy on *relative* believability – that in the absence of all other factors, some alibis are more believable when compared to other alibis.

The Creation of the Taxonomy

With relative believability as the focal construct, Olson and Wells (2004) began by examining a variable they believed essential to alibis – the type of corroborating evidence included in the alibi. In recognizing the complexity of the social contexts in which alibis arise (e.g., characteristics of a crime situation, the suspect, and the investigators), they intentionally and explicitly disconnected the content of the alibi statement – the narrative information – and the characteristics of the suspect from the alibi itself. They argued that these characteristics were unnecessary for the conceptual simplicity they were aiming for with the taxonomy. While this approach was necessary at the time, the literature has developed to address questions related to both the content of the alibi and characteristics of the suspect. The taxonomy may need updating, or additional models may be needed, to better explain and understand these more complex interactions.

In contrast to the extensive variation possible in surface characteristics, corroborating evidence for an alibi comes in one of two broad categories: physical evidence and person evidence. What distinguishes one alibi from another is the level of proof that can support the alibi – despite the burden being on the prosecution to disprove the claim. Because suspects could have physical and person evidence in any combination, Olson and Wells (2004) chose to create a factorial taxonomy with physical evidence and person evidence as the factors; they did not initially predict that one type of evidence would be considered more believable than the other. Physical evidence includes receipts, tickets, video recordings, or other physical records that demonstrate a person was at a particular location at a given time. One could argue this list is only increasing with the advent of new technologies, including wearable technology, location services, and doorbell cameras. Person evidence includes testimony from another person – relatives, friends, or strangers – who corroborate the alibi narrative that the suspect was at a particular place at a given time away from where the crime took place.

Olson and Wells identified one dimension, perceived ease-of-fabrication, on which both physical evidence and person evidence could vary. This dimension captures the evaluator's perception of how easily a suspect *could* create or orchestrate evidence to support the alibi – not only by manipulating physical evidence but the dimension could also include the willingness of corroborators to lie for them. More easily fabricated evidence was presumed to be less believable because a guilty suspect in the act of trying to escape detection may manipulate evidence in support of a false alibi. For example, a suspect may offer a social media post as proof of their whereabouts, but an evaluator may not find that particularly credible given that some social media apps allow a user to schedule posts ahead of time and there is no way to prove *who* posted or where they were at the time – thus, the evaluator perceives this kind of evidence as easy to fabricate. In contrast, it would be difficult for a corroborator to fabricate a dated and timed security video from a retail establishment; it is possible to tamper with video footage but the relative difficulty of fabrication should lead evaluators to rate that evidence as considerably more believable compared to the aforementioned social media example, though not completely foolproof. For his alibi, Steven Avery offered a receipt that showed he was in a ShopKo in Green Bay, just over an hour after the assault occurred. Detectives in the case demonstrated that it was possible to drive the distance from the crime scene and check out from ShopKo in 57 minutes, but they admitted they had driven 10 miles over the speed limit and did not account for possible delays from taking along Avery's five children (Lautenschlager, 2003).

Ease-of-fabrication for person evidence relates to an evaluator's perception of how easily a suspect could orchestrate corroboration (i.e., how easily could a suspect convince another person to corroborate an alibi – even if it is untrue). This discussion led Olson and Wells to differentiate the distinct relationships a suspect and alibi corroborator may have. An alibi corroborator with emotional ties to the suspect (i.e., a relative or close friend) could be perceived as *motivated* to keep a suspect out of legal trouble – and thus, an evaluator would perceive that corroborator as motivated to lie for the suspect, making their testimony less believable. Olson and Wells called this type of person-evidence corroboration "motivated familiar other" as the corroborator presumably has the familiarity, and therefore, the motivation to lie for the suspect. Several of Steven Avery's corroborators were family members, including his wife, and they could have been perceived as willing to lie to keep him from trouble. However, a suspect would likely have a difficult time convincing a stranger to lie for them, which an evaluator would perceive as difficult-to-fabricate corroboration and would find more believable. Steven Avery also offered as corroborators ShopKo employees who confirmed that he had been in the store on the day of the attack – which could be perceived as difficult for Avery to have orchestrated. A lack of familiarity with the suspect would significantly decrease the motivation of a potential corroborator to lie – they do not know the suspect, or their character, personality, or typical behaviors, let alone their actions in this specific instance. Therefore, Olson and Wells called these corroborators "nonmotivated strangers."

They also identified a third dimension related to person evidence, which perhaps comes from their background in eyewitness identification research: That some alibi corroborators may be more likely to be innocently mistaken than other corroborators – affecting the credibility and believability of the witness-corroborator. While close friends and relatives are highly unlikely to mistake that the suspect is the person they were talking with, a complete stranger is far more likely to mistakenly identify the suspect (see Wells et al., 2020). Thus, for person evidence, the ease-of-fabrication dimension is negatively correlated to ease-of-identification; strangers may be perceived as less likely to lie, but may have a greater risk of being mistaken. Therefore, Olson and Wells added a "nonmotivated familiar other" category to encompass those who would recognize a suspect's face but not have the motivation to lie for the suspect. In other words, a person who would be in all other ways a stranger but would have a regular, professional, and otherwise superficial relationship with the suspect, decreasing their likelihood of a mistake (e.g., a bus driver on a regular route or a front entrance attendant at a place where a suspect may frequent) and conceptually making them an ideal alibi corroborator.

Empirical Validity of and Updates to the Taxonomy

Testing of the alibi taxonomy in the initial Olson and Wells (2004) paper revealed that naïve participant-evaluators handled the theoretical dimensions of ease-of-fabrication and perceived likelihood of mistake somewhat differently than expected. Participants were largely sensitive to perceived ease-of-fabrication on the part of alibi corroborators, judging close friends and family as more likely to lie on a suspect's behalf (and rendering the alibi relatively less believable). However, participants largely ignored the risk of mistake inherent in stranger-corroborator statements and regarded them as highly believable. Nonmotivated familiar others were rated equally as believable as strangers, although Olson and Wells did not advocate the removal of that corroborator category at that point. A separate group of manipulation-check participants had rated stranger-corroborators as more likely to make a mistake than nonmotivated familiar others; in recognition of the theoretical distinction between the two categories, Olson and Wells advocated that they both remain as part of the taxonomy. Similarly, Olson and Wells' (2004) participants did not differentiate along the ease-of-fabrication dimension for physical evidence, regarding all types of physical evidence as similarly believable. This may have been an effect of the particular exemplars of physical evidence chosen in Olson and Wells' (2004) initial test of the taxonomy.

Culhane et al. (2008) provided support for ease-of-fabrication as a conceptual dimension for the taxonomy. They asked participants to identify what kinds of physical and person evidence they could potentially fabricate, if they had found themselves in a position to need to create an alibi. Nearly 34% of their participants reported that they could generate false physical evidence, largely ticket stubs and cash receipts, which reinforces that evaluators may judge them easy to fabricate. Also, a majority of participants (61%) believed they could convince a person to lie on their behalf – and 98% of those individuals identified were motivated familiar others.

Olson and Charman (2012) collected alibis from participants to assess the quality of innocent suspects' alibis, allowing for testing of the taxonomy's ability to classify more ecologically valid alibis. They discovered that classifying physical evidence required a re-working of the taxonomy: Olson and Wells (2004) had not identified the specific features of physical evidence that would make a piece of evidence "easy to fabricate" or "difficult to fabricate," which made operationalizing a classification system difficult. Olson and Charman (2012) chose to sort physical evidence according to both its direct connection to the suspect and its time and place information (when and where the evidence was generated); this relates to the ease-of-fabrication dimension of the initial taxonomy in that evidence without those features should be perceived as easier to fabricate than evidence that does directly connect to time, place, and the suspect. In Olson and Charman's (2012) updated taxonomy, the weakest physical evidence did not have any time or place information (e.g., a drawing reportedly done during the time in question, but with no indication as to when or where it was actually made). Moderate physical evidence contained time or place information but no direct connection with the suspect (e.g., a cash receipt, which has time and place information but no record of who actually made the purchase), and the strongest physical evidence both directly connected to the suspect and established the time and place the suspect had been (e.g., a credit-card receipt signed by the suspect). It is important to note that due to technological updates in society, the perception of these particular example pieces of evidence is ever-changing (e.g., the advent of photo and video editing software now makes these likely less believable than they once were).

Similar to Olson and Charman (2012), Nieuwkamp et al. (2017) collected alibis from a large community sample to establish patterns of alibi evidence among innocent suspects. A relatively small number of participants (about 1% of their sample) offered what Nieuwkamp and colleagues termed "knowledge evidence," wherein a participant reported knowledge that they could only have if they had been engaged in the activity they reported for their alibi, for example, a participant reported being home alone but was able to report the content of the television shows he had watched during that evening. Knowledge evidence, while relatively rare, offers a promising addition as a third evidence dimension in the taxonomy; it could be classified as "weaker" or "stronger" depending on the time-specificity of the knowledge opportunity. Knowledge of commonly available, on-demand video programming may not be considered by an evaluator to be particularly convincing, as one could watch such video at any time, but knowledge of a live-streamed community lecture, with no way to access a subsequent recording, may be rated as more believable since the only way to know what was said was to have been watching the lecture while it occurred. Additional research is needed to establish how knowledge evidence might interact with physical and person evidence.

Olson and Wells (2004) introduced the taxonomy with two major goals: First, to offer a basic, heuristic tool to differentiate types of corroborating alibi evidence and as a means to compare alibis to one another, and second, to generate research into alibis and the alibi process, including the ways alibis fit into the wider investigative and criminal system. In the first goal, they largely succeeded, and the taxonomy has served as a means to classify how well innocent suspects can support their alibis. Several studies have demonstrated that innocent suspects largely report alibis with relatively weak corroborating evidence or none at all (Culhane et al., 2008; Olson & Charman, 2012; Nieuwkamp et al., 2017). Nieuwkamp et al. (2017) also were able to document base-rate information for the likelihood of different types of evidence depending on time of day; corroborating evidence of any kind was considerably rarer during nighttime hours compared to afternoons. Weekend afternoons were more likely to allow suspects to generate both physical and person evidence for their alibis.

In their second goal, Olson and Wells also succeeded – this book is ample evidence of how researchers have examined alibi believability relating to the taxonomy as well as additional variables relating to how alibis operate in the justice system. The basic nature of the taxonomy means that it cannot account for the infinitely complex ways that narrative and suspect/evaluator characteristics interact with alibi evidence and incriminating evidence in a given case. However, the taxonomy has provided a framework for evaluating and comparing alibis within some of those situations to identify patterns in how alibis can be used. For example, Culhane and Hosch (2012) used motivated familiar others and nonmotivated familiar others from the taxonomy to operationalize changes to alibi strength: In some cases, the alibis switched from a motivated other to a nonmotivated familiar other (thus getting stronger), and others switched from a nonmotivated familiar other to a motivated other (thus getting weaker). Culhane and Hosch (2012) demonstrated that such changes can result in reduced alibi believability – even when alibis change to stronger evidence (see Chap. 4).

Future Directions

In creating the taxonomy, Olson and Wells (2004) made several assumptions that have only indirectly been empirically tested, and more thorough testing of these assumptions would be a fruitful future direction for alibi research. For example, the taxonomy assumed that everyone involved in an alibi situation – the suspect, investigators, and other evaluators – would have a similar evaluative strategy for the believability of different types of evidence. However, anecdotal evidence (Olson & Charman, 2012, for example) suggests that innocent suspects, much like innocent people who waive their Miranda rights and are thus in danger of giving false confessions, may believe the fact of their innocence renders whatever evidence they provide an inherent believability – if they feel the need to provide evidence at all due to the overestimation of their innocence protecting them. Suspects may show high confidence in their ability to provide alibi corroboration, but that corroboration may be physical or person-based "proof" that in fact substantiates very little. Olson and Charman (2012) noted one participant who offered as "proof" the bottlecaps he said he had been collecting in a parking lot at the relevant time, which should be viewed as extremely weak evidence with no time or location attached, not to mention the lack of proof the bottlecaps were even his. Nieuwkamp et al. (2017) reported one participant offering an alibi of running in a forest during the relevant time frame, and the evidence he had was the mud on his running shoes – which could support a claim that the shoes had been in a particular location, but there would be no way to establish a timeframe. Similarly, an appointment note on a calendar does not actually prove that a suspect was at that appointment, just as a class schedule does not prove a student was in that particular class on that particular day. Innocent suspects may offer these items believing that they constitute high-quality evidence or that other corroborations will coincide with the claim, increasing its believability and/or strength in combination.

Olson and Wells (2004) also based their differentiation of better-quality evidence from lesser-quality evidence on evaluators' perceptions, which may be more malleable than first assumed. Do different kinds of evaluators – defense attorneys, prosecutors, investigators – have different evaluations of alibi evidence? It is possible that perceptions of physical evidence as easy to fabricate or difficult to fabricate may depend on an evaluator's experience with that kind of evidence; for example, while a suspect may view their timecard as strong physical evidence, a juror who regularly punches in for his friend may view this evidence with justifiable skepticism. Olson and Wells (2004) note that when manipulation check participants were asked specific questions about the likelihood of mistake, they rated the nonmotivated strangers as less likely to be mistaken. A nonmotivated stranger, while believable due to lack of motivation to lie, is potentially quite unreliable due to the lack of relationship with the suspect – and this kind of argument could cause a juror to re-evaluate the quality of a corroborator's testimony. More broadly, with the increasing ubiquity of cameras – including cell phone cameras and neighborhood surveillance from doorbell cameras or home security systems – would evaluators have unrealistically high expectations about the quality and quantity of physical evidence suspects could potentially procure?

Additionally, many real-world alibis may be offered with either multiple corroborators, multiple pieces of physical evidence, or both. Steven Avery's alibi may have been an outlier for sheer number of corroborators, but evidence suggests that multiple corroborators are common: A majority of participants (64%) in Nieuwkamp et al.'s (2017) study offered multiple alibi corroborators to support their alibis, and nearly 18% offered multiple pieces of physical evidence. Currently, the taxonomy does not account for how multiple pieces of evidence interact. In classifying the alibis from their participants, Olson and Charman (2012) chose to use only a single piece of each type of evidence, taking the strongest of each in an attempt to classify a "best case" scenario – an approach which may or may not accurately reflect the relative believability of an alibi that contains multiple pieces of the same type of evidence.

Multiple alibi corroborators may show similar effects as multiple eyewitnesses (e.g., a bolstering effect; Slane & Dodson, 2019) such that multiple "weak" corroborators would be considered more believable than a single "strong" corroborator. Similarly, multiple pieces of weak physical evidence may show an additive effect, where the evidence, and therefore the alibi, are rated as more believable compared to those with a single piece of evidence. The relative strength changes of multiple pieces of evidence could be perceived differently for person corroborators and physical evidence; for example, multiple corroborators with similar stories may be perceived as having rehearsed a lie, but multiple pieces of physical evidence may be perceived as corroborating each other and creating a coherent story of the suspect's whereabouts. However, a complex alibi with multiple pieces of evidence may suffer a paradoxical reduction in believability – if an evaluator perceives the offered evidence is "too good," the evaluator may decide that such strength is the result of a guilty suspect attempting to fabricate their alibi. The effects of multiple corroborators and multiple pieces of evidence on alibi believability have not been empirically tested; however, the heuristic simplicity of the taxonomy should allow for its expansion into testing these effects.

Beyond testing underlying assumptions and expanding or modifying the taxonomy, future researchers in the field will continue find the taxonomy a useful tool. The taxonomy can help classify if innocent and guilty suspects produce systematically different alibis. How do evaluators' assessments shift when faced with a suspect who is excessively confident of their alibi, only to discover corroborators are considerably less certain – or perhaps even unwilling to serve as corroborators? Do suspects who have prior experience with the criminal justice system approach providing alibis differently than suspects who have no such experience? Do repeated alibi stories garner shifts in evaluator judgments, especially as they start to "sound" more rehearsed?

Early alibi research, like all new literatures, has taken some time to develop its terminology and understanding of the scope of the problem to be studied. Work is needed to address how alibi research can be useful for practitioners. For example, how do investigators use alibis, and how might they be failing to use alibis as useful parts of a criminal investigation? This interdisciplinary work can also be strengthened by explicitly connecting to basic research in psychology, particularly in stereotyping, memory, cognition, and decision-making. How do stereotypes and motivation affect the ways investigators evaluate suspects or integrate information into their development of a case? How do defense attorneys decide whether an alibi could be brought as a formal alibi defense at a trial, and when do they decide an alibi would be less useful? Are jury instructions, where a judge reminds jurors that the burden of negating an alibi is on the prosecution, sufficient to give alibis enough exculpatory weight that they could overcome incriminating evidence?

These questions and the many others referenced elsewhere in this text demonstrate the continuing potential richness of alibi research discussed in Olson and Wells (2004), and the taxonomy promises to continue as a useful heuristic tool for researchers. This is an exciting time to be part of alibi research: The field has tackled some basic questions and is moving toward a more integrated, connected understanding of how alibis operate not only on their own, but in the larger context of the criminal justice system.

References

Burke, T. M., Turtle, J.W., & Olson, E. A. (2007). Alibis in criminal investigations and trials. In M. P. Toglia, J. D. Read, D. F. Ross, & R. C. L. Lindsay (Eds.), *The handbook of eyewitness psychology* (*Memory for events*) (Vol. 1, pp. 157–174). Lawrence Earlbaum Associates.

Culhane, S. E., & Hosch, H. M. (2012). Changed alibis: Current law enforcement, future law enforcement, and layperson reactions. *Criminal Justice and Behavior, 39*, 958–977. https://doi.org/10.1177/0093854812438185

Culhane, S. E., Hosch, H. M., & Kehn, A. (2008). Alibi generation: Data from U.S. Hispanics and U.S. non-Hispanic Whites. *Journal of Ethnicity in Criminal Justice, 6*, 177–199. https://doi.org/10.1080/15377930802243395

Epstein, D. M. (1964). Advance notice of alibi. *The Journal of Criminal Law, Criminology, and Police Science, 55*, 29–38.

Ferak, J. (2016, January 28). *Update: Steven Avery Case Timeline.* Post Crescent. https://www.postcrescent.com/story/news/local/steven-avery/2016/01/28/steven-avery-case-timeline/79450680/

Friedman, J. P. (1998). Alibi instructions and due process of law. *Western New England Law Review, 20*, 343–386.

Lautenschlager, P. A. (2003, December 17). *Avery review* [Memorandum]. Wisconsin Department of Justice. https://isthmus.com/downloads/31173/download/Steve%20Avery%20review%20memo%20121703.pdf

Nieuwkamp, R., Horselenberg, R., & Van Koppen, P. J. (2017). The illusion of the perfect alibi: Establishing the base rate of non-offenders' alibis. *Journal of Investigative Psychology and Offender Profiling, 14*, 23–42. https://doi.org/10.1002/jip.1470

Nolan, J. R. (1990). *Black's law dictionary* (6th ed.). West Publishing.

Olson, E. A., & Charman, S. D. (2012). "But can you prove it?" Examining the quality of innocent suspects' alibis. *Psychology, Crime, and Law, 18*, 453–471. https://doi.org/10.1080/1068316X.2010.505567

Olson, E. A., & Wells, G. L. (2004). What makes a good alibi? A proposed taxonomy. *Law and Human Behavior, 25*, 204–294. https://doi.org/10.1023/B:LAHU.0000022320.47112.d3

Slane, C. R., & Dodson, C. S. (2019). Two eyewitnesses are more persuasive than one except when they remember a suspect's feature. *Journal of Applied Research in Memory and Cognition, 8*(1), 60–67.

Sommers, S. R., & Douglass, A. B. (2007). Context matters: Alibi strength varies according to evaluator perspective. *Legal and Criminological Psychology, 12*(1), 41–54.

The Innocence Project. (n.d.). *Steven Avery case profile*. https://innocenceproject.org/cases/steven-avery/

Wells, G. L., Malpass, R. S., Lindsay, R. C. L., Fisher, R. P., Turtle, J. W., & Fulero, S. M. (2000). From the lab to the police station: A successful application of eyewitness research. *American Psychologist, 55*(6), 581–598. https://doi.org/10.1037/0003-066X.55.6.581

Wells, G. L., & Olson, E. A. (2001). The other-race effect in eyewitness identification: What do we do about it? *Psychology, Public Policy, and Law, 7*(1), 230–246.

Wells, G. L., Kovera, M. B., Douglass, A. B., Brewer, N., Meissner, C. A., & Wixted, J. T. (2020). Policy and procedure recommendations for the collection and preservation of eyewitness identification evidence. *Law and Human Behavior, 44*(1), 3.

Wells, G. L., Small, M., Penrod, S., Malpass, R. S., Fulero, S. M., & Brimacombe, C. A. E. (1998). Eyewitness identification procedures: Recommendations for lineups and photospreads. *Law and Human Behavior, 22*, 603–647. https://doi.org/10.1023/A:1025750605807

Chapter 3
Generating Alibi Statements

Scott E. Culhane

"Where were you at 9:00 last night?" The hallmark of an alibi is the understanding that the suspect was not at the scene of the crime. Instead, the suspect was "in another place" per the Latin origin of the word alibi. The alibi is a frequently resorted to defense for criminal accusations (Gooderson, 1977). And why should not it be the most common defense? After all, what could be simpler than being in another part of the town, the state, the country, or the world when a crime occurs? Someone cannot be in two places at once. The ability to produce an alibi corroborator and/or physical evidence material to prove that someone was elsewhere should give police and prosecutors pause in pursuing a case against a suspect further. Why should one's alibi not be enhanced in the eyes of evaluators when another person can verify the veracity of the statement, or the suspect can produce documentation of their whereabouts?

Instead, attempting to discredit the veracity of an alibi and alibi corroborators has a long history in the legal literature. Take the following account from Corneluis (1929) on cross-examination of alibi corroborators, "An alibi witness can be effectively discredited if he is testifying falsely and goes into too much detail in narrating the facts and circumstances which took place on the day in question" (p. 154). Corneluis goes on to state that this is particularly true for long delays between the crime and court proceedings. Steele (2020) questions the defense use of an alibi as potentially "a risky gambit with a high likelihood of backfiring" (p. 1). According to Steele, defense attorneys may be leery of calling upon alibi corroborators because of the risks associated with cross-examinations. Solid alibis should actually work in the favor of the suspect. An investigator or a prosecutor who is presented with a strong and believable alibi should serve as a stop-gap measure in the criminal justice system and simply refuse to bring charges forward. The prosecutors are the best

S. E. Culhane (✉)
Department of Criminal Justice, Austin Peay State University, Clarksville, TN, USA
e-mail: culhanes@apsu.edu

J. D. Behl, M. R. Kienzle (eds.), *Alibis and Corroborators*,
https://doi.org/10.1007/978-3-030-95663-9_3

chance of stopping criminal proceedings, as judges have shown that issues of witness credibility are in the purview of the jury (Morales-Hurtado v. Reinoso, 2020).

This chapter covers a summation of the literature and theories of alibi generation. Subsequent chapters in this book discuss the issues of deception detection (Chap. 9) and evaluation and believability (Chap. 4) of alibi statements. Thus, the studies, data, and results of such examinations are only presented minimally here. The chapters of this book are an important step toward bolstering the research output in the alibi field.

Richard Rosario

A person would feel quite comfortable answering the aforementioned question of where they were when a crime occurred, if their answer really was "another state." Such was the case for Richard Rosario, who noted that he (a) had never met the victim and (b) was not only in another state on the night of the murder of Jorge Collazo, but he was in a state that was 1000 miles away. When he was notified about being wanted for the murder in New York, Richard was naturally surprised but voluntarily surrendered to authorities and was arrested on July 1, 1996.

When confronted by police, Mr. Rosario informed the officers of his whereabouts, and what should have been even more convincing of his innocence was that Mr. Rosario noted 13 alibi corroborators who could attest to the fact that he was in Florida the night a murder took place in New York (Slepian, 2019). Included in this large count of alibi corroborators was a woman who went into labor the same date as the shooting (certainly a highly robust memory for the witness). Like other cases in the fight for the exoneration of the innocent [see, e.g., the case of Temujin Kensu (Rappleye, 2021)], the police did not put forth much effort to verify the suspect's alibi. At least five NYPD officers investigated the murder, yet none were able to adequately account for Mr. Rosario's seemingly solid alibi statement, and none of them contacted the 13 alibi corroborators.

In addition, the performance of Mr. Rosario's defense attorney was less than stellar (see the full discussion of potential flaws in attorney behavior in Chap. 8). At trial, the State of New York relied on three eyewitnesses to the crime, all of whom were introduced to Mr. Rosario's face by police photographs. The State had no physical or forensic evidence, no evidence that the victim and defendant knew each other, and no motive. Only two of the three eyewitnesses identified Richard Rosario as the shooter in court. Two and a half years after the murder, Richard Rosario was convicted in a New York Criminal Court. Justice did not come by way of the appellate courts, as numerous appeals, including one with seven alibi corroborators' statements were denied. It would take the State of New York another 20 years to set Mr. Rosario free with a vacated conviction after a review of the case by the City District Attorney's Office (Rosario v. City of New York, 2019). Mr. Rosario's case was the subject of a popular podcast titled "13 Alibis" and without the coverage of his case, he could have died in prison an innocent man.

The Innocence Project (www.innocenceproject.org) alone has been responsible for hundreds of innocent individuals finally seeing freedom from the prison system. Many of the cases featured on their website talk about the exoneree's alibi. The truth of the matter is that *every* wrongfully convicted person had an alibi. In an examination of early exonerees by Wells et al. (1998), victim misidentification was the most prevalent reason for wrongful conviction (this was the thrust of the paper itself), but a significant number (more than 1 in 4) of these individuals also had "weak" or "no" alibi evidence. They might have been unable to recall their memories, they might have made mistakes with their recall, they may have been alone at the time, their alibi may not have been believed by the fact finders, and/or the justice system simply failed these men and women. However, the fact remains that every one of them *had* an alibi for the time of the crime because they were somewhere else. At some point in the judicial process, the alibi simply failed to stop the proceedings (for a more detailed discussion, refer back to Chap. 1).

The Literature on Alibi Generation

"At its most basic level, alibi generation is a memory test: we must have some memory for the time in question (encoding phase) to be able to recall that information later when asked by the police (retrieval phase)" (Crozier et al., 2017, p. 7). When a suspect is asked to recall their whereabouts for a particular time, place, and activities, the individual is generating autobiographical memory. When reported, this is what Burke et al. (2007) refer to as the "Story Phase." This is the fundamental start of the alibi process as a suspect is claiming they were somewhere else at the time of the crime. The person is asked to recall memory for the time, which is prone to a variety of possible errors (Burke et al., 2007). The process in a legal sense now requires proof of this story. This is referred to as the "Validation Phase." The suspect must provide evidence to show they were somewhere else at the time of the offense. The burden often lies with the suspect, contrary to the legal doctrine of "innocent until proven guilty" by the State. The validation phase can be difficult if their evidence is missing or contrary to the story provided at step one of the alibi generation.

The generation of memories has a lengthy history, and research on autobiographical memories is incredibly robust, as a cursory search of the topic produces over 10,000 PsycInfo results at the time of this publication. However, the same cannot be said of research on the autobiographical memories of a criminal suspect. The latter pales in comparison. Indeed, data and published research on alibis as a whole, much less the specific subarea of alibi generation, is far surpassed in the literature by other key topics in legal psychology, such as eyewitnesses and deception detection (Sauerland, 2017).

The Alibi Taxonomy

The Olson and Wells (2004) alibi taxonomy distinguishes between alibis that are the least and most believable (see the discussion in Chap. 2). There are potential corroborators to a suspect's alibi (person evidence), and there are receipts, video surveillance cameras, computer logs, phone records, or other pieces of evidence that could substantiate his or her statement (physical evidence). In their taxonomy, the authors identified the additional possibility of having nothing, neither physical evidence nor person evidence, as one's alibi (i.e., I was home alone). This is the least believable alibi a person could present. For all other possibilities, the authors divided the remaining scenarios into three types of person evidence and two types of physical evidence.

Person Evidence

The person evidence (aka one's alibi corroborator) categories consisted of one group who could be perceived as having a motivation to lie for the suspect and two groups who had no such motivation. This distinction had been presented decades before as considerations for the presentation of the defense's case in court (Sullivan, 1971). The alibi corroborator with reason to lie on behalf of the suspect was labeled motivated familiar other in the taxonomy (Olson & Wells, 2004). In their study, one example of this type of corroborator was the suspect's brother. Most strong familial relationships could be placed in this category (e.g., siblings, parents, grandparents, cousins). Likewise, many romantic relationships (e.g., married partners, fiancées, or boy/girlfriends) and strong social relationships (e.g., good or best friends) could also be perceived as having a motivation to lie for the suspect. According to the taxonomy, this group is the least believable outside of having no witness at all. There is no confusion about whether such a person could correctly identify the suspect, but a fact finder would have a skepticism for such corroborators and rate them accordingly.

The other two groups of corroborators were identified as nonmotivated (i.e., lacking a motivation to lie on the suspect's behalf and also referred to as unmotivated; Culhane et al., 2008), and only differed in their association with the suspect. The first of these two groups is the nonmotivated stranger. People encounter strangers nearly every day. When in public this is all but guaranteed. However, the likelihood of one of these strangers substantiating a lie on behalf on someone they do not know to the police or court is very low. Therefore, these individuals are more believable than the close family and friends of the suspect. Without a memorable moment, many stranger interactions do not strongly encode in our memories (Charman et al., 2017). A stranger could be mistaken about their memories for when they could have seen a suspect, or more importantly, if they could remember the suspect at all. This casts doubt in the eyes of an evaluator and thus makes them conceptually (though perhaps not realistically) less believable than the other nonmotivated group.

Charman et al. (2017) work supported this idea. When a student participant interacted with naïve university employees, the goal was to understand the accuracy of a stranger's subsequent identification for purposes of alibi corroboration in a real-world scenario. When participants were called on to provide support as an alibi witness, the majority of university employees could not accurately identify the student they had interacted with only 1 day earlier. Charman et al. (2017) concluded that it is difficult for a person to generate an accurate and believable alibi, and their work is particularly true for alibis involving nonmotivated strangers.

According to Olson and Wells (2004), the best-case scenario (i.e. most believable) for a suspect is the ability to generate a nonmotivated familiar other. A person who knows you, but is not so close to you as to cast a doubt on their honesty, was the best scenario in the taxonomy for one's alibi person evidence. In their study, Olson and Wells (2004) used a store clerk who had multiple interactions with the suspect in the past as their example, while other studies have used a neighbor (Culhane & Hosch, 2004). This narrows the scope of our social relationships as to whom would fit into such a category.

Herbert Alford

The other side of the alibi generation coin is what physical evidence you can produce to support your alibi statement. In 2016, Herbert Alford was wrongfully convicted of murder and was sentenced to 30 years to life when, in fact, he had rented a car and was miles away at the time of the murder. Unlike Mr. Rosario, Mr. Alford did know the victim and had been in the victim's vehicle prior to the murder. Therefore, Mr. Alford's DNA was present at the crime scene. The police and prosecution were aided by a series of police informants and plea deals from other criminals to build their case against Mr. Alford (Possley, 2021). Included in these deals was an alleged financial payment offer to one informant for a positive identification, a claim denied by the lead detective.

The rental car company was subpoenaed for the records but failed to respond to the court. Likewise, a company official had been ordered to appear in court but did not. The judge did not hold the company in contempt of court. After nearly 18 months of pretrial work, the rental car company still did not comply with the court orders, but the criminal trial of Mr. Alford proceeded. Unable to produce his car rental receipt for the initial trial, the end result was a conviction on December 13, 2016, carrying with it a 30 years to life sentence.

In 2018, the Michigan Appellate Court granted a remand back to the trial court to force the rental car company to comply with the court order to produce the receipts. In a written statement, the rental car company initially claimed all receipts from the time of the crime had been purged from their system. It was only after company officials were due to finally show up in court that the rental car company produced the evidence requested by the defense. The receipt showed that Mr. Alford was an approximate drive of 19 minutes from the crime scene with only 5 minutes between the dispatch of police and the time of the car rental. With the newly produced evidence, the prosecution reevaluated the case and declined to retry Mr. Alford. A factor in that decision, as noted by the prosecutor, was the evidence from the car rental company. In the end, the State's attorney did not believe they could prove culpability with the new evidence brought to light (Brest, 2021). At the time of this writing, Mr. Alford and his team were engaged in a civil lawsuit against the rental car company (Rivas, 2021).

Physical Evidence

Olson and Wells' alibi taxonomy divides physical evidence into two categories, easy to fabricate and difficult to fabricate. Physical evidence can include, but is not limited to, receipts, computer logs, GPS, surveillance or CCTV video, and phone logs. Not surprisingly, the ability to generate difficult-to-fabricate (convenience store security camera footage as one example) evidence would be the most believable.

The data collected by Olson and Wells to test their taxonomy would fall more into the evaluation category, so it is only mentioned briefly here (see Chap. 4 for a broader discussion). Olson and Wells found that the physical evidence was more believable by their mock evaluators. In that respect, their model was supported. However, when examining the person evidence, data from the believability of stranger alibis suggested a powerful effect. The stranger alibi corroborator's lack of motivation was sufficient enough to offset or compensate for the uncertainty of a positive identification by the alibi corroborator.

Types of Corroborators

When generating an alibi, one must consider how much time we spend with others who are particularly close to us, or in the aforementioned taxonomy motivated familiar others. Culhane et al. (2008) asked college students to generate an alibi in an effort to better understand the differences of alibis in Hispanic and Non-Hispanic populations, but to also better understand what a false alibi would look like. Students were asked if they could say they were with someone for a certain time and date, as well as any physical evidence that would support this statement. They were then asked about their ability to find someone to lie for them and if the participant could generate fabricated physical evidence.

In their examination of honest alibis, the majority of participants (88%) reported having at least one alibi corroborator. Of those participants, 28% claimed they had multiple alibi corroborators. In both ethnic groups, the motivated alibi corroborators (84.2%) far exceeded unmotivated alibi corroborators (15.8%). While the two groups were very likely to rely on motivated alibi corroborators, they did differ on the relationship held with that person. Hispanic participants were more likely to report a family member as a possible alibi corroborator, while White participants relied on friends.

These findings were replicated in a study by Culhane and colleagues (2013) again using students from two distinct regions of the United States. Again, students in a predominately Hispanic region were more likely to rely on family members as alibi corroborators and students in a predominately White, non-Hispanic region were more likely to rely on friends. Still, both groups were using motivated individuals as alibi corroborators. Kienzle and Levett (2018) have argued that friends are much more probable to serve as corroborators than are strangers, but their motivations are more likely to be called into question. The two studies by Culhane and his colleagues (2008, 2013) do lead to questions about the average age and lifestyle of the participants. College students lead very different social lives than do older adults or those in different life stages/environments. The increased reliance on family would only seem to expand as one ages. Furthermore, the types of witnesses expand to categories and characteristics not generally seen in college samples (e.g., young children as alibis; Fawcett & Winstanley, 2018; see Chap. 7 for this discussion).

The statements made by participants in Culhane et al. (2013) were also consistent. Wholesale changes to the alibi statement were seen in less than 4% of participants. However, consistency does not necessarily translate to accuracy. Leins and Charman (2013), discussed in greater detail below, found that accuracy was quite low for participants when examining their stated whereabouts for a particular time. Strange et al. (2014) found contrary evidence of consistency in alibi statements to that of Culhane et al. (2013). That is, university students in Loftus' study were very much inconsistent; the percentage of participants who were completely consistent in their alibi generation at a 1-week follow-up was less than 50%. This would not have been too concerning without the addition of partially consistent statements also near 50%. Instead, wholesale changes to a variety of features of the alibi statement was seen in one out of five participants. The authors noted that the recall for the action itself was more consistent than the time people were doing it. In fact, the greatest errors in consistency were seen for time, as 44% of participants were inconsistent about the timing of events in their day 1 week later (Strange et al., 2014). With time being such a crucial factor to the alibi statement, this would not bode well for innocent suspects, particularly in combination with what we learn about believability of changed alibi statements in Chap. 4 next.

Types of Physical Evidence

The generation of physical alibi evidence is a mixed bag. In essence, research on the types of physical evidence is going to be outpaced by the technological advances made in society. As technology continues to increase, there is a greater chance of being tracked by one's cellular phone for police surveillance purposes (Curtis et al., 2014; Rothstein, 2012). However, the same technology could be recreated to support an innocent individual's alibi statement. For example, research has utilized the global positioning system (GPS) capabilities in cellular telephones to monitor the whereabouts and societal exposures of adolescents (Byrnes et al., 2015). It is important to note that these are active or purposeful tracking systems. The historical data sent by cellular phones takes more effort to collect, but the amount of data collected by smartphones and their apps is dizzying (Thompson & Warzel, 2019). "Anything from weather apps to local news apps to coupon savers" have code and location tracking software (Thompson & Warzel, 2019, np). This largely unknown system of data captured by the technology industry could actually serve to assist a suspect's physical alibi evidence. The downside is the sheer mountain of roadblocks one would need to navigate to obtain such information.

The increased reliance on technology for transactions has also changed the landscape of physical evidence. With mobile pay, banking apps, and QR Codes there has been a substantial reduction in the use of paper receipts, ticket stubs, credit card transactions, etc. The logs of these purchases may be more accessible to suspects, than trying to find a single piece of paper. In their paper, Culhane et al. (2008) asked students about what physical evidence could be generated for their honest alibi statements. Most of the reported evidence would fall in Olson and Wells' easy-to-fabricate category, with receipts resulting in the largest count. A decade later, a mobile pay receipt from the same store could possibly be seen as difficult to fabricate. This changing landscape of physical evidence warrants further investigation.

Generation of False Alibi Statements

The generation of false alibi statements has been examined in a limited number of studies. In the law, a fabricated or manufactured alibi is sometimes referred to as a "hip pocket" defense (Fedeli, 1970). The research thus far has shown a consistent message: the true and false alibi corroborator often have the same relationship to the suspect. The data reported by Culhane et al. (2013) show a nearly mirror image for the generation of a corroborator when comparing true and false alibis. The minimal differences were seen with friends serving as corroborators, as participants were slightly more apt to call upon a friend as a false alibi corroborator. In that study, the researchers concluded that "it may be difficult to distinguish between honest and false alibi claims when considering the type of alibi provided" (Culhane et al., 2013, p. 626).

There were two notable findings of the comparison for true and false statements in Culhane et al. (2013). First, falsely generated alibi statements had significantly more changes made to the alibi statement when the participant returned with their "evidence" of a supported alibi. Second, the false alibi statements were more "long winded" than truthful statements. The participant had put more effort into spinning the story of a false alibi than the truth tellers. These findings supported the anecdotal expectations of a practicing trial attorney from almost 100 years ago by Cornelius (1929; see Chap. 8). Furthermore, trial attorneys may not be the only ones to discriminate between truth tellers and liars. While, Cardenas et al. (Chap. 9 of this text) go into more detail about detection of true and false alibis, it is important to note that police who wish to verify an honest alibi may have some clues. Nahari and Vrij (2014) found high degrees of success in classifying those who were truthful and those who were lying. This is a two-way street though, as a truth teller is vulnerable without verifiable details to support their alibi.

Nieuwkamp et al. (2018) recently replicated the research of Culhane et al. (2013) with "more representative participants" (p. 902). The subjects in this replication and expansion paper were recently arrested male suspects. These individuals are also more ecologically valid as participants with a vested interest in the criminal justice system. When generating true and false alibi statements, truth tellers and liars reported alibis in a very similar fashion. At 40.8% of the sample, the top alibi for both groups was "At home." This was equally divided between both the true and false groups (see Table 1 in Nieuwkamp et al., 2018). The next most common statements involved motivated alibi corroborators for truth tellers. Forty percent of the truth tellers were "in a bar with friends," "with family," or "with friends," respectively. Liars were very similar as 33% of them were "with friends," "with partner," "with family," and "in a bar with friends."

The vast majority of participants in both groups said they could support their alibi statement. There was no difference for whether the suspects would rely on person evidence only, physical evidence only, or a combination of the two for liars or truth tellers. However, their small sample size may have accounted for a nonsignificant finding for the differences in ability to produce viable physical evidence. Truth tellers reported physical evidence at a rate of 62.5%, but only 37.5% of liars were able to do so. Additionally, an examination of their data (Nieuwkamp et al.'s Table 2) does suggest that 75% of liars' physical evidence would fit in the easy-to-fabricate category.

Not only are false alibis generated, but they are also corroborated. In a sample of students, the strongest support for a possible corroborator's willingness to lie is seen in biologically related samples (Hosch et al., 2011). This was followed by affinal relationships and social relationships, respectively. Even when the person is not familiar to the suspect, Marion and Burke (2013) found that nearly one in four students corroborated a false alibi for a confederate of the study. Participants in this study were given the opportunity to build upon a friendship with the confederate or not. In both instances, a subset of participants corroborated a falsely generated alibi statement. There was no significant difference between the groups (termed "friendship-enhancing (FE)" or "stranger-maintaining (SM)") for the corroboration of a false alibi statement. There was an important reduction, albeit not an elimination, of false alibi corroboration when evidence of the mock crime was presented to the participants. Still, the researchers were surprised by the finding of how often alibi corroborators were willing to lie, *and* that their data exceeded previous estimates of how often participants reported they would allegedly lie for strangers (Hosch et al., 2011).

Research is mixed with respect to which group, liars or truth tellers, have higher motivations to be believed, although given the stakes in real world situations, both groups should be highly motivated to be believed. In a Norwegian sample, research suggests that false alibi providers have a significantly higher motivation to be believed (Sakrisvold et al., 2017). Sakrisvold and colleagues did not find that long windedness was indicative of liars or truth tellers by traditional statistical significance cutoff values. They did find that lying pairs of participants had more consistency than truth tellers and that there was an interaction such that truth tellers were even less consistent when considering the level of attention paid to the smallest of details.

Contrary to Sakrisvold and colleagues, research with a sample of English university students found innocent participants were more motivated to appear innocent than guilty ones (Dhammaperra et al., 2020). Furthermore, the lying participants can become so wrapped up in their creation of a false alibi, that it could implant a new autobiographical memory for the event, making them seem just as convincing as a truth teller. Dhammaperra and colleagues found this to be true even when attempting to test those providing false alibis using the autobiographical implicit association test (aIAT; Sartori et al., 2008). The innocent participants rated their memories for the task as less vivid than the guilty condition participants. Dhammaperra et al. found that when participants were given an opportunity to spend time thinking up a false alibi, the aIAT could not distinguish between the true and false alibi providers.

The research on false alibi generation does not bode well for the innocent. Intuitively, an evaluator should expect the innocent to be consistent and liars to be caught via the details of the story. However, neither the findings of consistency nor the findings of depth in one's story actually fit those anecdotal expectations.

The Schemas of Alibi Generation

Crozier and colleagues' (2017) aforementioned explanation of alibi generation leaves a multitude of follow-up logistical questions for the real-world application of a criminal suspect's memory of events. Under what circumstances would an innocent person richly encode the memories surrounding a random night in their life (Olson & Charman, 2012)? Is the default response a generalization of what someone typically does on a Tuesday (aka a script or schema: Crozier et al., 2017)? The idea of schemas as an autobiographical memory crutch for alibis has received attention by many researchers (Burke et al., 2007; Crozier et al., 2017; Leins & Charman, 2013). While usual activities and days may capture the majority of what actually occurred for an alibi statement, many important nuances can be lost or even wrong. Leins and Charman (2013) found that alibi generation can be hampered by schema reliance. More specifically, when participants were cued for a time factor, their accuracy was very low, much lower than when questioned about being in a certain location. Therefore, the question "Where were you at 9:00?" results in the lowest of accuracy and may actually hurt the suspect's chances of a correct alibi statement. The authors also found confidence to not be a robust predictor of accuracy as is often believed by law enforcement and other triers of fact, similar to other psycho-legal findings (e.g., eyewitnesses). For a further discussion on the erroneous link between confidence and accuracy, see Chap. 4.

Charman et al. (2019) identify schema-based responding as a hindrance for alibi generation. In their attempt to identify theoretical underpinnings for the alibi generation, an "overreliance on schema-based responding" was noted as an obstacle to the innocent suspect's alibi generation (p. 49). The authors subsequently proposed a new theory for alibi generation in the innocent: *The Schema Disconfirmation Model*, discussed in detail in Chap. 5.

A person's schema for what they "remember" can interfere with the actual details of the time in question. For example, as many studies have used college students as subjects, a question of "Where were you at noon on Monday?" could elicit a response based on the likelihood that the student was in a university class at the time. The autobiographical memory interference comes in the way of a regular event or expectation of what one was doing such as, "Well, I have class from 12-12:50 on Mondays, Wednesdays, and Fridays, so I must have been in class." Suddenly, the reported alibi is based on what the suspect was *likely* doing and not based on an actual retrieved memory for the day and time in question. The student in this case has nearly 4 months of Monday "memories" in this case for noon. Without an expansion on this, what the authors note as "memories that disconfirm schema," there are two possibilities in the generation of an alibi: reporting a schema or failing to report an alibi (p. 53; see Fig. 1 in Charman et al., 2019). Under the model proposed, suspects should engage in a memory search regardless, often with an eye toward disconfirming their schema, as opposed to a search for confirmation. This could be explored in future research, considering other stages of life and consistent versus varied schedules (e.g., 9–5 workers, temporary workers, or those with inconsistent daily schedules).

Charman and colleagues note that there is an opportunity for self-reflection of one's autobiographical memories while also using schema. In their example, a student might have typically been in class during a specific time, but there are other academic calendar issues. Their example notes a Spring Break day, thus taking the suspect out of the classroom and into a further dive of their memories, *or* a newly developed schema ("When I'm not at school, I do XYZ usually"). In order to break through the schema reliance and prevent the use of schema as an alibi or fail to report an alibi, a person must be able to access memories that disconfirm the schema. When such a process takes place, multiple possibilities exist.

A core component in the model is the person's belief criterion. Charman et al. define belief criterion as "the minimum judged probability that the event occurred that is required before reporting the event as having occurred" (p. 54). This component has two possible outcomes when an individual is evaluating the schema for disconfirmation. If the person cannot generate memories to disconfirm the schema *and* the likelihood of the schema is deemed accurate beyond the belief criterion, then the suspect will report their schema as an alibi. However, if the belief criterion surpasses the likelihood of the schema, the person will fail to provide an alibi. Charman et al. (2019) noted that schemas are often reported as alibis when the schemas tend to be what the suspect generally does at that time and the belief criterion threshold is low.

The actual accessing and reporting of memory must surpass a memory criterion, or "the minimum assessed likelihood that a memory is correct before the person is willing to report it as a memory" (Charman et al., 2019, p. 53). This can happen at the initial stage of memory generation (before a schema is developed) or after disconfirming information has triggered a memory. In the former, the memory must surpass the memory criterion to prevent schema from being accessed and instead report the memory as an alibi. In the latter (post-schema disinformation), the memory must also surpass the memory criterion to be reported as an alibi; otherwise, it would be a failure to report. The Schema Disconfirmation Model shows promise as a theoretical underpinning to alibi generation, and future generation projects should take such considerations under advisement.

The Courts and Generation of Alibis

An area often overlooked by psychology and law in alibi research is the law (see the discussion in Chap. 8). Both the United States and Canadian courts have wrestled with the alibi generation issue, particularly the need to report an alibi statement to the authorities in order to use it as a defense. In the case of Williams v. Florida (1970), the United States Supreme Court upheld a criminal procedure rule by the State of Florida requiring defendants to disclose alibi corroborators' names to the prosecution prior to trial. Florida was not alone in their establishment of such a requirement (Fayette, 2009). For decades, other states had statutes dictating not only the required notice to the prosecuting attorney that an alibi defense will be used, but also restricting the number of days the defendant had to provide such notice (Millar, 1934).

Today, the United States Federal Government requires upon written demand the right to discover a defendant's alibi and alibi corroborators (Federal Rules Crim P. 12.1; Irish, 1984) and state or local prosecution will often include an alibi demand as part of the pretrial packets. Failure to notify the prosecution in criminal cases (at both the Federal and State level) can result in the exclusion of alibi corroborators. At the Federal level, the defense has 10 days to disclose "the specific place or places at which [he] claims to have been at the time of the alleged offense and the names and addresses of the witnesses upon who[m] he intends to rely to establish such alibi" (Federal Rules Crim P. 12.1 630).

The Courts of Canada are different with respect to their procedures and alibi notifications. Craig (1996) has argued that the Canadian alibi rules could not coexist with a Canadian citizen's constitutionally protected right to remain silent (see R. v. Cleghorn, 1995). It is important to note that scholars (e.g., Burchill, 2018) have deemed the Canadian system to be more flexible with the time of disclosure. However, waiting too long to disclose the alibi may lead to judicial instructions diminishing the importance of the alibi (Burchill, 2018).

The advanced notice requirement puts the defense in an awkward position. The alibi must be accurate or the information could be utilized against the defendant during trial, as the prosecution can call rebuttal witnesses to refute the alibi statement. While alibi errors do occur, people may be slow to accept this fact similar to the errors made in the eyewitness literature (Crozier et al., 2017). The defense lawyers need to spend time and energy insuring a complete and detailed alibi evidence statement is presented (Burchill, 2018). The criminal justice system punishes mistakes in alibi statements, even those that potentially improve the motivation of the alibi corroborator (e.g., Motivated to Unmotivated; Culhane & Hosch, 2012). Thus, the error of incorrectly identifying where you were and whom you were with can be costly.

The United States Federal Court of Appeals have gone so far as to recommend that trial judges not use the word "alibi" in their instructions to the jury, as it would require a definition and subsequent instruction (US Court of Appeals 7th Circuit, 1998). The recommended language, if used at all,[1] in jury instructions is "You have heard evidence that the defendant was not present at the time and place where the offense charged in the indictment is said to have been committed. The government must prove beyond a reasonable doubt the defendant's presence at the time and place of the offense" (p. 82).[2]

Conclusion

Under the calmest of circumstances, the generation of autobiographical information is problematic in many respects. Under the pressure and scrutiny of a police interview or interrogation, the problems would only seem to be exacerbated. It is genuinely amazing that "weak alibi" or "no alibi" is not listed as a contributing factor of conviction for 99% of Innocence Project and other organization's exonerees.

The autobiographical memories of an alibi statement are fraught with problems. The memory for your average day is not cataloged sufficiently to account for what you were doing at a given time without a memorable occurrence (Strange et al., 2014). Is it the case that a suspect would consider themselves lucky that the crime occurred on the same date a monumental occasion happened to them, including committing other crimes, or so-called salacious alibis (Allison et al., 2013)? Are there penalties for the improper retrieval of these memories, only to have self-corrected them on one's own (Culhane & Hosch, 2012)? The answers to these and

[1] In the comments section of the recommendations for alibi instructions the higher court actually suggests that it is "appealing" to give no instruction on the topic at all.

[2] In some cases, the courts have noted that an additional line is part of standard instructions "If, after a full and fair consideration of all the facts and circumstances in evidence, you find that the government has failed to prove beyond a reasonable doubt that the defendant was present at the time when, and the place where, the offense charged was allegedly committed, you must find the defendant not guilty" (U.S. v. Cicero, 1994).

many other questions will take time and substantially more research but may provide much needed understanding for how alibis work (and do not work) in our current system of justice.

The criminal justice system (i.e., police, prosecutors, judges, and juries) is simply not equipped to overlook their biases of change or errors as an indicator of lying or guilt (Culhane & Hosch, 2012). Without substantial recognition of alibi generation research by the actors of the system, suspects and defendants like Mr. Rosario and Mr. Arnold are actually the lucky ones when it comes to an alibi. How many innocent defendants were convicted because they were home alone and could not accurately account for what TV show was on, or what book they were reading?

As the literature focusing on alibis nears two decades of a substantially increased pace, this author agrees with the sentiments of Charman et al. (2019). There is a "paucity of alibi generation research" (p. 56). In fact, there remains a paucity of alibi research entirely. It is mind boggling how one of the most fundamental aspects of criminal investigation was ignored for so many decades of legal psychological research. For a century, the criminal trial courts have criticized alibi defense and dubbed it a means of escape for guilty parties (Irish, 1984). It is time to accelerate the work done in this field at a pace that far exceeds the previous publication rate, but it is also time to focus attention on educating the practitioners of the criminal justice system.

References

Allison, M., Jung, S., Sweeney, L., & Culhane, S. E. (2013). The impact of illegal alibi activities, corroborator involvement and corroborator certainty on mock juror perceptions. *Psychiatry, Psychology, and Law, 21*(2), 191–204. https://doi.org/10.1080/13218719.2013.803275

Brest, M. (2021, March 13). *Man sues Hertz over lost receipt that overturned his murder conviction after five years in prison*. Washington Examiner. Retrieved 4 July 2021 from https://www.washingtonexaminer.com/news/man-sues-hertz-wrongful-conviction-michigan

Burchill, J. W. (2018). Alibi evidence: Responsibility for disclosure and investigation. *Manitoba Law Journal, 41*(3), 99–126. CanLIIDocs 202. https://canlii.ca/t/2btn

Burke, T. M., Turtle, J. W., & Olson, E. A. (2007). Alibis in criminal investigations and trials. In M. P. Toglia, J. D. Read, D. F. Ross, & R. C. L. Lindsay (Eds.), *The handbook of eyewitness psychology* (*Memory for events*) (Vol. 1, pp. 157–174). Lawrence Erlbaum Associates Publishers.

Byrnes, H. F., Miller, B. A., Wiebe, D. J., Morrison, C. N., Remer, L. G., & Wiehe, S. E. (2015). Tracking adolescents with global positioning system-enabled cell phones to study contextual exposures and alcohol and marijuana use: A pilot study. *Journal of Adolescent Health, 57*, 245–247. https://doi.org/10.1016/j.jadohealth.2015.04.013

Charman, S. D., Matuku, K., & Mosser, A. (2019). The psychology of alibis. In B. H. Bornstein & M. K. Miller (Eds.), *Advances in psychology and law* (Vol. 4, pp. 41–72). Springer.

Charman, S. D., Reyes, A., Villalba, D. K., & Evans, J. R. (2017). The (un)reliability of alibi corroborators: Failure to recognize races of briefly encountered strangers puts innocent suspects at risk. *Behavioral Sciences & the Law, 35*, 18–36. https://doi.org/10.1002/bsl.2264

Cornelius, A. L. (1929). *The cross-examination of witnesses: Rules, principles, and illustrations*. The Bobbs-Merrill Company.

Craig, J. D. R. (1996). The alibi exception to the right to silence. *Criminal Law Quarterly, 39*(2), 227–249.
Crozier, W. E., Strange, D., & Loftus, E. F. (2017). Memory errors in alibi generation: How an alibi can turn against us. *Behavioral Sciences & the Law, 35*(1), 6–17. https://doi.org/10.1002/bsl.2273
Culhane, S. E., & Hosch, H. M. (2004). An alibi witness's influence on juror's decision making. *Journal of Applied Social Psychology, 34*, 1604–1616. https://doi.org/10.1111/j.1559-1816.2004.tb02789.x
Culhane, S. E., & Hosch, H. M. (2012). Changed alibis: Current law enforcement, future law enforcement, and layperson reactions. *Criminal Justice and Behavior, 39*(7), 958–977. https://doi.org/10.1177/0093854812438185
Culhane, S. E., Hosch, H. M., & Kehn, A. (2008). Alibi generation: Data from U.S. Hispanics and U.S. non-Hispanic Whites. *Journal of Ethnicity in Criminal Justice, 6*(3), 177–199. https://doi.org/10.1080/15377930802243395
Culhane, S. E., Kehn, A., Horgan, A. J., Meissner, C. A., Hosch, H. M., & Wodahl, E. J. (2013). Generation and detection of true and false alibi statements. *Psychiatry, Psychology and Law, 20*, 619–638. https://doi.org/10.1080/13218719.2012.729018
Curtis, R. C., Gizzi, M. C., & Kittleson, M. J. (2014). Using technology the founders never dreamed of: Cell phones as tracking devices and the Fourth Amendment. *University of Denver Criminal Law Review, 4*, 61–102. https://digitalcommons.du.edu/crimlawrev/vol4/iss1/3/
Dhammaperra, P., Hu, X., & Bergström, Z. M. (2020). Imagining a false alibi impairs concealed memory detection with the Autobiographical Implicit Association Test. *Journal of Experimental Psychology: Applied, 26*, 266–282. https://doi.org/10.1037/xap0000250
Fawcett, H., & Winstanley, K. (2018). Children as alibi witnesses: The effect of age and confidence on mock-juror decision making. *Psychiatry, Psychology and Law, 25*(6), 957–971. https://doi.org/10.1080/13218719.2018.1482573
Fayette, J. (2009). "The judge said, 'son, what is your alibi…?'" A survey of Alaska criminal discovery principles. *Alaska Law Review, 26*(1), 47–96.
Fedeli, N. C., Jr. (1970). The alibi witness rule: Sewing up the hip pocket defense. *Santa Clara Law Review, 11*(1), 155–168. http://digitalcommons.law.scu.edu/lawreview/vol11/iss1/1C
Gooderson, R. (1977). *Alibi*. Heinemann Educational Books Ltd..
Hosch, H. M., Culhane, S. E., Jolly, K. W., Chavez, R. M., & Shaw, L. H. (2011). Effects of an alibi witness's relationship to the defendant on mock jurors' judgments. *Law and Human Behavior, 35*(2), 127–142. https://doi-org.ezproxy.lib.apsu.edu/10.1007/s10979-010-9225-5
Irish, L. A. (1984). Alibi notice rules: The preclusion sanction as procedural default. *The University of Chicago Law Review, 51*(1), 254–285. https://www.jstor.org/stable/1599607?seq=1
Kienzle, M. R., & Levett, L. M. (2018). A novel paradigm for examining alibi corroboration and evidence interaction: Does a confession affect the likelihood of alibi corroboration for friends and strangers? *Psychology, Public Policy, and Law, 24*(3), 353–364. https://doi.org/10.1037/law0000173
Leins, D. A., & Charman, S. D. (2013). Schema reliance and innocent alibi generation. *Legal and Criminological Psychology, 21*(1), 111–126. https://doi.org/10.1111/lcrp.12035
Marion, S. B., & Burke, T. M. (2013). False alibi corroboration: Witnesses lie for suspects who seem innocent, whether they like them or not. *Law and Human Behavior, 37*(2), 136–143. https://doi-org.ezproxy.lib.apsu.edu/10.1037/lhb0000021
Millar, R. (1934). Statutory notice of alibi. *The Journal of the American Institute of Criminal Law and Criminology, 24*(5), 849–859.
Morales-Hurtado v. Reinoso (2020). 241 N.J. 590.
Nahari, G., & Vrij, A. (2014). Can I borrow your alibi? The applicability of the verifiability approach to the case of an alibi witness. *Journal of Applied Research in Memory and Cognition, 3*(2), 89–94. https://doi-org.ezproxy.lib.apsu.edu/10.1016/j.jarmac.2014.04.005

Nieuwkamp, R., Horselenberg, R., & van Koppen, P. (2018). True and false alibis among prisoners and their detection by police detectives. *Psychiatry, Psychology and Law, 25*(6), 902–921. https://doi.org/10.1080/13218719.2018.1482570

Olson, E. A., & Charman, S. D. (2012). 'But can you prove it?'—Examining the quality of innocent suspects' alibis. *Psychology, Crime & Law, 18*(5), 453–471. https://doi.org/10.1080/1068316X.2010.505567

Olson, E. A., & Wells, G. L. (2004). What makes a good alibi? A proposed taxonomy. *Law and Human Behavior, 28*(2), 157–176. https://doi-org.ezproxy.lib.apsu.edu/10.1023/B:LAHU.0000022320.47112.d3

Possley, M. (2021, March 10). *Herbert Alford.* The National Registry of Exonerations. https://www.law.umich.edu/special/exoneration/Pages/casedetail.aspx?caseid=5904

R. v. Cleghorn (1995). 3 S.C.R. 175.

Rappleye, H. (2021, March 21). Is Temujin Kensu a 'ninja killer' or wrongfully convicted man? *NBC News.* Retrieved 4 July 2021 from https://www.nbcnews.com/news/all/temujin-kensu-ninja-killer-or-wrongfully-convicted-man-n1260983

Rivas, A. (2021, March 15). Man suing Hertz over receipt corroborating murder alibi says being innocent and imprisoned was 'surreal'. *ABC News.* https://abcnews.go.com/US/man-suing-hertz-receipt-corroborating-murder-alibi-innocent/story?id=76476841

Rosario v. City of New York (2019). 18 Civ. 4023 (LGS) (S.D.N.Y.).

Rothstein, J. H. (2012). Track me maybe: The Fourth Amendment and the use of cell phone tracking to facilitate arrest. *Fordham Law Review, 81*, 489–535. Available at: https://ir.lawnet.fordham.edu/flr/vol81/iss1/9

Sakrisvold, M. L., Granhag, P. A., & Giolla, E. M. (2017). Partners under pressure: Examining the consistency of true and false alibi statements. *Behavioral Sciences & the Law, 35*, 75–90. https://doi.org/10.1002/bsl.2275

Sartori, G., Agosta, S., Zogmaister, C., Ferrara, S. D., & Castiello, U. (2008). How to accurately detect autobiographical events. *Psychological Science, 19*, 772–780. https://doi.org/10.1111/j.1467-9280.2008.02156.x

Sauerland, M. (2017). Alibis: Generation, consistency, corroboration, believability, and detection – Introduction to this special issue. *Behavioral Sciences & the Law, 35*, 3–5. https://doi.org/10.1002/bsl.2289

Slepian, D. (2019, May 17). A reporter's notebook: I have yet to investigate a case that astounds me more than '13 Alibis'. *NBC News.* https://www.nbcnews.com/dateline/reporter-s-notebook-i-have-yet-investigate-case-astounds-me-n1006986

Steele, L. J. (2020). Investigating and presenting an alibi defense. *Criminal Law Bulletin, 56*, 1–43. https://doi.org/10.2139/ssrn.3572102.

Strange, D., Dysart, J., & Loftus, E. F. (2014). Why errors in alibis are not necessarily evidence of guilt. *Zeitschrift für Psychologie, 222*, 82–89. https://doi.org/10.1027/2151-2604/a000169

Sullivan, T. P. (1971). Presentation of the defense. *The Journal of Criminal Law, Criminology, and Police Science, 62*, 153–172.

Thompson, S. A. & Warzel, C. (2019, December 19). Twelve million phones, one dataset, zero privacy. *New York Times.* https://www.nytimes.com/interactive/2019/12/19/opinion/location-tracking-cell-phone.html

US Court of Appeals 7th Circuit (1998). Pattern criminal federal jury instructions for the Seventh Circuit. http://www.ca7.uscourts.gov/pjury.pdf

U.S. v. Cicero (1994). 22 F.3d 1156 (D.C. Cir.).

Wells, G. L., Small, M., Penrod, S., Malpass, R. S., Fulero, S. M., & Brimacombe, C. A. E. (1998). Eyewitness identification procedures: Recommendations for lineups and photospreads. *Law and Human Behavior, 22*, 603–647. https://doi.org/10.1023/A:1025750605807

Williams v. Florida (1970). 399 U.S. 78.

Chapter 4
Alibi Believability

Meredith Allison

Ronald Cotton was a suspect in two rape cases in Burlington, North Carolina, in 1984 (Thompson-Cannino et al., 2009). Cotton heard that the police were investigating him and went to the police station to "clear everything up." The officers asked about his whereabouts for Saturday night, July 28th, several days earlier. Cotton wrote in 2009 that as a 22-year-old he did not pay particular attention to which days were which. He answered that he was with his brother and then with friends at their house, and eventually he went to a bar. He stated that he had received a ride home from a friend at 2:30 in the morning. The police informed Mr. Cotton that they had evidence against him (foam found at the scene that seemed to match his shoes, a flashlight similar to the one the perpetrator used, one victim had identified him in a photo lineup). Cotton was taken to the county jail where he phoned his mother. She told him he had mixed up the weekends and was in fact at home, asleep on her couch, on the night in question (Thompson-Cannino et al., 2009). Two trials led to Mr. Cotton serving 10 years in prison. He was exonerated in 1995 when DNA evidence showed that he had not committed the crime.

There was a confluence of factors that led to Mr. Cotton's wrongful conviction, including eyewitness error and racism on the part of some of the officers. But Mr. Cotton's alibi was not believed when it should have been. This chapter will focus on research on the believability of alibis. Alibis are judged by several triers-of-fact: law enforcement, attorneys, judges, and jurors. These individuals' assessments of alibis can lead to positive views of the suspect or defendant and can potentially be exonerating (Burke et al., 2007). However, if these assessments are negative, then there is the potential for conviction. One major contributing factor when it comes to alibi believability is the strength of the alibi evidence, whether it is physical evidence like video footage or person evidence like the testimony of alibi corroborators (Olson &

M. Allison (✉)
Elon University, Elon, NC, USA
e-mail: mallison5@elon.edu

J. D. Behl, M. R. Kienzle (eds.), *Alibis and Corroborators*,
https://doi.org/10.1007/978-3-030-95663-9_4

Wells, 2004). This chapter will connect the research back to Ronald Cotton's case, first by analyzing the corroborative evidence he had in support of his alibi and how that might have been perceived. Another significant factor was that Mr. Cotton mixed up the dates and gave the wrong alibi information to officers when first questioned about his whereabouts. Does such inconsistency negatively affect perceptions of alibis and suspects? This chapter will also address multiple contextual factors that can affect alibi believability, like defendant characteristics, the salaciousness of the alibi story, and the type of crime. Finally, this chapter will end with a brief focus on methodological issues and future directions for research in this area.

Alibi Corroborators

The most researched area in the alibi believability domain concerns the alibi corroborator. In particular, researchers have focused on the relationship between the corroborator and defendant or suspect. Some corroborators are closely related to the defendant (relative, romantic partner, or spouse), while others are less closely related (coworker or boss, regular server at a restaurant, stranger). Hosch et al. (2011) reasoned that people are more likely to help close others due to the desire to help others (altruism) or due to shared genes (when confirming an alibi for a relative). For example, people are most likely to want to help close biological relatives, then relatives through marriage, then nonkin (Hosch et al., 2011). In many contexts, helping others is a good thing, but in the alibi context, helpers may not always be honest. Corroborators who are close to the defendant may be motivated to lie about the alibi because they wish to keep their close friend or relative out of trouble.

Mock jurors are skeptical of alibis provided by close relatives and friends. Research has shown this consistently: alibi believability ratings are lower when the alibi was corroborated by a relative versus a nonrelative (e.g., Allison et al., 2012; Hosch et al., 2011; Lindsay et al., 1986; Eastwood et al., 2016, 2020). Corroborators themselves are seen as less reliable when they are more motivated to lie (girlfriend versus neighbor, Fawcett, 2016). This skepticism has also affected guilt ratings and verdicts. Alibis corroborated by nonmotivated people like a stranger or store clerk lead to better outcomes for defendants in terms of verdicts (e.g., Culhane & Hosch, 2004; Lindsay et al., 1986; Pozzulo et al., 2012). Having an alibi corroborator helps defendants when compared to having no alibi corroborator at all, but often only when that corroborator is nonmotivated (Hosch et al., 2011; Olson & Wells, 2004; Pozzulo et al., 2012). That is, in some contexts, it may be better to have no alibi witness at all than to have a close relative (mother, spouse) support the alibi.

Mock jurors are not the only group of participants that are skeptical of some types of alibi corroborators. Studies wherein participants acted as mock police investigators have similarly found that alibis corroborated by motivated people are viewed negatively (e.g., Bruer et al., 2017; Dahl & Price, 2012; Dahl et al., 2009; Olson & Wells, 2004; Snow & Eastwood, 2020). For example, mock officers have viewed alibis provided by a brother as less credible than alibis provided by a coworker (Dahl et al., 2009). They were also more likely to decide to arrest the suspect when the alibi was provided by the brother rather than the neighbor (Dahl et al., 2009). Olson and Wells (2004) noted that alibis supported by nonmotivated corroborators had higher believability ratings compared to motivated corroborators (recall the discussion in Chap. 2). But they were surprised to find that alibis corroborated by strangers were more believable than alibis corroborated by nonmotivated but familiar others (like regular server in a restaurant). They had hypothesized that participants would doubt the ability of strangers to identify someone they did not know well, while a regular server would be able to identify someone they had seen multiple times before. However, it seems that participants may have cared less about the ability to identify the suspect and instead cared more about the relationship between the corroborator and the suspect (with strangers being less motivated than a regular server in a restaurant).

Police officers similarly are skeptical of corroborators who are relatives or close friends of the suspect. For example, in Eastwood et al. (2016), police officers' decisions about alibis were affected by the relationship between the suspect and the corroborator. In that study, students, law enforcement students, and police officers evaluated 32 alibis for 32 armed robberies. The alibis were statements from corroborators, and these statements varied in terms of the degree of relationship between the corroborator and the suspect (family member or stranger), the age of the corroborator (child or adult), the number of corroborators (1 or several), the corroborator's confidence (low or high), and salience (mundane or unique, such as a funeral or wedding). After reading each statement, the participants rated the alibi's believability and the likelihood that the suspect was guilty. They then completed an open-ended question where they described how they made these decisions. An analysis of the police officers' decision-making showed that the number of corroborators was the strongest predictor of police officer decision-making, with the corroborator relationship to the defendant as the second strongest predictor. The police officers rated alibis involving more corroborators and those that were from nonmotivated corroborators as the most believable. Similarly, Dysart and Strange's (2012) survey of law enforcement found that acquaintances and strangers are the most believable corroborators, while relatives, romantic partners, and friends are least believable.

Other corroborator characteristics have also been found to affect views of the suspect/defendant and alibi. The age of the corroborator affects participant views and is discussed in Chap. 7. In several studies, child corroborators were viewed more positively compared to adult corroborators (e.g., Bruer et al., 2017; Dahl & Price, 2012; Fawcett & Winstanley, 2019; Snow & Eastwood, 2020). However, in one study, both undergraduates and law enforcement students found alibis corroborated by adults to be more believable than alibis corroborated by children (Eastwood et al., 2016). Another corroborator characteristic that affects participant views is confidence and credibility (see Chap. 3). Not surprisingly, corroborators who were more confident were viewed more positively (Allison et al., 2012, 2014; Fawcett & Winstanley, 2019).

The number of corroborators may matter when it comes to believability (Allison et al., 2020; Eastwood et al., 2020). Dysart and Strange (2012) asked police officers to describe a believable alibi. The authors found that 18% of participants described that having statements from multiple corroborators would make an alibi believable (and this answer was second to 63.9% who mentioned physical evidence). Eastwood et al.'s (2016) policy-capturing study described above similarly found that the number of corroborators mattered when it came to alibi believability. Eastwood et al. (2020) also noted that alibis that were corroborated by 7 or 14 people were more believable than alibis corroborated by 1 person. Allison et al. (2020) did not find that the number of corroborators affected alibi believability but having 2 corroborators (versus 1) led to higher defendant intelligence and likeability ratings. Given that there are only four studies addressing the impact of the number of corroborators, more research is needed. Ronald Cotton's case as described earlier included multiple corroborators, albeit they were all friends and family members. Clearly, having many corroborators does not always lead to positive views.

While the extant research clearly shows people's reluctance to believe close friends and relatives when it comes to alibi corroboration, the fact is that people spend most of their time with friends and family or are alone. Indeed, Dysart and Strange's (2012) law enforcement participants confirmed that most suspects they had dealt with had friends, family members, and romantic partners as corroborators. In Mr. Cotton's case, in both of his alibi claims (original mistaken alibi and later, correct alibi), he stated that he was with a combination of his mother, brother, sister, friends, and his mother's boyfriend (Thompson-Cannino et al., 2009). Mr. Cotton was in fact at his mother's house on the night in question and several relatives saw him there. It is perhaps rare for suspects and defendants to have strangers corroborate their alibis as this may be very difficult evidence to gather. For example, store clerks deal with many individuals on a typical day. If asked weeks or months later about a regular customer's presence in the shop on a particular day, it would be very difficult to confirm this unless something unusual happened or if there is physical evidence like a receipt or videotape to provide confirmation.

Physical Alibi Evidence

People can corroborate alibis, but there is also the possibility that suspects may have some kind of physical evidence to support their alibi claim. Corroborative physical evidence can be easy to fabricate, like a receipt, or more difficult to fabricate, like video footage (Olson & Wells, 2004). The officers mentioned before in Dysart and Strange's (2012) study were asked to provide examples of physical evidence that would be difficult to fabricate. Participants stated that jail/prison records would be the hardest to fabricate, followed by video (especially if the suspect had no control over the video), a time card from work, cell phone records, and so on.

Participants from several other studies that did not include law enforcement have found similar results. Olson and Wells (2004) systematically examined perceptions of alibis that varied according to physical evidence (none, receipt, or video) and person evidence (motivated and familiar corroborator like mother, nonmotivated familiar corroborator like a regular server, and stranger corroborator like a store clerk). They found that alibi believability was strongly affected by physical evidence, with higher believability ratings when there was a receipt or video footage versus when there was no physical evidence. Physical evidence also affected guilt ratings in the predicted direction (lower guilt ratings when there was a receipt or video compared to no physical evidence). The authors noted that physical evidence overwhelmed person evidence – when physical evidence was present, it was much more important to believability and guilt than person evidence. Thus, having any kind of physical evidence, even if it is easy to fabricate, helps boost alibi believability ratings and lowers guilt ratings.

More recently, another study similarly found that an alibi that lacked physical evidence was seen as less believable than an alibi that was corroborated by a receipt and that in turn was less believable than an alibi corroborated by video (Allison et al., 2020). Positive views of the alibi spread to positive views of the defendant's character, as they were seen as more intelligent, honest, etc., when they had videotaped alibi evidence than when they did not. Participants were also more certain of their verdicts when the defendant had either kind of physical evidence. Other studies have found that guilt ratings are also affected by the quality of the physical alibi evidence (e.g., Jung et al., 2013; Pozzulo et al., 2015; Sargent & Bradfield, 2004). These studies found that having physical evidence like a receipt or movie ticket (Jung et al., 2013; Pozzulo et al., 2015) or video (Sargent & Bradfield, 2004) led to fewer guilty verdicts.

Although physical evidence is very powerful when it comes to evaluating alibis, its use as corroborative evidence by suspects and defendants is rare (Burke & Turtle, 2003). As mentioned earlier, law enforcement officers noted that most alibis are supported by people (Dysart & Strange, 2012). Alibi generation studies similarly have shown that participants have trouble finding corroborative physical evidence (e.g., Olson & Charman, 2012; Strange et al., 2014). Thus, it is perhaps not surprising that Ronald Cotton's alibi relied solely on alibi corroborators; he did not have any physical evidence to support his claims of being at his mother's house on the night of the crimes. In 1984, most people did not have cell phones, and photography and videography were not as readily available as they are today. And even then, law enforcement may be skeptical of at-home video because it could be tampered with. Clearly physical evidence, particularly video from an outside source, is persuasive but difficult to obtain.

Alibi Consistency

While the evidence that supports an alibi affects perceptions of suspects and defendants, another central feature in alibi believability is whether the alibi is consistent across time. A suspect's story of where they were at the time of a crime may change because of a memory mistake as occurred with Ronald Cotton. For example, early in the investigation when first asked about their whereabouts, people may misremember which day they did which activity. But later on, as the investigation continues and they have had the opportunity to check their records and check with corroborators, that story may change due to legitimate memory mistakes. Of course, it is also possible that the alibi story can change over time because of purposeful fabrication where the suspect may be trying to derail the investigation and avoid arrest. Guilty suspects may at first state they were home alone, but when they realize the investigation is narrowing in on them, they may fabricate a legitimate-sounding alibi, like being at the store or out for a walk.

In general, people are skeptical of changes to the alibi (Culhane & Hosch, 2012). For example, police officers were asked why an alibi story might change from its initial telling 1 week earlier (Dysart & Strange, 2012). They found that 81.4% of participants stated that the change was due to the suspect lying. When asked to consider other factors that could lead to the inconsistency, they mentioned alcohol and drug use and the fact that people have poor memories. Experimental research has supported the finding that people are skeptical of changed alibis. Culhane and Hosch's (2012) participants were undergraduates and current or recent law enforcement officers. Participants evaluated several alibis that were either strengthened, weakened, or unchanged. Strengthened alibis moved from a motivated to unmotivated corroborator (best friend to neighbor), no corroborator to motivated corroborator (girlfriend), and no corroborator to unmotivated corroborator (coworker). Weakened alibis moved in the other direction (e.g., unmotivated corroborator to motivated corroborator) and consistent alibis maintained the type of corroborator (consistently no corroborator or neighbor or half-sister). Consistent alibis had higher alibi believability ratings than changed alibis. Interestingly, alibis that were changed and strengthened were viewed with suspicion. The authors' second and third studies confirmed the findings from the first study, but ratings of guilt were also affected in the predicted direction: there were fewer guilty verdicts when the alibi was consistent. Any change, even a seemingly positive change involving a new, less motivated corroborator, did not improve alibi believability.

The skepticism of inconsistent alibi statements was also found in Price and Dahl (2017). In their first study, the alibi corroborator was filmed (supposedly) 1 week after the crime or 5 years later in a mock case. The two videos were either consistent or contained minor or major contradictions. When the videos included major contradictions, guilt ratings and arrest rates were highest compared to most other conditions (Price & Dahl, 2017). The second study similarly showed that consistency led to reduced guilt ratings and arrest rates compared to inconsistency. However, inconsistency does not always lead to negative views. In Nieuwkamp et al. (2016), a suspect claimed to be at work until 9 pm. In some conditions, the police found that he had actually left work at 7:30 pm. In these conditions, the suspect either stated he had made a mistake or stated that he had initially lied. He then stated that he was in fact either with his mistress (salacious alibi) or with his cousin (nonsalacious alibi). Interestingly, when the suspect's alibi was changed from its initial telling because of a lie, it was seen as more believable than when it was due to a memory mistake.

Further, salacious alibis were more believable than nonsalacious alibis when there was inconsistency (Nieuwkamp et al., 2016). Thus, changing the initial work alibi to the salacious alibi involving the mistress helped suspects. Not all alibi change is detrimental to suspects and defendants, and surprisingly, people may be more tolerant of purposeful lies than unintentional mistakes.

How well do people do at discriminating between true and false alibis? Participants who watch videos of other participants giving true or false information about their whereabouts at a particular time are not good and gauging who is actually telling the truth and who is not (Culhane et al., 2013). Most studies show that participants perform close to chance when deciding which alibis are true and which are false (Verigin et al., 2020), even when trained individuals like detectives are the ones evaluating the alibis (Nieuwkamp et al., 2018). These studies confirm what has been found in the detecting deception literature, namely that people tend to believe what others say and so exhibit a truth bias (e.g., Vrij, 2000). Thus, when people tell the truth, evaluators are generally accurate because they tend to believe that the statements are the truth. However, problems arrive when faced with liars because people tend to believe them too, and so accuracy at detecting deception declines (e.g., Strömwall et al., 2003).

One recent study found that its participants were able to detect deception in alibis quite well, performing well above chance (Vernham et al., 2020). In this study, evaluators assessed alibi statements using a verifiability approach. The alibi statements came from pairs of individuals who had either done an activity together and told the truth about it, or had performed it separately and were lying about being together. The participant-evaluators examined statements either from one member of the pair or from both members of the pair. The evaluators were trained to look for checkable and uncheckable details in the alibi statements. Checkable details were statements that could be verified, like when the pair claimed to have run into a friend at the park. Uncheckable details were statements that were not so easily verified, like seeing the leaves fall off the trees in the park. When assessing statements from both members of the pair using the verifiability approach, participants were accurate at identifying truth (82.8%) and lies (75%). However, the authors noted that although participants often used the verifiability approach that aided deception detection, they still relied on nondiagnostic cues like consistency when they had multiple statements to evaluate from the members of the pair (Vernham et al., 2020).

Others have found that lie detectors weigh consistency heavily. In Stromwall et al. (2003), evaluators looked for consistency between two individuals who claimed to be together at the time in question. However, the use of consistency as a gauge to accuracy did not help them as it was not diagnostic of accuracy (Strömwall et al., 2003). That is, both true and false statements can be consistent or inconsistent, again indicating that consistency is not a sign of purposeful deception. Relating back to the Cotton case, alibi change did not help Mr. Cotton. His first telling of his alibi story to investigators at the police station involved a description of a night out with friends. His mother later reminded him that he had been at her house and not with his friends at all. It is likely that this accidental mix up of weekends led to the police being skeptical of his claims. But to a young person with an active social life, it is easy to mix up the dates when questioned in a high-stress environment like a police station. The night in question did not stand out for Mr. Cotton because nothing of particular significance had happened so it was easy to make a mistake (Burke et al., 2007). As shown through several studies, innocent memory mistakes do not seem to be tolerated in the alibi context.

Contextual Factors

Issues of evidence and consistency aside, there are several other factors that alibi researchers have investigated within the alibi context: the incriminating evidence; the order of the presentation of information; the salaciousness of the alibi activities; the timing of the alibi's disclosure; the type of crime; defendant characteristics; and juror motivation.

Incriminating Evidence Alibi evidence is one piece of evidence presented at trial. Although some of the studies presented here have asked participants to evaluate alibis separate from other case information (e.g., Olson & Wells, 2004), many have presented incriminating evidence as well, so that participants must consider the alibi in the face of conflicting evidence. The most studied evidence is that of eyewitness identification. Lindsay et al. (1986) first pitted an alibi corroborator against a victim-witness in a simulated videotaped trial. Having one or two prosecution eyewitnesses led to a lot of guilty votes, but the number of guilty votes dropped dramatically when there was an alibi corroborator for the defense. When there was no identification made and a stranger corroborated the alibi, the number of guilty votes was also low (Lindsay et al., 1986). Culhane and Hosch (2004) similarly found that guilty verdicts were reduced when an eyewitness was not 100% certain that the defendant was the perpetrator versus when the witness was 100% certain.

Some studies have examined the effect of the eyewitness' age and corroborative evidence on mock juror and investigator decisions. Pozzulo et al. (2012) manipulated the eyewitness' age in a mock homicide case. The eyewitness made a positive identification and the defendant either was home alone, with his girlfriend, or at the store. The researchers found that when the nonmotivated store clerk corroborated the alibi and the eyewitness to the crime was 4 years old, guilty votes decreased. Thus, the young child eyewitness was doubted only when faced with strong alibi evidence from a nonmotivated corroborator.

Another study compared alibi witnesses and crime eyewitnesses in a mock investigator context. Participants in Dahl et al. (2009) were presented with testimony from an eyewitness or an alibi witness (corroborator). The corroborator was either a coworker (not motivated to lie) or brother (motivated to lie). While the authors had hypothesized that the participants always would believe an eyewitness over a corroborator, their results showed that their mock investigators' decisions were not affected by the eyewitness more so than by the alibi corroborator when the alibi was provided by a coworker (versus brother). There was some evidence of skepticism regarding alibis, however, in that the alibi providers were generally rated as not particularly credible, and guilt ratings were unaffected when the alibi was corroborated by the brother (Dahl et al., 2009).

Two studies have moved beyond the eyewitness paradigm and included DNA and alibi evidence (Charman et al., 2016; Ribeiro et al., 2020). In Ribeiro et al. (2020), online participants read a case scenario where a homicide occurred. DNA from the victim was either in the process of being analyzed or participants were given information on a likelihood ratio regarding the victim sample and a sample from a suspect. The suspect's alibi was either weak (on a walk) or strong (overseas acting as a groomsman in a friend's wedding, time-stamped photos). Interestingly, when the alibi was strong rather than weak, participants felt the suspect was less likely to be the source of the DNA. They also felt that an error was more likely to have occurred in the DNA analysis when the alibi was stronger rather than weaker. Charman et al. (2016) found that DNA evidence (either exonerating or incriminating) affected guilt ratings when it was presented to officers last rather than first, suggesting that more recent evidence affects decision-making.

Taken together, these studies suggest that mock jurors and investigators may be sensitive to eyewitness and DNA evidence in the alibi context. While more research is needed, these studies show that strong alibi evidence can lead participants to question eyewitness evidence (e.g., young children) and even DNA evidence in some situations. In Ronald Cotton's case, there was very compelling eyewitness evidence against him from Jennifer Thompson, one of the victims. She had identified him in a photo lineup and in a live lineup, and also identified him confidently in open court. As stated, Mr. Cotton's alibi corroborators were comparatively weak being that they were his family members, so it is likely that the strong eyewitness evidence against him could not compete against the alibi evidence. There was no DNA evidence against Mr. Cotton because the technology at the time was not sophisticated, and in fact it was the DNA evidence that eventually exonerated Mr. Cotton.

Investigator Factors Another contextual factor that can affect alibi believability is the order in which investigators received various pieces of evidence. As stated, some researchers have found a recency effect, so that the last piece of evidence seen drives decision-making (Charman et al., 2016; Dahl et al., 2009; Price & Dahl, 2014). When mock investigators viewed both eyewitness and alibi testimony in the study described earlier, investigators lowered the suspect guilt ratings when the alibi was seen last and the alibi was strong (Dahl et al., 2009). Price and Dahl (2014) also found a recency effect in that investigators thought the suspect was less likely to have committed the crime when they saw the alibi video last versus first, but only in the condition in which a child was the alibi corroborator.

Investigator expectations also can affect their views of alibis (Olson, 2013). Participants in Olson's (2013) study were informed they would watch a video. Some were told ahead of the viewing that the video was an alibi, but others only learned this fact after watching it. Further, some were told that the person was innocent and others that he was guilty of the crime. Participants who presumed innocence recalled little alibi information. Participants who presumed guilt before viewing found the alibi to be less believable and thought it was weaker compared to those who presumed innocence. The author suggested that participants shifted into an interrogation perspective when they presumed guilt and remembered less information about the alibi, saw the alibi as less believable, and viewed the suspect more negatively (Olson, 2013). Interestingly, the idea that people are skeptical of alibis in general was not supported. Participants who thought they were viewing an alibi versus those who thought they were viewing a story did not evaluate the alibi any differently. Thus, the term "alibi" alone may not elicit a presumption of guilt as Olson and Wells (2004) had suggested.

Others have examined the timing at which mock jurors learn about the alibi. Participants in Sommers and Douglass (2007) read about an alibi in either a police investigation or trial. Their two studies showed that participants found the alibi to be more believable, stronger, and credible when it was presented in the investigation rather than at trial. More recently, Fawcett (2016) found a few differences in perceptions of alibis when presented in an investigation versus at trial. The alibi corroborator was seen as more reliable when the alibi was disclosed in the investigation rather than at trial. Allison et al. (2020) manipulated whether the alibi was disclosed to the prosecution early (right after the case was set for trial) or late (19 days after the case was set for trial). The timing manipulation did not affect alibi believability ratings, but early alibi disclosure led to higher defendant trustworthiness and confidence ratings when compared with the late alibi disclosure condition.

These studies suggest that the context in which alibi researchers present the alibi (investigation or trial) may affect views of the alibi and suspect/defendant. Note that Ronald Cotton gave up his alibi to law enforcement right away (although he was mistaken). In this one case, early disclosure in the investigation did not appear to help Mr. Cotton. Thus, the timing of when one learns the alibi story may not matter when faced with a mistaken or changed alibi that has been shown to be seen negatively by law enforcement (Dysart & Strange, 2012), but this has yet to have been investigated empirically.

Salaciousness The qualities of the alibi story itself are another contextual factor that has been studied by several researchers. While the literature described earlier shows that the supportive evidence provided by corroborators and physical evidence are especially important, the surface traits of the alibi can also affect perceptions of the alibi (Olson & Wells, 2004). Specifically, alibi researchers have investigated how the salaciousness of the defendant's alibi activities have affected mock juror views. Salaciousness refers to morally questionable acts, often of a scandalous or sexual nature. The salacious activities may or may not be illegal (e.g., watching illegal pornography or having an affair with a consenting adult while married to someone else). Several studies have found that salacious alibis lead to more negative views of the alibi and the defendant. For example, Jung et al. (2013) found that defendants with salacious alibis were viewed negatively on several character trait measures compared to defendants with nonsalacious alibis, but only when the defendant had no physical evidence to corroborate his alibi. Similarly, Keeping et al. (2017) found that people who admitted to engaging in other illegal activities at the time of the crime had lower alibi believability ratings. In one condition in Nieuwkamp et al. (2016), when the alibi was presented immediately, the nonsalacious alibis were more believable than the salacious alibis. These findings suggest that suspects or defendants who claim not to have committed the crime because they were elsewhere doing something salacious leads to a negativity bias. That is, the negative and salacious acts that suspects admit to engaging in at the time of the crime may be weighed heavily against them (Keeping et al., 2017).

However, other studies have shown that in some cases, alibi salaciousness can improve views of the suspect or defendant. Defendants in Allison et al. (2012) who claimed to have been watching a pornographic movie (versus watching a movie) had alibis that were viewed as more believable, were seen positively on several character trait ratings (less suspicious, more honest), and had lower guilt ratings. Alibi corroborators in Allison et al. (2014) were seen as more believable when they were 100% certain they were with the defendant and the defendant was illegally downloading movies to sell. And finally, in Nieuwkamp et al. (2016), suspects whose salacious alibis were presented a second time because the first alibi was found to be incorrect were more believable than suspects who had nonsalacious alibis. Thus, salaciousness sometimes helps and sometimes does not help defendants. In Mr. Cotton's case, his alibi was nonsalacious (with friends or family). More research is needed to further understand when and how salaciousness affects juror views.

Type of Crime The type of crime is another contextual factor that can affect perceptions of alibis. Snow and Warren (2018) manipulated crime seriousness and victim age in an online study. The crime was a mugging or mugging with assault. The victim was described as either a 25-year-old woman or a 70-year-old woman. The alibi was held constant: the suspect's girlfriend corroborated the alibi. Alibi believability was negatively correlated with negative affect, so participants who were more worried as a result of reading about the crime viewed the alibi as less believable. Participants believed the alibi more when the crime was less serious and the victim was older (versus younger). They also believed the alibi more when the crime was serious and the victim was younger (versus older). The authors explained these findings by referring to the Belief in a Just World measure (Snow & Warren, 2018). They suggested that their participants, who were predominantly young adults, were threatened by the idea of another young person being the victim of serious crime. The participants may have reasoned that the young victim somehow deserved her fate and so viewed the suspect's alibi more positively. Or on the flip side, these results show that when the victim was older and the crime was serious, the alibi was less believable; the participants were more punitive here because the victim was more vulnerable. These results are interesting because the alibi did not change and was constant across conditions. It must be noted that other alibi studies have not found that the type of crime affects views of alibis, but crime seriousness does affect the length of suggested sentences (Hosch et al., 2011; Jung et al., 2013). For example, sexual assault led to longer sentences than physical assault and theft (Jung et al., 2013). Allison et al. (2020) found that misdemeanor versus felonious assault did not affect any of the dependent measures, including verdicts and sentencing. More research is needed to determine when the type of crime may lead to changes in alibi believability and guilt ratings.

Defendant Characteristics and Juror Motivation The final contextual factors to be overviewed are defendant characteristics and juror motivation. One study included defendant gender identity (male or female) and whether the proffered alibi included gender stereotype-consistent activities or gender stereotype-inconsistent activities (Maeder & Dempsey, 2013). The male stereotype-consistent activity was shopping for tools at a hardware store, and the female stereotype-consistent activity was shopping for skin-care products at the mall. The stereotype-inconsistent activities were when the male defendant was shopping for skin-care products and the female defendant was shopping for tools at the hardware store. While there was no direct impact of the independent variables on guilt, they did indirectly influence guilt ratings through ratings of the defendant's femininity, credibility, and likeability (Maeder & Dempsey, 2013). More positive scores on these three measures led to lower guilt ratings. More feminine defendants received higher scores on credibility and likeability and received lower guilt ratings. More positive views of female defendants have been found in other studies outside of the alibi context (e.g., Rogers & Davies, 2007).

Defendant race and juror motivation have also been studied in the alibi context (Sargent & Bradfield, 2004). In Sargent and Bradfield (2004), participants were White and evaluated a defendant who was either White or Black. Alibi strength was also manipulated: in one condition the defendant had videotaped footage, and in the other there was no video and the waitress in the restaurant where he was eating could not be found. And finally, participants were either in a high motivation condition (they were told this was a real case and they would be compensated $5 only if their decisions were close to the actual jurors) or they were in a low motivation condition (this was a pilot study, given $5 right away). Overall, the participants felt the White defendant was more guilty than the Black defendant. When in the high motivation condition, guilt ratings were affected by alibi strength in the predicted direction (with higher guilt ratings when the alibi was weak). Interestingly, in the low motivation condition, defendant race moderated the effect of alibi strength on guilt ratings. Here, the Black defendant was more likely to be guilty when his alibi was weak rather than strong, but the White defendant's guilt was not affected by alibi strength. This suggests that when participants are not motivated, they scrutinized the alibi evidence only when the defendant was Black. An extralegal factor like race should not influence guilt ratings, but this study shows that in some situations it does.

Juror motivation was also studied in Allison and Brimacombe (2010), along with defendant prior convictions. In this study, participants listened to a description of a theft of a convenience store and then listened to a police interview with a suspect. The alibi strength varied (strong, weak, or no physical evidence). The suspect admitted to a prior conviction for robbery (prior conviction-same crime) or physical assault (prior conviction-different crime) or perjury (prior conviction-perjury).

Finally, half of the participants heard a judge's instructions concerning the correct, legal use of prior conviction evidence (as information on credibility, not guilt). Rather than manipulating juror motivation using situational features as occurred in Sargent and Bradfield (2004), these authors instead administered the Need for Cognition (NFC) Scale which measured participants' underlying propensity to enjoy thinking and engage in effortful scrutiny of information (high NFC) or whether they tend to avoid thinking deeply (low NFC, Caccioppo & Petty, 1982).

The authors found that strong alibis were more believable than weak alibis (Allison & Brimacombe, 2010). Defendants who had been convicted of a dissimilar crime in the past (physical assault) had more believable alibis than defendants who had been previously convicted of perjury. Defendants convicted of the same crime in the past were more likely to be guilty than those convicted of a dissimilar past crime (physical assault). Participants who heard the judge's instructions found the alibi to be more believable than those who did not hear the instructions. There were a few effects of participant motivation as measured using the NFC Scale. Participants lower in NFC rated the defendant higher on suspiciousness than participants higher in NFC. Participants higher in NFC also rated themselves as being more motivated to listen to the alibi. When it came to the judge's instructions, participants higher in NFC felt they understood the judge's instructions better and actually recalled more of the instructions when compared to those lower in NFC (Allison & Brimacombe, 2010). However, NFC did not affect alibi believability or guilt ratings. The authors theorized that the situational context (a legal case) caused all participants to listen to the case information quite carefully and scrutinize the evidence, regardless of their underlying NFC levels.

These studies show that in some situations, defendant characteristics and juror motivation can affect views of the alibi and subsequent guilt ratings. The fact that defendant race and past convictions can affect views of the defendant has relevance to Mr. Cotton's case. Ronald Cotton was a Black man who lived in a small southern town. His history of dating White women seemed to anger one of the officers involved in his case (Thompson-Cannino et al., 2009), a confederate monument sits outside the Alamance County Courthouse where the trials took place, and indeed 60% of those exonerated due to DNA evidence are Black (Innocence Project, 2020). Racism clearly played a part in Cotton's case. Mr. Cotton also had prior convictions, although not for rape. As a 16-year-old, Mr. Cotton was drunk and entered his friend's house, hoping to "fool around" with his friend's younger sister who he liked. The girl was startled and yelled, and her mother pointed a shotgun at Cotton and asked him to leave (Thompson-Cannino et al., 2009). Mr. Cotton was later charged with breaking and entering and served 18 months in prison. He served time again after that for breaking and entering and was released a few months before the 1984 rapes. Having these past offenses on his record, even though the first was a misunderstanding (Thompson-Cannino et al., 2009), did not help Cotton in his dealings with local law enforcement. One of the victims, Jennifer Thompson, was told of Cotton's past crimes by an officer who said Cotton had tried to rape a 14-year-old who was also White. The officer explained that Cotton liked White women and was a "real scumbag" (Thompson-Cannino et al., 2009). Clearly, Cotton's past crimes were used against him.

Methodological Issues and Future Directions

Alibi believability has been studied sporadically since the 1980s, but renewed interest in the 2000s has prompted many researchers to study how various factors influence people's perceptions. Several studies have used mock jurors (e.g., Fawcett & Winstanley, 2019; Jung et al., 2013; Sommers & Douglass, 2007) and mock investigators (Bruer et al., 2017; Eastwood et al., 2016, 2020; Olson & Wells, 2004) as participants. How well do these participants represent the actual jurors from the community and actual police investigators? The participants often were young (university age) and White, although participant race was sometimes not reported (e.g., Olson & Wells, 2004). Recent movements toward online data collection through crowdsourcing have resulted in a bit of movement away from traditional undergraduate populations as participants (e.g., Eastwood et al., 2020). Clearly, more representative participant pools are necessary so that studies can generalize to the broader community. Many studies are North American-based, but there are several European researchers whose work is adding to the field (e.g., Nieuwkamp et al., 2016; see Chap. 6). Continued effort is needed to include participants from diverse backgrounds, ages, and geographic regions.

The activities that the participants engage in are also important to address. How well do these studies resemble what jurors and investigators do in the real world? Questions of ecological validity arise given that participants often read written vignettes, act as individuals rather than as a part of a jury or investigative team, and view limited pieces of evidence, often in isolation. Some studies have attempted to capture participant motivation (e.g., Allison & Brimacombe, 2010; Sargent & Bradfield, 2004), but studies that have included actual law enforcement officers better capture the views of the individuals working with suspects in investigations. More studies of actual investigators are warranted as they are few and far between, likely due to the challenges of collecting these kinds of data. More studies that ask mock jurors to evaluate alibis as one piece of evidence in a trial can help to increase ecological validity as well.

Researchers should continue to examine key factors, like physical evidence, corroborator characteristics, and consistency. For example, studies have shown that triers-of-fact find videotaped evidence to be highly believable, but with continued improvements in video editing it is often difficult to distinguish between altered video and unaltered video. Are jurors aware of this fact? More research into the incriminating evidence that conflicts with the alibi evidence is also needed, as most studies have included eyewitness evidence and few have included stronger evidence like DNA (e.g., Ribeiro et al., 2020). Researchers also should continue to be inspired by real-life cases involving alibis, like Ronald Cotton's. In what ways have alibis been believed and disbelieved historically and contemporarily? How has law enforcement investigated alibi claims and how has evidence driven investigator decision-making? Had Mr. Cotton's alibi been believed, then perhaps his interactions with the criminal justice system would have been different. It is hoped that continued research into alibi believability will help to understand and prevent such miscarriages of justice.

References

Allison, M., & Brimacombe, C. A. E. (2010). Alibi believability: The effect of prior convictions and judicial instructions. *Journal of Applied Social Psychology, 40*(5), 1054–1084. https://doi.org/10.1111/j.1559-1816.2010.00610.x

Allison, M., Jung, S., & Benjamin, A. C. (2020). Alibi believability: Corroborative evidence and contextual factors. *Behavioral Sciences & the Law, 38*(4), 337–354. https://doi.org/10.1002/bsl.2473

Allison, M., Jung, S., Sweeney, L., & Culhane, S. E. (2014). The impact of illegal alibi activities, corroborator involvement and corroborator certainty on mock juror perceptions. *Psychiatry, Psychology and Law, 21*(2), 191–204. https://doi.org/10.1080/13218719.2013.803275

Allison, M., Mathews, K. R., & Michael, S. W. (2012). Alibi believability: The impact of salacious alibi activities. *Social Behavior and Personality, 40*(4), 605–612. https://doi.org/10.2224/sbp.2012.40.4.605

Bruer, K. C., Price, H. L., & Dahl, L. C. (2017). When an alibi is not enough: Judgments of evidence needed to lay charges in a burglary case. *Journal of Police and Criminal Psychology, 32*, 94–104. https://doi.org/10.1007/s11896-016-9209-6

Burke, T. M., & Turtle, J. W. (2003). Alibi evidence in criminal investigations and trials: Psychological and legal factors. *The Canadian Journal of Police and Security Services, 1*, 193–201.

Burke, T. M., Turtle, J. W., & Olson, E. A. (2007). Alibis in criminal investigations and trials. In M. P. Toglia, J. D. Read, D. F. Ross, & R. C. L. Lindsay (Eds.), *The handbook of eyewitness psychology* (Memory for events) (Vol. 1, pp. 157–174). Erlbaum. https://doi.org/10.4324/9781315086309

Cacioppo, J. T., & Petty, R. E. (1982). The need for cognition. *Journal of Personality and Social Psychology, 42*(1), 116–131. https://psycnet.apa.org/doi/10.1037/0022-3514.42.1.116

Charman, S. D., Carbone, J., Kekessie, S., & Villalba, D. K. (2016). Evidence evaluation and evidence integration in legal decision-making: Order of evidence presentation as a moderator of context effects. *Applied Cognitive Psychology, 30*(2), 214–255. https://doi.org/10.1002/acp.3181

Culhane, S. E., & Hosch, H. M. (2004). An alibi witness's influence on mock jurors' verdicts. *Journal of Applied Social Psychology, 34*(8), 1604–1616. https://doi.org/10.1111/j.1559-1816.2004.tb02789.x

Culhane, S. E., & Hosch, H. M. (2012). Changed alibis: Current law enforcement, future law enforcement, and layperson reactions. *Criminal Justice and Behavior, 39*(7), 958–977. https://doi.org/10.1177/2F0093854812438185

Culhane, S. E., Kehn, A., Horgan, A. J., Meissner, C. A., Hosch, H. M., & Wodahl, E. J. (2013). Generation and detection of true and false alibi statements. *Psychiatry, Psychology and Law, 20*(4), 619–638. https://doi.org/10.1080/13218719.2012.729018

Dahl, L. C., Brimacombe, C. A. E., & Lindsay, D. S. (2009). Investigating investigators: How presentation order influences participant-investigators' interpretations of eyewitness identification and alibi evidence. *Law and Human Behavior, 33*, 368–380. https://doi.org/10.1007/s10979-008-9151-y

Dahl, L. C., & Price, H. L. (2012). "He couldn't have done it, he was with me!": The impact of alibi witness age and relationship. *Applied Cognitive Psychology, 26*(3), 475–481. https://doi.org/10.1002/acp.2821

Dysart, J. E., & Strange, D. (2012). Beliefs about alibis and alibi investigations: A survey of law enforcement. *Psychology, Crime and Law, 18*(1), 11–25. https://doi.org/10.1080/1068316X.2011.562867

Eastwood, J., Lively, C. J., Snook, B., & Snow, M. (2020). Quality vs. quantity: The effect of relationship and number of corroborators on alibi assessments. *Psychiatry, Psychology and Law.* https://doi.org/10.1080/13218719.2020.1754956

Eastwood, J., Snook, B., & Au, D. (2016). Safety in numbers: A policy-capturing study of the alibi assessment process. *Applied Cognitive Psychology, 30*(2), 260–269. https://doi.org/10.1002/acp.3200

Fawcett, H. (2016). The effect of evidence timing and witness motivation upon juror evaluations of alibi witnesses and defendants. *Psychiatry, Psychology and Law, 23*(4), 575–587. https://doi.org/10.1080/13218719.2015.1081317

Fawcett, H., & Winstanley, K. (2019). Children as alibi witnesses: The effect of age and confidence on mock-juror decision making. *Psychiatry, Psychology and Law, 25*(6), 957–971. https://doi.org/10.1080/13218719.2018.1482573

Hosch, H. M., Culhane, S. E., Jolly, K. W., Chavez, R. M., & Shaw, L. H. (2011). Effects of an alibi witness's relationship to the defendant on mock juror's judgments. *Law and Human Behavior, 35*(2), 127–142. https://doi.org/10.1007/s10979-010-9225-5

Innocence Project. DNA exonerations in the United States. Retrieved 11 Dec 2020 from https://innocenceproject.org/dna-exonerations-in-the-united-states/

Jung, S., Allison, M., & Bohn, L. (2013). Legal decision-making on crimes involving an alibi. *Applied Psychology in Criminal Justice, 9*(1), 45–58. https://doi.org/10.1037/t04698-000

Keeping, Z., Eastwood, J., Lively, C. J., & Snook, B. (2017). Don't stop believing: The relative impact of internal alibi details on judgments of veracity. *Psychology, Crime & Law, 23*(9), 899–913. https://doi.org/10.1080/1068316X.2017.1338700

Lindsay, R. C. L., Lim, R., Marando, L., & Cully, D. (1986). Mock-juror evaluations of eyewitness testimony: A test of metamemory hypotheses. *Journal of Applied Social Psychology, 16*(5), 447–459. https://doi.org/10.1111/j.1559-1816.1986.tb01151.x

Maeder, E. M., & Dempsey, J. L. (2013). A likely story? The influence of type of alibi and defendant gender on juror decision-making. *Psychiatry, Psychology and Law, 20*(4), 543–552. https://doi.org/10.1080/13218719.2012.727066

Nieuwkamp, R., Horselenberg, R., & van Koppen, P. J. (2016). A lie and a mistress: On increasing the believability of your alibi. *Psychiatry, Psychology and Law, 23*(5), 733–745. https://doi.org/10.1080/13218719.2016.1142934

Nieuwkamp, R., Horselenberg, R., & van Koppen, P. (2018). True and false alibis among prisoners and their detection by police detectives. *Psychiatry, Psychology and Law, 25*(6), 902–921. https://doi.org/10.1080/13218719.2018.1482570

Olson, E. A. (2013). "You don't expect me to believe that, do you?" Expectations influence recall and belief of alibi information. *Journal of Applied Social Psychology, 43*(6), 1238–1247. https://doi.org/10.1111/jasp.12086

Olson, E. A., & Charman, S. D. (2012). 'But can you prove it?' Examining the quality of innocent suspects' alibis. *Psychology, Crime and Law, 18*(5), 453–471. https://doi.org/10.1080/1068316X.2010.505567

Olson, E. A., & Wells, G. L. (2004). What makes a good alibi? A proposed taxonomy. *Law and Human Behavior, 28*(2), 157–176. https://doi.org/10.1023/B:LAHU.0000022320.47112.d3

Pozzulo, J. D., Pettalia, J. L., Dempsey, J. L., & Gooden, A. (2015). Juvenile offenders on trial: Does alibi corroboration evidence and defendant age interact to influence jurors' perceptions and verdicts? *Psychiatry, Psychology and Law, 22*(2), 224–234. https://doi.org/10.1080/13218719.2014.937518

Pozzulo, J. D., Pettalia, J. L., Dempsey, J. L., & Melo, C. M. (2012). Influential factors in jurors' decisions: Eyewitness age and alibi corroboration. *American Journal of Forensic Psychology, 30*(4), 63–79.

Price, H. L., & Dahl, L. C. (2014). Order and strength matter for evaluation of alibi and eyewitness evidence. *Applied Cognitive Psychology, 28*(2), 143–150. https://doi.org/10.1002/acp.2983

Price, H. L., & Dahl, L. C. (2017). Investigator sensitivity to alibi witness consistency after a long delay. *Behavioral Sciences & the Law, 35*(1), 60–74. https://doi.org/10.1002/bsl.2276

Ribeiro, G., Tangen, J., & McKimmie, B. (2020). Does DNA evidence in the form of a likelihood ratio affect perceivers' sensitivity to the strength of a suspect's alibi? *Psychonomic Bulletin & Review, 27*, 1325–1332. https://doi.org/10.3758/s13423-020-01784-x

Rogers, P., & Davies, M. (2007). Perceptions of victims and perpetrators in a depicted child sexual abuse case: Gender and age factors. *Journal of Interpersonal Violence, 22*(5), 566–584. https://doi.org/10.1177/2F0886260506298827

Sargent, M. J., & Bradfield, A. L. (2004). Race and information processing in criminal trials: Does the defendant's race affect how the facts are evaluated? *Personality and Social Psychology Bulletin, 30*(8), 995–1008. https://doi.org/10.1177/2F0146167204265741

Sommers, S. R., & Douglass, A. B. (2007). Context matters: Alibi strength varies according to evaluator perspective. *Legal and Criminological Psychology, 12*(1), 41–54. https://doi.org/10.1348/135532506X114301

Snow, M. D., & Eastwood, J. (2020). Assessing the credibility of child alibi corroborators. *Journal of Forensic Psychology Research and Practice*. https://doi.org/10.1080/24732850.2020.1840000

Snow, M. D., & Warren, K. L. (2018). Emotions, crime seriousness, and alibi believability. *Psychiatry, Psychology and Law, 25*(1), 19–31. https://doi.org/10.1080/13218719.2017.1347938

Strange, D., Dysart, J., & Loftus, E. F. (2014). Why errors in alibis are not necessarily evidence of guilt. *Zeitschrift für Psychologie, 222*(2), 82–89. https://doi.org/10.1027/2151-2604/a000169

Strömwall, L. A., Granhag, P. A., & Jonsson, A. (2003). Deception among pairs: Let's say we had lunch and hope they will swallow it! *Psychology, Crime, and Law, 9*(2), 109–124. https://doi.org/10.1080/1068316031000116238

Thompson-Cannino, J., Cotton, R., & Torneo, E. (2009). *Picking cotton: Our memoir of injustice and redemption*. St. Martin's Press.

Verigin, B. L., Meijer, E. H., & Vrig, A. (2020). A within-statement baseline comparison for detecting lies. *Psychiatry, Psychology and Law*, https://doi.org/10.1080/13218719.2020.1767712

Vernham, Z., Vrij, A., Nahari, G., Leal, S., Mann, S., Satchell, L., & Orthey, R. (2020). Applying the verifiability approach to deception detection in alibi witness situations. *Acta Psychologica, 204*, https://doi.org/10.1016/j.actpsy.2020.103020

Vrij, A. (2000). *Detecting lies and deceit: The psychology of lying and implications for professional practice*. Wiley.

Chapter 5
Towards a System Variable Approach to Improving the Quality of Alibi Evidence

Steve D. Charman and Laura Shambaugh

On the morning of August 12, 2003, Juan Catalan was arrested for first-degree murder of 16-year-old Martha Puebla, a young woman who had recently testified against Catalan's older brother in another murder case. Facing a possible death sentence, Catalan retained criminal defense attorney Todd Melnik, who set to work establishing Catalan's whereabouts on the night Martha was killed. In his initial alibi statement, Catalan reported that he had attended a Dodgers baseball game with his daughter, his cousin, and a friend. Catalan's girlfriend was able to locate the physical ticket that Juan used to enter the game, but neither possession of this ticket nor testimony from his various corroborators was sufficient proof to the prosecutor that Juan had actually attended the game. Using Juan's seat location, Melnik reviewed game footage that may have captured Juan in the stands. Sure enough, Melnik found Catalan in a few frames; unfortunately, the resolution of those captured images was too low to be admissible in court.

Melnik pressed Catalan to remember any other evidence that would place him at the Dodgers game during the murder. Eventually, Catalan recalled seeing a film crew in his section of the stadium and believed he may have been caught on camera at one point. After some investigation, Melnik discovered that, in fact, HBO was at the same Dodgers game filming an episode of the TV show *Curb Your Enthusiasm*. After obtaining access to the footage, Melnik finally found what he was looking for: Juan and his daughter walking down the stadium aisle right in front of the camera.

But even this evidence was not sufficient to support Catalan's alibi: The last scene featuring Catalan was filmed at 9:15 pm, but Martha's murder took place at 10:32 pm, providing Catalan with a window of 1 hour and 17 minutes to kill Martha. Fortunately, Catalan also remembered speaking to his girlfriend on his phone as he left the game that night, a conversation that was later verified by his cellphone

S. D. Charman (✉) · L. Shambaugh
Department of Psychology, Florida International University, Miami, FL, USA
e-mail: charmans@fiu.edu; lsham005@fiu.edu

J. D. Behl, M. R. Kienzle (eds.), *Alibis and Corroborators*,
https://doi.org/10.1007/978-3-030-95663-9_5

records as having occurred at 10:12 pm. This call pinged a cellphone tower that was located right next to Dodger stadium and had a radius of only one mile. On the basis of this evidence, the judge at Catalan's pre-trial hearing ruled to dismiss the case on grounds of insufficient evidence. After spending 6 months in a maximum-security prison where he had been awaiting trial, Juan Catalan was freed.

Not all innocent suspects are as fortunate as Juan was to have been able to produce corroborative evidence in support of an alibi. Consider an analysis of the first 40 people exonerated by DNA for crimes they did not commit: 28% had "no alibi" or "weak alibi" listed as a cause for their conviction (Wells et al., 1998). These findings are not surprising in light of the myriad hurdles an innocent suspect must overcome to generate a believable alibi (see Charman et al., 2019 for an overview, or Chaps. 3 and 4 of this text for additional details). A falsely accused person must (a) accurately remember one's whereabouts during a time period that could have occurred days, weeks, or months prior, and during which the innocent suspect had no reason to know they would have to later remember it; (b) provide verifiable corroborative evidence for one's claim, which may never have existed, or which may have become lost or forgotten in the interim; and (c) convince skeptical evaluators who are generally motivated to discount any evidence of the validity of the alibi. Unfortunately, research has demonstrated that people frequently fail at each of these tasks. People commonly misremember their whereabouts for specific times in the past, leading them to report mistaken alibis (Olson & Charman, 2012; Leins & Charman, 2016; Chap. 9 of this text). Even if they do accurately recall their whereabouts, people are often unable to provide corroborative evidence to support their claims (Culhane et al., 2008, 2013; Strange et al., 2014), whether because the evidence does not exist (e.g., if one was at home alone watching television), because their potential alibi corroborators fail to remember them (Charman et al., 2017), or because they fail to recall the existence of corroborative physical evidence (Matuku & Charman, 2020). Even if innocent suspects are able to overcome these obstacles and provide a strong, corroborated alibi, evaluators tend to be (a) highly skeptical of alibis in general (Culhane & Hosch, 2012; Dysart & Strange, 2012; Olson & Wells, 2004), (b) dismissive of the types of corroborative evidence innocent suspects are most likely to produce (e.g., corroborative evidence from friends and family; Olson & Wells, 2004; Eastwood et al., 2016; Hosch et al., 2011), (c) biased by a multitude of factors when evaluating the strength of alibis (e.g., Charman et al., 2016; Sargent & Bradfield, 2004), and (d) generally poor at discriminating true from false alibis (Culhane et al., 2013).

Although alibi research has clearly demonstrated the difficulty innocent suspects face in providing a strong alibi defense (see Chap. 9), the field has been much less successful in developing recommendations for *how* to improve alibi evidence. In their overview of the extant alibi research, Charman et al. (2019) recently advocated for alibi researchers to adopt what is known as a *system variable* approach (Wells, 1978) to alibi evidence, which involves developing and testing interventions aimed at improving the quality of alibi evidence, with the ultimate goal of being able to make empirically based recommendations to the legal system. With this goal in mind, the primary purpose of the current chapter is to review the relatively small corpus of research on system variable approaches to improving the quality of alibi evidence. In doing so, we first consider how suspects who provide alibis can be most appropriately classified into three categories and how an understanding of this tripartite classification informs three general strategies aimed at improving alibi evidence in different ways. Studies that have adopted a system variable approach to alibi evidence are discussed within the context of those strategies.

A Tripartite Classification of Alibi-Providing Suspects

Broadly speaking, many subfields of legal psychology involve classifying people into two categories. Eyewitness researchers, for instance, are concerned with classifying witnesses who make lineup identifications as being either correct or mistaken; notably, because witnesses are assumed to be engaged in good faith efforts to identify the perpetrator, the field is largely unconcerned with purposefully deceptive eyewitnesses. Taking a system variable approach with respect to eyewitness identification is thus primarily focused on improving memory *accuracy*. Deception detection researchers, in contrast, are concerned with classifying suspects as being either truth-tellers or liars; notably, because truth-tellers are assumed to know what the truth is, the field is largely unconcerned with truth-tellers who mistakenly provide erroneous statements. Taking a system variable approach with respect to deception detection is thus primarily focused on improving evaluators' abilities to correctly discriminate between liars and truth-tellers based on cues to *veracity*.

Alibi researchers are also concerned with classifying people into categories. Clearly, we wish to improve innocent suspects' abilities to generate accurate alibis, and thus a system variable approach should focus on improving our ability to classify alibi-providing suspects as being correct or mistaken. To that extent, we are concerned with memory *accuracy*. However, alibi-providing suspects are not limited to being either accurate or mistaken; the existence of purposefully deceptive suspects who generate false alibis means we must also be concerned with evaluators' abilities to correctly classify suspects as truth-tellers (i.e., innocent suspects) or liars (i.e., guilty suspects). A system variable approach therefore also needs to be concerned with *veracity*.

Consequently, suspects who provide alibis can be categorized into not two but three categories: deceptive (i.e., guilty suspects), honest/accurate (i.e., innocent suspects who provide an accurate alibi), and honest/mistaken (i.e., innocent suspects who provide an honestly mistaken alibi).[1] Appreciating this tripartite classification of alibi-providing suspects is important for developing a system variable approach

[1] We could also consider a fourth category: innocent suspects who lie about their whereabouts, perhaps because their actual alibi would incriminate them in another transgression. However, it is unclear how often innocent suspects provide deliberately false alibis in the real world, and consequently we do not discuss it in this chapter. For a more detailed discussion of salacious alibis, see Chap. 4 on believability.

to alibi evidence, as interventions must be sensitive to both accuracy and veracity concerns. Imagine, for instance, a hypothetical accuracy-based intervention that improves suspects' memories for their whereabouts (e.g., allowing suspects to discuss their whereabouts with friends and family before officially reporting their alibi). Such an intervention will help innocent suspects generate accurate alibis, effectively shifting some suspects from the honest/mistaken category to the honest/accurate category. But because alibi-providing suspects can be not only mistaken, but also deceptive, this intervention may not be suitable for use within an alibi context, as it does not address veracity concerns: Perhaps our hypothetical intervention also increases the ability of guilty suspects to generate a believable alibi (e.g., by allowing them to coordinate their alibi story with false corroborators), resulting in increased misclassifications of guilty suspects as being honest. If so, our intervention could improve accuracy among innocent suspects while simultaneously harming evaluators' abilities to discriminate between guilty and innocent suspects based on veracity.

Alternatively, imagine a hypothetical veracity-based intervention in which evaluators are led to determine veracity based on the consistency of the alibi with known facts (e.g., an intervention similar to the Strategic Use of Evidence Technique—a strategy for the questioning of suspects that involves using inconsistencies between a suspect's story and case evidence as a proxy for deception; Granhag and Hartwig 2015). This intervention will allow for much improved discrimination between deceptive and honest/accurate suspects. However, because even the best-intentioned innocent suspects can mistakenly generate inaccurate alibis, this intervention will result in the inaccurate classification of many honest/mistaken suspects as being guilty. Indeed, law enforcement often fails to consider the possibility of innocent people providing mistaken alibis: When asked why someone might change an alibi story, senior law enforcement overwhelmingly interpreted it as indicative of lying (81%), as opposed to a memory error (19%; Dysart & Strange, 2012), despite innocent people commonly changing their alibi stories (Olson & Charman, 2012; Strange et al., 2014).

Due to the tripartite classification of alibi-providing suspects, the goal of improving the quality of alibi evidence requires a multi-pronged strategic approach. To address accuracy concerns, one approach is to investigate strategies that can be implemented prior to a suspect providing an alibi with the ultimate goal of transforming honest/mistaken suspects into honest/accurate suspects (Strategy 1). However, producing an accurate alibi is insufficient if that alibi cannot also be verified. An alternative approach is therefore to investigate strategies that can improve honest/accurate suspects' abilities to produce corroborative evidence (Strategy 2). To address veracity concerns, a third approach is to devise strategies that can be used to improve evaluators' abilities to discriminate between honest and deceptive alibis (Strategy 3). Each of these strategies is discussed in turn, along with empirical examples of techniques that have attempted to leverage each strategy to improve the quality of alibi evidence.

Strategy 1: Transforming Honest/Mistaken Suspects into Honest/Accurate Suspects

Clearly, one of the main goals of alibi research is to minimize the existence of honest but mistaken suspects by transforming them into honest and accurate suspects. To improve the accuracy of innocent suspects' alibis, we must first understand why innocent suspects generate mistaken alibis in the first place.

Why Do Innocent Suspects Generate Mistaken Alibis?

Numerous studies using a variety of methodological approaches have shown that innocent suspects are highly susceptible to providing mistaken alibis (Leins & Charman, 2016; Olson & Charman, 2012; Strange et al., 2014). When later investigated and shown to be false, these honestly mistaken alibis tend to be perceived as highly suspicious by evaluators, even if they are subsequently corrected (Dysart & Strange, 2012; Culhane & Hosch, 2012). Yet despite the risks associated with providing an honestly mistaken alibi, people seem to be highly willing to provide an alibi nonetheless, even though many of those alibis are later proven to be incorrect (Culhane et al., 2008, 2013; Olson & Charman, 2012).

Mistaken alibis are, however, not simply random guesses as to one's whereabouts. Rather, research suggests that mistaken alibis often arise when innocent suspects' activities deviate from their usual activities (Leins & Charman, 2016). When suspects lack a memory for their whereabouts for a specific time in the past, they do not simply fail to report an alibi. Instead, they tend to resort to a back-up strategy: They assess their *schemas*—their beliefs about what they normally do during the critical time period. An innocent suspect, asked to provide an alibi for three Tuesdays ago at 12:30 pm, might reason that they normally eat lunch in their workplace's cafeteria at that time. They report their typical lunchtime activity as their alibi—critically forgetting that on that specific day they were actually attending a doctor's appointment. Using a schema-based strategy to generate alibis is thus prone to error. Fortunately, schema-based responding is not inevitable: According to the schema-disconfirmation model—a theoretical account of how innocent people provide alibis—innocent suspects only tend to rely on their schemas when reporting their alibis if they lack a memory of their whereabouts for the critical time period (Charman et al., 2019). According to this model, then, one way to potentially improve the accuracy of innocent suspects' alibis is to facilitate their reliance on their memories for their whereabouts and to discourage reliance on their schemas.

Improving Alibis by Reducing Reliance on Schemas

One simple strategy aimed at reducing reliance on schemas involves intervening before innocent suspects generate a schema, by explaining to them the difference between a memory and a schema and instructing them to only report alibis based on memories. This is, in fact, an approach we have tried in the lab; unfortunately, this instruction failed to improve the accuracy of people's alibis. In retrospect, it is easy to see why this strategy failed: Because schemas represent activities that people normally engage in, innocent suspects should have numerous memories of actually engaging in schema-consistent behavior. In other words, suspects *are* relying on memories when reporting their schema—just the *wrong* memories. Furthermore, according to the schema disconfirmation model, innocent suspects tend to rely heavily on schemas when generating alibis because a time cue (e.g., "What were you doing three Tuesdays ago at 12:30 pm?") fails to trigger a memory of their whereabouts (see also Leins & Charman, 2016). Simply instructing people to ignore their schemas is missing an important facet of accurate alibi generation: It does not tell people *how* to access that missing memory.

Given this failure to prevent schema reliance via an instruction, perhaps a superior strategy to improve alibi accuracy would be to assist innocent suspects in accessing their original memory, obviating their need to access their schemas. With this goal in mind, Cardenas et al. (2020) tested whether they could increase the accuracy of innocent suspects' alibis by instructing them, prior to providing an alibi, to visualize their physical environment (e.g., their physical location and actions) as well as their psychological environment (e.g., how they felt) during the critical time period. This *mental reinstatement of context* (MRC) instruction is aimed at helping recall by increasing the number of retrieval cues available to the rememberer (Tulving & Thomson, 1973) and is considered to be one of the critical components of the Cognitive Interview, the gold standard of eyewitness interviewing protocols (Dando et al., 2009; Memon et al., 2010). By helping uncover retrieval cues, MRC might be expected to improve innocent suspects' memories for their whereabouts, in turn decreasing their reliance on schemas when reporting their alibis.

Cardenas et al. (2020) tested this idea by first prompting participants via text at various points over approximately 2 weeks to report on what they were doing, where they were, and who they were with. Following this 2-week reporting period, participants were asked to provide alibis for four time periods for which the researchers had the participants' self-reported data. Critically, two of these alibis were prompted without first instructing the participant to mentally reinstate the context, and two were prompted by having participants first mentally reinstate the context. However, contrary to the authors' predictions, alibis elicited using MRC were no more likely to be accurate than alibis elicited without MRC, a null effect that was replicated in a second study.

Why did MRC fail to improve alibi accuracy, especially given the technique's notable success at improving eyewitness memory? Although null effects are difficult to interpret, one likely possibility is that the effectiveness of MRC depends on the rememberer knowing what the critical event is in the first place. MRC instructions involve telling people to visualize what happened in their mind and to think about what they were feeling, who they were with, etc. To eyewitnesses who know that the critical event they are trying to remember is the witnessed crime, these MRC instructions can trigger additional memory cues that help them provide additional crime details. But to innocent suspects, who do not even know what the critical event is they are attempting to recall, it is difficult to imagine how these MRC instructions might help. If innocent suspects are unaware of the event they are trying to recall, how would instructions to think about what they were feeling or who they were with help their memories? It seems to us that MRC can only improve memory output among people who already know what the critical event is that they are attempting to remember and is thus doomed to fail to improve innocent suspects' memories for their whereabouts.

Improving Alibis by Improving Memory for Disconfirming Information

If strategies to intervene prior to the formation of a schema have failed, what other strategies might we use to transform honest/mistaken suspects into honest/accurate suspects? A key aspect of the schema disconfirmation model (Charman et al., 2019) is that once a schema is accessed, people do not mindlessly report it, but first engage in a memory check in an attempt to uncover a memory that might disconfirm the schema. Perhaps, then, we can increase people's abilities to disconfirm their schemas once they are accessed, preventing them from being reported as the alibi. For instance, allowing suspects access to physical memory aids—materials that might contain information as to their whereabouts such as planners, diaries, phones, and calendars—prior to generating an alibi might help them uncover information that disconfirms their schemas.

Recall that due to the tripartite classification of alibi-providing suspects, an intervention that improves the accuracy of innocent suspects' alibis may also increase the believability of guilty suspects' alibis. Fortunately, there is reason to believe that memory aids should disproportionately help innocent, rather than guilty, suspects. When asked to provide an alibi, innocent suspects are faced with a memory task, which should become easier with memory aids. Guilty suspects, however, are not faced with a memory task; their inability to provide corroborative evidence in support of their fabricated alibi is not due to a lack of a memory for that evidence, but rather to its inherent unavailability. We might expect, then, that allowing access to memory aids should not only help innocent people generate alibis but should do so without simultaneously helping guilty people generate alibis, thus increasing evaluators' abilities to discriminate between innocent and guilty suspects.

We are currently in the process of empirically testing the effectiveness of this simple strategy to improving alibi evidence by allowing suspects—both innocent and guilty—access to their phones for 3 minutes prior to providing an alibi (Matuku

& Charman, 2021). Presumably, some proportion of innocent suspects will be able to uncover information on their phones (via calendars, social media posts, texts, etc.) that would disconfirm their schemas of where they were during the critical time period. Preliminary analyses are consistent with this reasoning: allowing innocent suspects access to their phones for a mere 3 minutes more than tripled the percentage of people who provided accurate alibis (from 16% to 51%). Although it is important to show that phone access does not also increase the believability of deceptive alibis (a possibility we are currently testing), allowing suspects to access their phones prior to providing an alibi could be an easily implemented system variable approach to improving alibi evidence.

Strategy 2: Improve Honest/Accurate Suspects' Abilities to Produce Corroborative Evidence

Although the development of strategies that successfully transform honest/mistaken suspects into honest/accurate suspects would certainly be useful, they are nonetheless insufficient by themselves. Investigators may attempt to verify suspects' alibis (though see Chap. 8 for an opposing viewpoint); even completely accurate alibis will likely be regarded with high suspicion if no corroborative evidence is uncovered to support them (Olson & Wells, 2004). Unfortunately, research suggests that honest/accurate suspects commonly lack corroborative evidence that could help exonerate them (Culhane et al., 2008, 2013; Olson & Charman, 2012; Strange et al., 2014). Consequently, a second general strategy for improving alibi evidence is to improve the quality of corroborative evidence that can support an innocent suspect's alibi. Because this strategy is aimed at improving memory for corroborative evidence among suspects who have already provided an accurate alibi, it is focused only on honest/accurate suspects.

Improving the Quality of Corroborative Person Evidence

Alibis that are corroborated by other people are found to be more believable than alibis that lack such corroboration, especially if those alibi corroborators are not perceived as motivated to lie for the suspect (Culhane & Hosch, 2004; Eastwood et al., 2016; Olson & Wells, 2004). Increasing the number of corroborators should therefore help exonerate innocent suspects. There are two general strategies to accomplish this goal. First, strategies can be aimed at improving innocent suspects' memories for people with whom they interacted during the critical time period who could support their alibi. For instance, an innocent suspect whose alibi is that they were shopping might forget having interacted with a cashier who might later be able to corroborate their story. For that suspect, remembering the cashier might be the difference between exoneration and a lengthy prison sentence.

How might we increase innocent suspects' memories for potential person corroborators? Although we are unaware of any research that has specifically examined this question in an alibi context, related research from other areas might help to shed light on this question. For instance, the Cognitive Interview (Fisher & Geiselman, 1992), which has consistently been shown to improve memory output among eyewitnesses (Memon et al., 2010), has recently been shown to also increase the number of people one reports having interacted with in an epidemiological context (Mosser & Evans, 2019). Given that innocent suspects are faced with roughly the same task (i.e., recalling interactions with other people during a designated time period), we might expect a similar finding if the Cognitive Interview were administered to alibi-providing suspects. There are, however, two caveats with generalizing these results to an alibi context. First, it would be important to show that the Cognitive Interview does not also increase the believability of deceptive alibis (e g., by allowing guilty suspects more time to plan an alibi) or decrease the believability of innocent/mistaken alibis (e.g., by increasing the amount of mistaken information provided). Second, Mosser and Evans were unable to verify the existence of the people their participants claimed to have interacted with, making it unclear whether the Cognitive Interview increased accurate or inaccurate recollections. Future alibi research should use methodologies that allow for the assessment of whether any additional corroborators reported during a Cognitive Interview are indeed people with whom the suspect interacted during the critical time period.

Of course, improving innocent suspects' memories for corroborators is insufficient if those potential corroborators themselves fail to remember having interacted with the suspect. Indeed, Charman et al. (2017) showed that almost two thirds of potential corroborators shown a photograph of a stranger with whom they had interacted only 24 hours previously failed to remember having interacted with that person. Consequently, a second strategy to improve the quality of corroborative person evidence is to improve potential corroborators' memories for the suspect. In fact, Charman et al. attempted to do just that by cueing potential corroborators who failed to remember having interacted with the stranger with the approximate time of day during which the interaction took place. Unfortunately, this manipulation failed to appreciably increase correct recognition rates.

Developing methods to improve corroborators' memories for a suspect is likely to be challenging. When interacting with someone who will later become a suspect, potential alibi corroborators are unaware that they will be asked about the future suspect at a later time and thus lack any motivation to attempt to remember their face. Additionally, investigators are likely to be hesitant to use interventions that improve corroborators' memories for the suspect if those interventions might also increase mistaken corroboration of guilty suspects. For instance, perhaps cueing possible alibi corroborators with the location that their purported interaction with the suspect took place could improve their memories for innocent suspects. If, however, this cueing also increases the likelihood of mistakenly corroborating a guilty suspect's alibi, investigators may not want to cue potential corroborators in this manner. Overcoming these challenges to develop a strategy that improves potential alibi corroborators' memories would be an important step towards developing a system variable approach to improving the quality of corroborative evidence.

Improving the Quality of Corroborative Physical Evidence

Perhaps the most important factor affecting the believability of an alibi is the physical evidence that exists to support it: Alibis with physical evidence are considered much more believable than alibis that lack it, whether evaluated by students (Olson & Wells, 2004), people in the general US population (Allison et al., 2020), or actual senior law enforcement (Dysart & Strange, 2012). Unfortunately, a survey of law enforcement indicated that only a minority (approximately 24%) of suspects provide leads that result in physical evidence (Dysart & Strange, 2012). Of course, that number is low in part due to the prevalence of guilty suspects who deliberately avoid providing physical evidence. Nonetheless, these results also suggest that there could be many innocent suspects who are unable to provide corroborative physical evidence that could help exonerate them. Consider the story of Juan Catalan, the man falsely accused of murder whose story opened this chapter. Although his alibi was that he was at a baseball game during the crime, he was initially unable to provide sufficient physical evidence to place him there. It was only after conversations with his attorney that he remembered the existence of a film crew that was also at the baseball game and the phone call he made to his girlfriend, which ultimately proved Catalan's innocence. Had he not remembered that physical evidence, he might never have been exonerated.

Juan Catalan's story demonstrates the importance of developing strategies to improve innocent suspects' memories for the existence of corroborative physical evidence. To date, we are aware of only a single study that has adopted this approach. Matuku and Charman (2020) tested whether two different manipulations, both of which could be implemented at the time that law enforcement ask suspects for their alibis, could increase the quantity of physical evidence that innocent suspects report. The first, based on research suggesting that autobiographical memories are organized chronologically (e.g., Anderson & Conway, 1993), involved explicitly telling participants to think about their activities in chronological order when reporting corroborative physical evidence, as opposed to having participants simply list the physical evidence in whatever order they wished. The second, based on research suggesting that taking another person's perspective while recalling an event can increase the amount of information recalled about that event (e.g., Anderson & Pichert, 1978), involved telling participants to consider the types of physical evidence to which someone else present during the critical time might have access.

Matuku and Charman (2020) had participants engage in a series of tasks at Time 1 that created 13 pieces of physical evidence that the participant could later report as supporting their alibi. At a later Time 2 session, these participants were individually interviewed about their Time 1 activities. Because the general strategy of improving recall of physical evidence can only work among honest/accurate suspects, all participants were first told that they had been engaged in Part 1 of this study (but were not reminded of their actual activities during that period). Participants were then randomly assigned to either receive the chronological recall instruction or not and to either receive a perspective-taking instruction (e.g., "consider the evidence that the experimenter would have access to") or not. Finally, all participants were asked to report the physical evidence that supported their alibi. Results were consistent with predictions: Both the chronological recall instruction and the perspective-taking instruction significantly increased the number of pieces of physical evidence that innocent suspects correctly recalled to support their alibis.

We view the general strategy of improving innocent suspects' memories for corroborative evidence as a particularly promising approach to improving the quality of alibi evidence. Nonetheless, this approach has its own limitations. First, it requires that innocent suspects accurately remember their whereabouts in the first place. Consequently, we view this strategy to work best in concert with strategies aimed at transforming honest/mistaken suspects into honest/accurate suspects. Second, the success of this strategy requires the existence of physical evidence that can corroborate the innocent suspect's alibi. We find it promising, however, that due to recent technological advancements, innocent suspects increasingly have physical evidence to support their alibis. Indeed, the ubiquity of cell phones with GPS tracking, the proliferation of high-definition cameras in public spaces, the increased use of social media sites, and many other technologies that leave a digital trace of one's whereabouts all contribute to the myriad types of physical evidence that might exist to support an alibi. Whether innocent people can remember these types of corroborative evidence is a critical question. As Juan Catalan's case illustrates, innocent people's freedom might hinge on their ability to do so.

Strategy 3: Improving Evaluators' Abilities to Discriminate Between Liars and Truth-Tellers

Unfortunately, even if researchers successfully develop strategies that (a) transform honest/mistaken suspects into honest/accurate suspects and (b) improve recall of corroborative evidence among innocent suspects, these strategies will certainly not work for every individual suspect—there will always be innocent people who nonetheless provide mistaken or uncorroborated alibis. At numerous points in the legal process, evaluators (detectives, jurors, etc.) must attempt to determine if a suspect is telling the truth or lying about their alibi without the luxury of being able to rely on the existence of strong, corroborative evidence. Consequently, a third general strategy to improve the quality of alibi evidence requires improving evaluators' abilities to discriminate between honest and deceptive suspects.

Discriminating Between Honest and Deceptive Suspects Who Lack Person Corroborators

People tend to be poor at discriminating between truthful and deceptive statements in general (Bond Jr. & DePaulo, 2006), as well as between truthful and deceptive alibis in particular (Culhane et al., 2013; Nieuwkamp et al., 2018). The reasons for this poor observed performance are numerous (e.g., see Vrij et al., 2010). As one example, people often base their judgments of deception on cues that are not diagnostic of actual deception. For instance, one of the primary cues that alibi evaluators believe signals a deceptive alibi is inconsistency: Changes to an alibi are generally perceived as indicative of dishonesty (Dysart & Strange, 2012; Culhane & Hosch, 2012). However, given the observed prevalence of honest/mistaken suspects who make changes to their alibi following investigation (e.g., Olson & Charman, 2012; Strange et al., 2014), this perception is often misplaced. Using inconsistency as a proxy for deception will thus result in many innocent suspects being mistakenly classified as deceptive. In general, behavioral cues to deception tend to be weak and unreliable (DePaulo et al., 2003). Other deception detection methods that rely on presumed differences between truth-tellers and liars, such as the assumption that liars tend to become more physiologically aroused than truth-tellers, have similarly been shown to be misguided (National Research Council, 2003).

Due to these observed failures to discriminate between truth-tellers and liars, researchers have recently shifted their focus towards a more cognitive approach to deception detection (Vrij, 2015). This approach is based on the underlying logic that guilty suspects are under greater cognitive demands than innocent suspects, as liars must not only remember their prefabricated lies but also ensure that they are consistent across numerous recountings, monitor their own behavioral cues, and monitor the interviewer's reactions to their stories (Vrij et al., 2006). Because truth-tellers, in contrast, should tend to simply rely on their memories when recalling events, they are not under the same cognitive load as liars. Numerous techniques have been developed that maximize discernible differences between liars and truth-tellers by capitalizing on these cognitive differences (e.g., see Giolla & Luke, 2021, and Vrij et al., 2017, for overviews).

Alibi researchers have also attempted to leverage this difference in cognitive demands between liars and truth-tellers to improve deception detection. Sauerland et al. (2019) reasoned that if suspects were later confronted with a version of their previously generated alibi that contained inconsistencies, guilty people should be less likely to notice those discrepancies than innocent people due to their greater cognitive demands. To test this idea, they had participants either engage in a "crime" (taking an envelope from an unattended jacket) or not. Prior to being questioned about their whereabouts, participants were instructed to be either truthful or deceptive about their activities. Participants then provided their alibi. Approximately 1 week later, participants returned and were interviewed again about their alibi; critically, the interviewer asked a number of questions regarding the initial alibi in which specific details had been altered. The researchers recorded whether participants noticed these discrepancies to their alibi during this interview, whether they were willing to sign an alibi statement that contained these discrepancies, and whether they reported noticing those discrepancies in retrospect. Their results, however, did not conform to their predictions: Guilty suspects were no less likely than innocent suspects to notice discrepancies to their alibi, whether during the interview, at the signing of the altered alibi, or in retrospect.

Dhammapeera et al. (2020) investigated a different approach to discriminating between innocent and guilty suspects. After either committing a mock crime (stealing a ring) or not, participants completed a computerized autobiographical implicit association test (aIAT). In an aIAT, participants are provided with a series of statements that vary according to whether they are true (e.g., "I am seated in front of a computer") or false (e.g., "I am in a restaurant") and whether they are guilt-related (e.g., "I stole a ring") or innocence-related (e.g., "I bought a ring"). Participants are tasked with classifying each statement as either true or false or as guilt-related or innocence-related as quickly as possible by pressing one of two computer keys. Critically, they do so in two different blocks. In the guilt-congruent block, participants classify true statements and guilt-related statements using the same key (and false statements and innocence-related statements using a different key); in the guilt-incongruent block, participants classify true statements and innocence-related statements using the same key (and false statements and guilt-related statements using a different key). The logic is that a guilty person has automatic implicit associations between the concepts of "guilt" and "truth" and that consequently, they should tend to find it easier to classify statements in guilt-congruent blocks than in guilt-incongruent blocks. Innocent people, in contrast, should have automatic implicit associations between the concepts of "innocent" and "truth," thus making it easier for them to classify statements in guilt-incongruent blocks than in guilt-congruent blocks. Therefore, guilty and innocent suspects should be able to be discriminated by looking at how long it takes people to make guilt-congruent classifications versus guilt-incongruent classifications (e.g., Agosta & Sartori, 2013; Sartori et al., 2008).

However, Dhammapeera et al. (2020) noted a potential critical limitation to this finding that undermines the practical use of the aIAT in discriminating between guilty and innocent alibi-providing suspects. Specifically, they reasoned that a guilty suspect who plans and rehearses a deceptive alibi is effectively creating and storing information in memory that makes the deceptive alibi similar (in terms of the neural characteristics of the stored information) to a truthful alibi. If so, then rehearsing a deceptive alibi would basically provide guilty suspects with a countermeasure to the aIAT, as the aIAT would be unable to discriminate between truthful alibis and rehearsed deceptive alibis. Indeed, their results were consistent with this logic. As shown in prior studies, guilty suspects who did not rehearse an alibi responded more quickly for guilt-congruent trials than guilt-incongruent trials, whereas innocent suspects responded more quickly for guilt-incongruent trials than for guilt-congruent trials. In other words, the aIAT could discriminate between innocent and guilty suspects. However, this difference was largely eliminated if guilty suspects had mentally rehearsed an alibi prior to the test: The aIAT was unable to substantially discriminate between innocent suspects and guilty suspects who rehearsed an alibi.

Discriminating Between Truthful and Deceptive Suspects Who Have Person Corroborators

Given that the deception detection literature generally shows that people are poor at discriminating truths from lies, it is probably not overly surprising that people are also poor at discriminating between true and false alibis. However, unlike typical deception detection participants, alibi-providing suspects have the opportunity to provide a person that can corroborate their alibi. Of course, that corroborator might be lying to cover for a guilty suspect—especially if a family member or a friend (e.g., Culhane et al., 2013; Marion & Burke, 2017; Hosch et al., 2011). Nonetheless, the existence of alibi corroborators opens the door for additional strategies to discriminate between honest and deceptive alibis. Alibi researchers have examined two such strategies.

The first strategy involves attempts to discriminate honest from deceptive alibis based on the consistency between the suspect's story and an alibi corroborator's story. For instance, Strömwall et al. (2003) had pairs of students (representing a suspect and an alibi corroborator) generate either true or false alibis, who were then interrogated about their alibi stories. Video recordings of those interrogations were then shown to participant-evaluators, who attempted to determine if each pair had provided an honest or a deceptive alibi. When later asked how they made their judgments, the most commonly mentioned cue by evaluators was the consistency of the alibi story within each pair: Greater consistency was associated with greater perceptions of honesty (see Chap. 4 for additional discussion on this link). However, consistency was only very poorly related to actual honesty, and consequently, evaluators' abilities to discriminate lying pairs from truth telling pairs were only slightly above chance. In fact, relying on consistency as a proxy for honesty can even backfire. Because lying pairs can plan an alibi ahead of time, whereas truth telling pairs will tend to instead rely on memory—which is prone to normal memory errors—lying pairs are often more consistent than truth telling pairs (Sakrisvold et al., 2017; Vredeveldt et al., 2014).

A second strategy for discriminating pairs of liars from pairs of truth-tellers, known as the verifiability approach (Nahari et al., 2014; Verschuere et al., 2020), involves noting that guilty suspects are faced with a dilemma: Although they should wish to provide a detailed alibi, as detailed accounts tend to be perceived as being more believable (Amado et al., 2016), they also clearly want to avoid providing any information that can be investigated and shown to be false, which would uncover their lie. To satisfy both of these goals, we might expect guilty suspects to provide primarily unverifiable information when reporting their alibis. In contrast, innocent suspects wish their alibis to be verified and should therefore provide primarily verifiable information when reporting their alibis. Consequently, truth-telling pairs, and lying pairs should be able to be discriminated by examining the proportion of verifiable and unverifiable information provided in their alibis. Indeed, using this approach, Nahari and Vrij (2014) were able to correctly classify an impressive 88% of alibi-providing pairs.

Vernham et al. (2020) also applied the verifiability approach to discriminating between guilty and innocent alibi-providing suspects specifically in the context of collective interviewing—when pairs of suspects are interrogated together. These researchers randomly assigned pairs of participants to be either truth-tellers or liars. Truth-tellers engaged in a series of tasks in a park, which would later serve as their alibi. Liars were split up: one participant, playing the role of a guilty suspect, engaged in a mock crime (stealing money from a purse), whereas the other, playing the role of a lying corroborator, engaged in the same series of tasks as the truth-telling pairs. Each pair was told that they would be interrogated for their role in the mock crime and that they should attempt to convince the interrogator that they were together performing the various tasks in the park. Thus, innocent pairs simply told the truth whereas liars had to deceive the interrogator about the guilty suspect's activities. All pairs were then given as much time as needed to prepare their alibis. Alibis were then collected in two ways. First, each individual participant separately provided their own written alibi statement. Second, each pair was reunited and together created a collective alibi statement.

Results were consistent with hypotheses: Lying pairs provided a significantly greater proportion of unverifiable details than truth-telling pairs, and truth-telling pairs provided a significantly greater proportion of verifiable details than lying pairs (Vernham et al., 2020). A follow-up study (reported in the same paper) indicated that evaluators who were informed of the verifiability approach were able to successfully discriminate truth-tellers from liars almost 80% of the time, but only if they were given just the pair's collective alibi statement. Evaluators given either individual alibi statements or the individual statements along with the collective alibi statement performed no better than chance. When given individual alibi statements, it seems that evaluators' natural tendency was to judge the veracity of those statements by their consistency; because greater consistency tended to be associated with liars, relying on consistency across alibi statements harmed evaluators' judgments.

Although a verifiability approach appears to be one of the more promising approaches to improving discrimination, three important practical limitations should be noted. First, this approach is limited to suspects who have a corroborator who supports their alibi, which may not be the case among many real-world suspects. Second, due to evaluators' tendencies to erroneously rely on consistency across alibi statements as a proxy for accuracy, the verifiability approach requires investigators to permit the suspect and corroborator to discuss and plan their alibi prior to providing a collective statement—something that law enforcement might not be willing to do out of fear of guilty suspects generating stronger false alibis. Third, the success of the verifiability approach should be limited to certain types of alibis: those that allow for truth-tellers to generate verifiable information. Assuming that a lack of verifiable information is indicative of lying will result in the mistaken classification of truth-telling pairs as liars among suspect pairs who simply have no verifiable information to provide in the first place (e.g., a husband and wife who were at home reading). Alternative approaches to improving discrimination that are not subject to these same limitations would be highly desirable.

Conclusions

Although an increasing amount of alibi research has documented the difficulties that innocent people have generating believable alibis, few studies have taken a system variable approach by attempting to develop strategies to improve the quality of alibi evidence—and even fewer have been successful. The difficulties in developing these strategies are substantial, as innocent suspects generally lack a memory of their whereabouts during the critical time period (instead often relying on their schemas to provide an alibi), which can undercut known memory-improvement strategies. Furthermore, discriminating between honest and deceptive alibis has been a difficult task, and attempts to improve that discrimination are only successful in limited circumstances.

In this chapter, we have argued that adopting a system variable approach to alibis and developing strategies to improve alibi evidence will require novel, multi-pronged solutions, in part because alibi-providing suspects are best characterized according to a tripartite classification, in which they can be deceptive, honest/mistaken, or honest/accurate. This tripartite classification means that a system variable approach to alibi evidence requires focusing both on accuracy concerns (i.e., helping innocent suspects generate accurate alibis) and on veracity concerns (i.e., improving evaluators' abilities to discriminate between truthful and deceptive suspects). We have laid out three broad strategies to accomplish these goals: (1) developing strategies to transform honest/mistaken suspects into honest/accurate suspects (e.g., by allowing them access to phones prior to providing an alibi: Matuku & Charman, 2021); (2) developing strategies to help innocent suspects recall evidence that might help to exonerate them (e.g., through chronological recall and perspective-taking instructions: Matuku & Charman, 2020); and (3) developing strategies to help evaluators discriminate between honest and deceptive alibis (e.g., by using a verifiability approach: Vernham et al., 2020). It is our hope that this chapter will inspire future alibi researchers to pursue additional strategies to improve the quality of alibi evidence.

References

Agosta, S., & Sartori, G. (2013). The autobiographical IAT: A review. *Frontiers in Psychology, 4*, 1–12. https://doi.org/10.3389/fpsyg.2013.00519

Amado, B. G., Arce, R., Fariña, F., & Vilariño, M. (2016). Criteria-based content analysis (CBCA) reality criteria in adults: A meta-analytic review. *International Journal of Clinical and Health Psychology, 16*, 201–210. https://doi.org/10.1016/j.ijchp.2016.01.002

Anderson, S. J., & Conway, M. A. (1993). Investigating the structure of autobiographical memories. *Journal of Experimental Psychology: Learning, Memory, and Cognition, 19*, 1178–1196. https://doi.org/10.1037/0278-7393.19.5.1178

Anderson, R. C., & Pichert, J. W. (1978). Recall of previously unrecallable information following a shift in perspective. *Journal of Verbal Learning and Verbal Behavior, 17*, 1–12. https://doi.org/10.1016/S0022-5371(78)90485-1

Allison, M., Jung, S., & Benjamin, A. C. (2020). Alibi believability: Corroborative evidence and contextual factors. *Behavioral Sciences & the Law, 38*, 337–354. https://doi.org/10.1002/bsl.2473

Bond, C. F., Jr., & DePaulo, B. M. (2006). Accuracy of deception judgments. *Personality and Social Psychology Review, 10*, 214–234. https://doi.org/10.1207/s15327957pspr1003_2a

Cardenas, S. A., Crozier, W., & Strange, D. (2020). Right place, wrong time: The limitations of mental reinstatement of context on alibi-elicitation. *Psychology, Crime & Law, 27*, 201–230. https://doi.org/10.1080/1068316X.2020.1798424

Charman, S. D., Carbone, J., Kekessie, S., & Villalba, D. (2016). Evidence evaluation and evidence integration in legal decision-making: Order of evidence presentation as a moderator of context effects. *Applied Cognitive Psychology, 30*, 214–225. https://doi.org/10.1002/acp.3181

Charman, S. D., Matuku, K., & Mosser, A. (2019). The psychology of alibis. In M. Miller & B. Bornstein (Eds.), *Advances in psychology and law*. Springer Nature.

Charman, S. D., Reyes, A., Villalba, D. K., & Evans, J. R. (2017). The (un)reliability of alibi corroborators: Failure to recognize faces of briefly encountered strangers puts innocent suspects at risk. *Behavioral Sciences & the Law, 35*, 18–36. https://doi.org/10.1002/bsl.2264

Culhane, S. E., & Hosch, H. M. (2004). An alibi witness' influence on mock jurors' verdicts. *Journal of Applied Social Psychology, 34*, 1604–1616. https://doi.org/10.1111/j.1559-1816.2004.tb02789.x

Culhane, S. E., & Hosch, H. M. (2012). Changed alibis: Current law enforcement, future law enforcement, and layperson reactions. *Criminal Justice and Behavior, 39*, 958–977. https://doi.org/10.1177/0093854812438185

Culhane, S. E., Hosch, H. M., & Kehn, A. (2008). Alibi generation: Data from U.S. Hispanics and U.S. Non-Hispanic whites. *Journal of Ethnicity in Criminal Justice, 6*, 177–199. https://doi.org/10.1080/15377930802243395

Culhane, S. E., Kehn, A., Horgan, A. J., Meissner, C. A., Hosch, H. M., & Wodahl, E. J. (2013). Generation and detection of true and false alibi statements. *Psychiatry, Psychology and Law, 20*, 619–638. https://doi.org/10.1080/13218719.2012.729018

Dando, C., Wilcock, R., & Milne, R. (2009). The cognitive interview: The efficacy of a modified mental reinstatement of context procedure for frontline police investigators. *Applied Cognitive Psychology, 23*, 138–147. https://doi.org/10.1002/acp.1451

DePaulo, B. M., Lindsay, J. J., Malone, B. E., Muhlenbruck, L., Charlton, K., & Cooper, H. (2003). Cues to deception. *Psychological Bulletin, 129*, 74–118. https://doi.org/10.1037/0033-2909.129.1.74

Dhammapeera, P., Hu, X., & Bergström, Z. M. (2020). Imagining a false alibi impairs concealed memory detection with the autobiographical IAT. *Journal of Experimental Psychology: Applied, 26*, 266–282. https://doi.org/10.1037/xap0000250

Dysart, J. E., & Strange, D. (2012). Beliefs about alibis and alibi investigations: A survey of law enforcement. *Psychology, Crime & Law, 18*, 11–25. https://doi.org/10.1080/1068316x.2011.562867

Eastwood, J., Snook, B., & Au, D. (2016). Safety in numbers: A policy-capturing study of the alibi assessment process. *Applied Cognitive Psychology, 30*, 260–269. https://doi.org/10.1002/acp.3200

Fisher, R. P., & Geiselman, R. E. (1992). *Memory enhancing techniques for investigative interviewing: The cognitive interview*. Charles C. Thomas.

Giolla, E. M., & Luke, T. J. (2021). Does the cognitive approach to lie detection improve the accuracy of human observers? *Applied Cognitive Psychology, 35*, 385–392. https://doi.org/10.1002/acp.3777

Granhag, P. A., & Hartwig, M. (2015). The strategic use of evidence (SUE) technique: A conceptual overview. In P. A. Granhag, A. Vrij, & B. Vershuere (Eds.), *Deception detection: Current challenges and new directions* (pp. 231–251). Wiley.

Hosch, H. M., Culhane, S. E., Jolly, K. W., Chavez, R. M., & Shaw, L. H. (2011). Effects of an alibi witness's relationship to the defendant on mock jurors' judgments. *Law and Human Behavior, 35*, 127–142. https://doi.org/10.1007/s10979-010-9225-5

Leins, D. A., & Charman, S. D. (2016). Schema reliance and innocent alibi generation. *Legal and Criminological Psychology, 21*, 111–126. https://doi.org/10.1111/lcrp.12035

Marion, S. B., & Burke, T. M. (2017). Altruistic lying in an alibi corroboration context: The effects of liking, compliance, and relationship between suspects and witnesses. *Behavioral Sciences & the Law, 35*, 37–59. https://doi.org/10.1002/bsl.2269

Matuku, K., & Charman, S. D. (2020). Enhancing innocent suspects' memories for corroborating evidence. *Psychology, Public Policy, and Law, 26*, 442–454. https://doi.org/10.1037/law0000264

Matuku, K., & Charman, S. D. (2021). Alibi generation: Improving innocent suspects' accuracy. Manuscript in preparation.

Memon, A., Meissner, C. A., & Fraser, J. (2010). The cognitive interview: A meta-analytic review and study space analysis of the past 25 years. *Psychology, Public Policy, and Law, 16*, 340–372. https://doi.org/10.1037/a0020518

Mosser, A., & Evans, J. (2019). Increasing the number of contacts generated during contact tracing interviews. *Memory, 27*, 495–506. https://doi.org/10.1080/09658211.2018.1529247

Nahari, G., & Vrij, A. (2014). Can I borrow your alibi? The applicability of the verifiability approach to the case of an alibi witness. *Journal of Applied Research in Memory and Cognition, 3*, 89–94. https://doi.org/10.1016/j.jarmac.2014.04.005

Nahari, G., Vrij, A., & Fisher, R. P. (2014). Exploiting liars' verbal strategies by examining the verifiability of details. *Legal and Criminological Psychology, 19*, 227–239. https://doi.org/10.1111/j.2044-8333.2012.02069.x

National Research Council. (2003). *The polygraph and lie detection. Committee to review the scientific evidence on the polygraph*. The National Academies Press.

Nieuwkamp, R., Horselenberg, R., & van Koppen, P. (2018). True and false alibis among prisoners and their detection by police detectives. *Psychiatry, Psychology and Law, 25*, 902–921. https://doi.org/10.1080/13218719.2018.1482570

Olson, E. A., & Charman, S. D. (2012). 'But can you prove it?' – Examining the quality of innocent suspects' alibis. *Psychology, Crime, and Law, 18*, 453–471. https://doi.org/10.1080/1068316X.2010.505567

Olson, E. A., & Wells, G. L. (2004). What makes a good alibi? A proposed taxonomy. *Law and Human Behavior, 28*, 157–176. https://doi.org/10.1023/B:LAHU.0000022320.47112.d3

Sakrisvold, M. L., Granhag, P. A., & Mac Giolla, E. (2017). Partners under pressure: Examining the consistency of true and false alibi statements. *Behavioral Sciences & the Law, 35*, 75–90. https://doi.org/10.1002/bsl.2275

Sargent, M. J., & Bradfield, A. L. (2004). Race and information processing in criminal trials: Does the defendant's race affect how the facts are evaluated? *Personality and Social Psychology Bulletin, 30*, 995–1008. https://doi.org/10.1177/0146167204265741

Sartori, G., Agosta, S., Zogmaister, C., Ferrara, S. D., & Castiello, U. (2008). How to accurately detect autobiographical events. *Psychological Science, 19*, 772–780. https://doi.org/10.1111/j.1467-9280.2008.02156.x

Sauerland, M., Krix, A. C., & Sagana, A. (2019). Deceiving suspects about their alibi is equally harmful to the innocent and guilty. *Applied Cognitive Psychology, 33*, 1238–1246. https://doi.org/10.1002/acp.3577

Strange, D., Dysart, J., & Loftus, E. F. (2014). Why errors in alibis are not necessarily evidence of guilt. *Zeitschrift Fur Psychologie, 222*, 82–89. https://doi.org/10.1027/2151-2604/a000169

Strömwall, L. A., Granhag, P. A., & Jonsson, A. C. (2003). Deception among pairs: "Let's say we had lunch and hope they will swallow it!". *Psychology, Crime, and Law, 9*, 109–124. https://doi.org/10.1080/1068316031000116238

Tulving, E., & Thomson, D. M. (1973). Encoding specificity and retrieval processes in episodic memory. *Psychological Review, 80*, 352–373. https://doi.org/10.1037/h0020071

Vernham, Z., Vrij, A., Nahari, G., Leal, S., Mann, S., Satchell, L., & Orthey, R. (2020). Applying the verifiability approach to deception detection in alibi witness situations. *Acta Psychologica, 204*, 1–14. https://doi.org/10.1016/j.actpsy.2020.103020

Verschuere, B., Bogaard, G., & Meijer, E. (2020). Discriminating deceptive from truthful statements using the verifiability approach: A meta-analysis. *Applied Cognitive Psychology, 35*, 374–384. https://doi.org/10.1002/acp.3775

Vredeveldt, A., van Koppen, P. J., & Granhag, P. A. (2014). The inconsistent suspect: A systematic review of different types of consistency in truth tellers and liars. In R. H. C. Bull (Ed.), *Investigative interviewing* (pp. 183–207). Springer.

Vrij, A. (2015). A cognitive approach to lie detection. In P. A. Granhag, A. Vrij, & B. Verschuere (Eds.), *Wiley series in the psychology of crime, policing and law. Detecting deception: Current challenges and cognitive approaches* (pp. 205–229). Wiley-Blackwell.

Vrij, A., Fisher, R., Mann, S., & Leal, S. (2006). Detecting deception by manipulating cognitive load. *Trends in Cognitive Science, 10*, 141–142. https://doi.org/10.1016/j.tics.2006.02.003

Vrij, A., Granhag, P. A., & Porter, S. (2010). Pitfalls and opportunities in nonverbal and verbal lie detection. *Psychological Science in the Public Interest, 11*, 89–121. https://doi.org/10.1177/1529100610390861

Vrij, A., Fisher, R. P., & Blank, H. (2017). A cognitive approach to lie detection: A meta-analysis. *Legal and Criminological Psychology, 22*, 1–21. https://doi.org/10.1111/lcrp.12088

Wells, G. L. (1978). Applied eyewitness-testimony research: System variables and estimator variables. *Journal of Personality and Social Psychology, 36*, 1546–1557. https://doi.org/10.1037/0022-3514.36.12.1546

Wells, G. L., Small, M., Penrod, S., Malpass, R. S., Fulero, S. M., & Brimacombe, C. A. E. (1998). Eyewitness identification procedures: Recommendations for lineups and photospreads. *Law and Human Behavior, 22*, 603–647. https://doi.org/10.1023/A:1025750605807

Chapter 6
Alibi Assessment and Believability Across Different Legal Systems and Cultural Contexts

Ricardo Nieuwkamp and Lore Mergaerts

An alibi can be considered as one of the strongest defenses for an innocent person to prove his innocence, as an alibi consists of a suspect's claim that he cannot have committed the alleged crime because he was elsewhere. One can simply not be in two locations at the same time. As such, an alibi can distinguish between innocents and perpetrators. In this regard, the importance of the assessment of the believability of an alibi can hardly be neglected.

There has been quite some academic research on alibi believability assessment (see Chap. 4 of this text). To date, most of the existing studies are, however, exclusively Anglo-Saxon, focusing on the alibi evaluation by (mock) jurors (i.e., undergraduate students). So far, research on the evaluation of alibis in the early stages of proceedings, such as during a police vs. prosecutorial investigation – which is important within civil law and more inquisitorial legal systems – is scarce. Because of the differences between legal systems – in particular adversarial and inquisitorial systems – it can be assumed that the assessment of alibi believability also varies depending on the nature of the legal system at stake. The results from the limited research in a non-Anglo-Saxon legal system indeed suggest some differences regarding the assessment of alibi believability across legal systems (e.g., Nieuwkamp et al., 2018; Sauerland et al., 2016). As such, this to some extent allows researchers to determine to what degree the existing Anglo-Saxon research is also applicable to a more inquisitorial context.

The aim of this chapter is to address both the differences and the robustness of alibi research across legal systems. First, we will briefly discuss the relevant differences between adversarial and inquisitorial systems. In the remainder of the chapter,

R. Nieuwkamp (✉)
Expert Research Data Management Competence Centre (RDM-CC), KU Leuven, Leuven, Belgium

L. Mergaerts
KU Leuven, Leuven, Belgium

J. D. Behl, M. R. Kienzle (eds.), *Alibis and Corroborators*,
https://doi.org/10.1007/978-3-030-95663-9_6

we turn to the similarities and differences coming forward in research on alibi assessment according to the two dominant domains of alibi assessment: (1) alibi generation and validation and (2) alibi believability and discrimination (Burke et al., 2007).

Background: Alibi Assessment in Different Legal Systems

In general, two types of legal systems exist in which the pretrial investigation is embedded: an inquisitorial or an adversarial system (P. J. Van Koppen & Penrod, 2003a). However, pure adversarial or inquisitorial systems do not occur. This implies that, within the civil law tradition, a mixed system may exist in which characteristics of both inquisitorial and adversarial criminal proceedings are expressed. As such, the importance of the adversarial model has increased in European legal systems. This is for instance happening under the influence of case law of the European Court of Human Rights (ECtHR) concerning the right to a fair trial, as guaranteed by Article 6 of the European Convention on Human Rights (ECHR). A striking example of this is undoubtedly the right of access to a lawyer for suspects during police interviews (e.g., see the Salduz v. Turkey ECtHR judgment). It is precisely this increasing interaction between the inquisitorial and adversarial model of criminal procedure that makes the findings from Anglo-American countries considerably relevant for continental countries and vice versa.

In most continental countries in Western Europe, however, the pre-trial investigation has a predominantly inquisitorial character, whereby the public prosecutor and by extension the police look for both inculpatory and exculpatory evidence, while the suspect has a rather passive role. In countries with an adversarial tradition, the suspect is pitted against the State, and the prosecution service may restrict itself to gathering only incriminating evidence, and the suspect and his lawyer are more active participants in the evidence gathering process (De Smet, 1999; Van den Wyngaert & De Smet, 2014; Van Koppen & Penrod, 2003a, 2003b). As an active participant in the criminal investigation, the suspect then has to organize his own defense (Baldwin, 1993; Norfolk & Stark, 2011).

In systems with a predominantly inquisitorial character during the pre-trial investigation, the role of police detectives is crucial and cannot be neglected. Indeed, in predominantly inquisitorial systems, the police interview of victims, witnesses, and suspects is a crucial part – if not the center piece – of a criminal investigation. In practice, police detectives are the ones to create a first impression of the believability of the suspect's alibi. The initial suspect interviews are a key investigative act in the criminal investigation (Baldwin, 1993; Norfolk & Stark, 2011; Walsh et al., 2017). The gathered information in those interviews is crucial to further develop the investigation in light of the evidence gathered. For example, if a suspect claims to be where CCTV footage may exist, those tapes should be collected as soon as possible to reduce the risk the evidence may no longer be available. Furthermore, witnesses may forget having seen the suspect as time increases between the alleged crime and the moment of questioning. This should provide insight into the involvement of certain persons in a criminal offense and the circumstances of what happened. However, victims, witnesses, and suspects do not always provide truthful statements, whether consciously or not and for various reasons (Redlich et al., 2016; Vredeveldt & Van der Zee, 2017). As such, interviewing suspects is a particularly complex task for investigators. After all, there are always two possible scenarios: the suspect is involved in the offense (guilty scenario) or has nothing to do with it (innocent scenario). In view of the court hearing, evidence collected throughout the course of the criminal investigation will determine the probability of either scenario (Crombag et al., 2006). From this point of view, in inquisitorial systems, detectives already try to assess the suspect's involvement during the interview.

The suspect's alibi can be an important starting point for an alternative scenario such that the suspect claims that he cannot be the perpetrator because he was somewhere else (Nieuwkamp, 2018). The suspect's alibi should then be assessed on its merits and compared with other inculpatory and exculpatory evidence, so it can contribute to assessing the likelihood of the alternative, innocent, or guilty scenario. This will avoid an innocent person being suspected and deprived of their liberty for longer than necessary, but will also avoid an offender being presumed innocent.

Alibi Generation and Validation

The importance of an alibi as a starting point for alternative scenarios becomes apparent when focusing on the initial stages of alibi assessment. This claim of innocence is referred to as alibi generation and can be supported by corroborating evidence, which is referred to as validation of the alibi (Burke et al., 2007; Olson, 2002). During the alibi generation and validation stages, the suspect or defendant explains that he cannot have committed the alleged crime as he was elsewhere during that time. The reported evidence should then be evaluated to determine whether the validation is accurate as suspects and defendants may report false supportive evidence (Culhane et al., 2013; Nieuwkamp et al., 2018).

The corroborating evidence typically consists of witness and/or physical evidence (Olson & Wells, 2004). More recently, researchers suggested that also the unique knowledge of a suspect or defendant could serve as corroborative alibi evidence (Nieuwkamp, 2018; Van Koppen & Nieuwkamp, 2017). Where witness evidence consists of a witness's testimony that the suspect or defendant was indeed somewhere else than where the alleged crime was committed, physical evidence refers to tangible evidence that supports the suspect's claim, such as CCTV recordings or a receipt. In general, witness evidence is considered as less believable evidence by evaluators compared to physical evidence (e.g., Olson & Wells, 2004) as witnesses can be mistaken or could lie in favor of the suspect (see Chaps. 2, 3, and 4 for more information on types of corroborating alibi evidence and how they are perceived by evaluators).

For the criminal investigation, it is crucial that the available evidence is gathered as soon as possible in order to determine the veracity of the alibi and corroborating evidence. When time passes, the chances increase that the evidence itself is altered or even erased or the quality weakened. For example, with physical corroborative evidence, the recording of surveillance cameras can be erased. For person corroborative evidence, the likelihood increases that witnesses' memories are more likely to be mistaken, and the suspect's unique knowledge of events away from the crime may be lost as time increases between the generation of the alibi and when the potential supportive evidence is investigated.

In an adversarial system, two main parties gather the evidence: the prosecution and the defense. Where the prosecution may have knowledge, means, and experience in how and where to collect the evidence, this may not always be the case for the defense. Consequently, this may lead to delays in gathering the necessary evidence, which might have negative impacts on potential supportive evidence for an alibi. On the contrary, in a predominantly inquisitorial system, the police collect both inculpatory and exculpatory evidence, mostly on behalf of the prosecutor. The defense may also bring forward pieces of evidence, but this usually only occurs if the criminal file is deemed incomplete by defense attorneys in preparation of the court hearings.

Alibi Evaluation and Discrimination

A Case Study: John Travolta

Once the suspect or defendant has reported his alibi and corresponding evidence, the believability and veracity of the claim of innocence need to be assessed. The importance and the impact an alibi can have for an innocent suspect cannot be underestimated. This importance is illustrated by the following case: on January 16, 2012, John Travolta was accused of sexually assaulting a male massage therapist. The therapist claimed that Travolta had grabbed his penis in the Beverly Hills Hotel in Los Angeles. The accusation was reported in the media for the first time on May 8, 2012 (D'Zurilla, 2012). The day after the news broke, Travolta told the media that he had been in New York when the alleged assault took place and therefore could not have committed the assault (Goodhand, 2012). Mr. Travolta's alibi was corroborated with three pieces of physical evidence: (a) flight records that indicated that his private jet flew from Los Angeles on January 15, 2012, at 9:00 PM and landed at 4:38 AM in New York on January 16, 2012; (b) a receipt printed at 11:38 PM on January 16 at a Chinese restaurant in New York, paid with a credit card and signed by John Travolta (Britney, 2012); and (c) at least two photographs of Travolta taken in the Greenwich Hotel in New York at 4:30 PM and at 5:21 PM that same day (D'Zurilla, 2012). These items of physical evidence demonstrated that Travolta was in New York and not in Los Angeles on January 16, 2012. In response to the alibi, the massage therapist explained to the media that he had been mistaken about the date of the sexual assault (Dillon, 2012). He withdrew his accusations against Travolta a few days later (Sinha-Roy, 2012). This shows that an alibi can lead to the withdrawal of an invalid claim, making prosecution no longer viable.

Alibi Evaluation in Inquisitorial and Adversarial Systems

In a predominantly inquisitorial system, the police (rather than the trier of fact) will determine the believability of an alibi, and a judge or jury will evaluate the alibi in light of all the evidence available – which implies taking into account both inculpatory and exculpatory evidence. The judge or jury will put all the evidence into balance and determine which scenario is more plausible than the other: a guilty scenario where the supportive alibi evidence is weak and is accompanied with strong incriminating evidence or an innocent scenario where the supportive alibi evidence is strong and the incriminating evidence is weak. In that sense, the judge or jury will not specifically determine the veracity of the alibi but will evaluate an alibi in light of all the presented evidence.

In inquisitorial systems, the determination of the alibi believability is a task for the police. Based on the reported alibi and supportive evidence, they may gather the reported exculpatory evidence (e.g., collect the recordings of surveillance cameras) and conduct investigative acts (e.g., questioning witnesses who may support the alibi or determine the uniqueness of the suspect's knowledge). In the Netherlands, one of the countries where the criminal proceedings have a predominantly inquisitorial character, very few alibis are presented at court (Nieuwkamp, 2015) as suspects with believable alibis are ruled out as a potential perpetrator and are not prosecuted. The alibis that are presented during trial often consist of alibis supported by weak evidence (Nieuwkamp, 2015).

In an adversarial system, both the prosecution and defense search for evidence that makes each of their cases as strong as possible. The veracity of each piece of evidence is determined during the trial where either the judge or a jury decides on the believability of the evidence and ultimately whether or not the defendant is guilty. Also, in adversarial systems, the timing of the alibi is important. A study from Sommers and Douglass (2007) already showed that if the alibi is presented early (i.e., during police questioning), it is considered to be more believable compared to when the same alibi is introduced late (i.e., during the trial; see Fawcett, 2016). In the United States and Canada, the prosecution must be notified in advance – normally 14 days before – but the timing differs between individual states in the United States (Allison et al., 2020; see also Chap. 8 of this text). This prior notice is needed for the prosecution to investigate the reported alibi. As the burden of proof rests on the prosecution, they must demonstrate that the reported alibi is false when the defendant is the actual perpetrator.

In adversarial systems, the (ultimate) alibi evaluation is predominantly conducted by judges and jurors who will determine the alibi believability and the strength of the corroborating evidence (see discussion of the alibi taxonomy in Chap. 2 of this text). When an alibi is presented during trial, mock jurors (i.e., students) tend to set high expectation in order to believe the defendant's alibi (e.g., Jung et al., 2013). But in practice, police detectives and prosecutors in adversarial systems may face a suspect who claims to be innocent and reports an alibi (Dysart & Strange, 2012). It appears that the timing of the alibi is important (i.e., the sooner, the better) and that the most believable alibis are those supported by (strong) physical evidence and/or an unmotivated witness. In contrast, police detectives in the Netherlands are less interested in the strength of the corroborating evidence. They tend to focus on the verifiability of the reported evidence (Nieuwkamp, 2018), whereas Dutch students – like student mock jurors in adversarial countries – also find the strength of the supportive evidence most important for the alibi evaluation.

The approach taken by Dutch police detectives aligns well with the verifiability approach (Nahari & Vrij, 2014). That approach shows that truth-tellers are more inclined to report information that is verifiable (e.g., I called my friend Kris yesterday evening), while liars will present information that is more difficult to verify (e.g., when I walked to my house, I saw a black Audi). The assumption of the verifiability approach is that truth-tellers will report more verifiable details and evidence than liars or suspects who provided a false alibi (Nahari & Vrij, 2014). The results from a recent meta-analysis (Verschuere et al., 2021) indeed demonstrate that truth-tellers report more verifiable details in absolute numbers and in higher proportions than liars do, especially when the statement consists of a suspect's alibi.

Different Systems or Different Research Participants?

This difference between Dutch and US detectives may stipulate an important difference between the approach taken in inquisitorial and adversarial legal systems. Where US detectives and prosecutors may restrict themselves to searching for incriminating evidence, they set high standards for an alibi to be believable. When the suspect wishes to change the initial reported alibi, 80% of the experienced detectives believe that the initial alibi was a lie (Dysart & Strange, 2012). Dutch detectives take another approach: they assume every reported alibi is true until proven otherwise (Nieuwkamp et al., 2018). As detectives in the Netherlands are trained to think in scenarios (i.e., a guilty scenario where the suspect is the perpetrator and an innocent scenario where the suspect is not involved in the crime), the suspect's alibi could be a good start for such innocent scenario. This difference could be explained due to the nature of the system – predominantly inquisitorial vs. adversarial – but it could also be explained by the background of the research participants. Most studies indeed include students as participants instead of practitioners. Therefore, we tend to believe that the contrary perspectives can be explained by the differential use of participants in research. For example, Eastwood et al. (2016) found that detectives in Canada are more likely to evaluate the reported alibi on the number of alibi witnesses rather than the relational distance to the suspect. This finding contradicts the original alibi taxonomy. Therefore, we want to stress the importance for future research with practitioners in all domains of legal psychology, but for alibi research in particular. This importance was recently also underlined by Cardenas et al. (2021).

As both (student) mock jurors and US detectives set high standards for an alibi to be believable, they could forget how difficult and unrealistic it may be to have such strong evidence for an alibi when you are innocent (Culhane et al., 2013;

Nieuwkamp et al., 2017; Olson & Charman, 2012). One way to alter these high expectations and make mock jurors realize how unlikely it is to have such strong evidence is by first asking mock jurors to generate an alibi for themselves prior to the evaluation of the defendant's alibi. This is referred to as the alibi generation effect (Olson & Wells, 2012). Although this effect has been demonstrated with mock jurors, it does not help police detectives to alter their expectations (Nieuwkamp, 2018). In fact, the alibis reported by the police are similar to those of laypeople, but when put in this position themselves, police detectives tend to report more physical evidence than laypeople. This could inflate their already high expectations, but it appears that this is not the case as detectives report to be more aware of the presence of physical evidence and the variety of forms it may take, whereas laypeople may forget to report such evidence (Dysart & Strange, 2012; Nieuwkamp, 2018). Dutch detectives in particular stipulated that they seek additional evidence to evaluate the suspect's alibi and, as mentioned above, that they focus on the verifiability of the evidence rather than the taxonomy's suggestion of strength of the reported and retrieved evidence.

One can also wonder when evidence can be considered to be strong. The taxonomy of Olson and Wells (2004) and the updated taxonomy in particular (Olson & Charman, 2012) provide some guidelines and have been validated over many years with predominantly (student) mock jurors (Allison et al., 2020). For example, for physical evidence to be considered strong, it must fulfill three criteria: it must be directly linked to the suspect and contain time and location information (e.g., a credit card receipt). However, in practice, often a distinction is made between evidence that is registered to the suspect and contains time and location information (such as the credit card receipt) and physical evidence that can be directly linked to the suspect (i.e., CCTV recordings).

The case of Patrick (name changed for privacy; Nieuwkamp, 2018) shows how important it can be to collect the evidence at the earliest stages of the proceedings and illustrates the potential danger of only focusing on the strength of the reported evidence. On Wednesday November 7, 2001, around 4:00 AM, Brigitte and her two children were killed in their house near Aalst, Belgium. Quite soon in the investigation, Patrick, the father of the family, became a suspect. However, Patrick had an alibi; he was a successful businessman and organized seminars on a regular basis in a conference hotel in Landgraaf, the Netherlands, about 165 km from his residence. He said that he was in the hotel Monday through Thursday of the week that his spouse and children were killed. There is only one entrance to the hotel, which is filmed by a CCTV camera 24 hours a day, 7 days a week. The records from that CCTV camera show that Patrick entered the hotel November 7 at 12:44 AM and left the hotel the following morning at 8:06 AM. The records thus provide strong corroborative evidence for Patrick's alibi because the CCTV records show that Patrick did not leave the hotel that night. His alibi, however, did not set Patrick free. At the crime scene, footprints covered in the victim's blood were found. We know that those footprints belong to Patrick because he has a very specific way of walking. So Patrick can be placed at the crime scene with a great level of certainty.

How can the footprint evidence be brought into agreement with the alibi? To answer that question, it is important to have some additional information about the conference hotel. No tourists were staying in the hotel because the company that organized the seminars rented the entire hotel. All attendees were checked into their rooms at the reception desk, but the keys of the spare rooms remained in the locks on the outside of the rooms, giving all attendees access to the spare rooms. Patrick had checked into a room on the first floor, B.14. On Wednesday November 7, the housekeeper noticed that room B.14 had not been used that night. The bed appeared to be untouched; the shower was dry and showed no signs of use. In the room below Patrick's room on the ground floor B.04 the shower was wet, although nobody was registered in that room. Later it became clear that Patrick snuck out of the window in room B.04 on the night of the murder, but used the shower in that room after he returned (through the same window) and later exited the hotel at 8:06 AM using the single entrance of the hotel (Nieuwkamp, 2018). This case demonstrates why only focusing on the strength of the reported evidence may be dangerous. In this case, Patrick's alibi was supported by the strongest type of supportive alibi evidence, and yet it was still false. Therefore, one should be cautious with drawing inferences from research with less ecologically valid samples, as they may hamper an adequate alibi assessment in practice.

Conclusions

To date, most of the existing studies are exclusively Anglo-Saxon, focusing on the alibi evaluation by (mock) jurors (i.e., undergraduate students). Further, the evaluation of alibis in the early stages of proceedings is mostly ignored in the literature. In most European countries (including the Netherlands), however, the emphasis of the proceedings, including the evidence gathering, lies in the pre-trial investigation. In addition, in most countries with inquisitorial systems, the role of police detectives is somewhat different than in countries with more adversarial systems. It is important to place the alibi research conducted to date in the right context to understand what we already know and how to understand and contextualize the results and to know in which direction the research could evolve in order to ultimately prevent wrongful convictions caused by non-believed alibis.

With regard to the alibi generation domain (i.e., the generation and validation phase), the results across both legal systems are quite robust: innocent people can report their alibi and support it with evidence (Culhane et al., 2013; Nieuwkamp et al., 2017). However, that evidence is most often considered weak for all timeframes of the day. This is true in both adversarial and inquisitorial systems. One should bear in mind that the lives of actual suspects are far less organized compared to the lives of students. The subsequent danger for reporting an alibi could be that one could be mistaken about his whereabouts, which has already occurred in known wrongful conviction cases (Thompson-Cannino et al., 2009).

With regard to the alibi evaluation domain (i.e., the evaluation and discrimination phase), the results across both legal systems are more complicated. The evaluation of an alibi is conducted by (mock) jurors in an adversarial system, whereas, in an inquisitorial system, police detectives determine the alibi believability, and an alibi rarely plays a central role in court. As such, the alibi's believability is predominantly assessed by different parties between the two systems. Police detectives can nevertheless be presented with suspect alibis and will also have to create a first impression of the suspect's alibi believability in adversarial systems as well (Dysart & Strange, 2012; Eastwood et al., 2016). However, in most alibi research to date, often students are asked to take on the role of a mock juror and to determine the alibi believability and/or veracity. The results of such studies show that students find the presence and strength of the evidence most important in determining alibi believability (e.g., Jung et al., 2013; Pozzulo et al., 2015). In such studies (e.g., Allison & Brimacombe, 2010; Hosch et al., 2011) the strength of the reported evidence is manipulated based on the alibi taxonomy (Olson & Wells, 2004). Although the efficacy of the taxonomy has been supported when students in both adversarial (e.g., Allison et al., 2020) and inquisitorial systems (e.g., Sauerland et al., 2016) were included as participants, its efficacy has not yet been demonstrated with practitioners.

Both students (Jung et al., 2013) and police detectives (Dysart & Strange, 2012) are very skeptical toward alibis in criminal proceedings in adversarial systems. They often expect a large amount of strong supportive evidence to find the alibi believable. However, as Culhane et al. (2008) point out, there is an irony in what evidence people find believable and what evidence non-offenders can actually present. The high expectations can be remediated for students via asking research participants to engage in their own generation activities (the so-called alibi generation effect; Olson & Wells, 2012). However, the effect does not apply in the same way to police detectives in inquisitorial systems (Nieuwkamp, 2018). Furthermore, in both legal systems, students find the strength of the supportive alibi evidence the most important factor to determine the alibi believability (Allison et al., 2020; Nieuwkamp et al., 2018).

As Eastwood et al. (2016) found that Canadian detectives focus more on the number of alibi witnesses than the relational distance between the suspect and the witness, the strength of the evidence is of less importance to detectives in inquisitorial systems. However, Dysart and Strange (2012) found that US detectives focus more on the strength of the reported supportive evidence of the alibi. This demonstrates that the differences in the evaluation of alibis in both systems can be explained by the investigative attitude of detectives in the inquisitorial system.

Depending on the nature of the criminal proceedings and the role of the police and judicial authorities within the system, future research should also include other practitioners, such as prosecutors, judges, jurors, and lawyers, when studying alibis. Furthermore, we recommend expanding the scope of future research to practitioners other than police detectives, regardless of the nature of the criminal proceedings. For instance, given that judges or jurors ultimately decide upon the guilt of the defendant, it is valuable to study to what extent the presence of an alibi and the evidence, or lack thereof, to support that alibi plays a role in their decision-making process. In addition, future researchers should examine whether and how defense lawyers use the presence or absence of an alibi in the defense strategy and to what extent they actively pursue evidence to support that alibi (see Chap. 8 of this text for an initial foray into this topic). This is of particular importance in legal systems with a pre-trial investigation that is more adversarial and in which the suspect and his defense lawyer play an active role in gathering the evidence.

References

Allison, M., & Brimacombe, C. (2010). Alibi believability: The effect of prior convictions and judicial instructions. *Journal of Applied Social Psychology, 40*, 1054–1084. https://doi.org/10.1111/j.1559-1816.2010.00610.x

Allison, M., Jung, S., & Benjamin, A. C. (2020). Alibi believability: Corroborative evidence and contextual factors. *Behavioral Sciences & the Law, 38*(4), 337–354.

Baldwin, J. (1993). Police interview techniques. Establishing truth or proof? *The British Journal of Criminology, 33*, 325–352.

Britney, F. (2012). John Travolta sex allegations contradicted by flight records? *The Hollywood Gossip*. Retrieved from http://www.thehollywoodgossip.com/2012/05/john-travolta-allegationscontradicted-by-flight-records/

Burke, T. M., Turtle, J. W., & Olson, E. A. (2007). Alibis in criminal investigations and trials. In M. P. Toglia, J. D. Read, D. F. Ross, & R. C. Lindsay (Eds.), *The handbook of eyewitness psychology: Memory for events* (Vol. 1, pp. 159–192). Lawrence Erlbaum Associates.

Cardenas, S. A., Crozier, W., & Strange, D. (2021). Right place, wrong time: The limitations of mental reinstatement of context on alibi-elicitation. *Psychology, Crime & Law, 27*, 201–230.

Crombag, H. F. M., Van Koppen, P. J., & Wagenaar, W. A. (2006). *Dubieuze zaken: De psychologie van strafrechtelijk bewijs [Dubious cases: The psychology of criminal evidence]*. Olympus.

Culhane, S. E., Hosch, H. M., & Kehn, A. (2008). Alibi generation: Data from U.S. Hispanics and U.S. Non-Hispanic Whites. *Journal of Ethnicity in Criminal Justice, 6*, 177–199.

Culhane, S. E., Kehn, A., Horgan, A. J., Meissner, C. A., Hosch, H. M., & Wodahl, E. J. (2013). Generation and detection of true and false alibi statements. *Psychiatry, Psychology, and Law, 20*, 619–638.

D'Zurilla, C. (2012). John Travolta accused by second man in sexual-battery lawsuit. *Los Angeles Times*. Retrieved from http://articles.latimes.com/2012/may/08/entertainment/le-et-mg-john-travoltasexual-battery-massage/

De Smet, B. (1999). *Internationale samenwerking in strafzaken tussen Angelsaksische en continentale landen [International cooperation in criminal cases between Anglo-Saxon and continental countries]*. Intersentia Rechtswetenschappen.

Dillon, N. (2012). John Travolta scandal: First accuser admits he got wrong date of alleged sexual assault as third man steps forward. New York Daily News. Retrieved from http://www.nydailynews.com/entertainment/gossip/john-travolta-scandalaccuser-admits-wrong-date-alleged-sexualassault-man-steps-article-1.1076518

Dysart, J. E., & Strange, D. (2012). Beliefs about alibis and alibi investigations: A survey of law enforcement. *Psychology, Crime & Law, 18*, 11–25.

Eastwood, J., Snook, B., & Au, D. (2016). Safety in numbers: A policy-capturing study of the alibi assessment process: Alibi assessment. *Applied Cognitive Psychology, 30*, 260–269. https://doi.org/10.1002/acp.3200

Fawcett, H. (2016). The effect of evidence timing and witness motivation upon juror evaluations of alibi witnesses and defendants. *Psychiatry, Psychology, and Law, 23*, 575–587.

Goodhand, A. (2012). John Travolta's attorney says he has flight & hotel records proving actor wasn't in LA. *Radar Online*. Retrieved from http://www.radaronline.com/exclusives/2012/05/john-travolta-attorney-saysproof-he-wasnt-la-time-sexual-harassment-lawsuit/

Hosch, H. M., Culhane, S. E., Jolly, K. W., Chavez, R. M., & Shaw, L. H. (2011). Effects of an alibi witness's relationship to the defendant on mock jurors' judgments. *Law and Human Behavior, 35*, 127–142. https://doi.org/10.1007/s10979-010-9225-5

Jung, S., Allison, M., & Bohn, L. (2013). Legal decision-making on crimes involving an alibi. *Applied Psychology in Criminal Justice, 9*, 45–58.

Nahari, G., & Vrij, A. (2014). Can I borrow your alibi? The applicability of the verifiability approach to the case of an alibi witness. *Journal of Applied Research in Memory and Cognition, 3*, 89–94. https://doi.org/10.1016/j.jarmac.2014.04.005

Nieuwkamp, R. (2015). De geloofwaardigheid van alibi's [the believability of alibis]. *Strafblad, 5*, 428–434.

Nieuwkamp, R. (2018). *Where I was and how I will prove it*. Academic dissertation Maastricht University. Enschede: Gildeprint.

Nieuwkamp, R., Horselenberg, R., & van Koppen, P. (2018). True and false alibis among prisoners and their detection by police detectives. *Psychiatry, Psychology, and Law, 25*, 902–921.

Nieuwkamp, R., Horselenberg, R., & Van Koppen, P. J. (2017). The illusion of the perfect alibi: Establishing the base rate of non-offenders' alibis. *Journal of Investigative Psychology and Offender Profiling, 14*. https://doi.org/10.1002/jip.1470

Norfolk, G. A., & Stark, M. M. (2011). Fitness to be interviewed. In M. M. Stark (Ed.), *Clinical forensic medicine. A physician's guide* (pp. 341–356). Springer.

Olson, E. A. (2002). *Where were you last night? Alibi believability and corroborating evidence: A new direction in psychology and law*. Unpublished master's thesis, Iowa State University.

Olson, E. A., & Charman, S. D. (2012). "But can you prove it?" – Examining the quality of innocent suspects' alibis. *Psychology, Crime & Law, 18*, 453–471.

Olson, E. A., & Wells, G. L. (2004). What makes a good alibi? A proposed taxonomy. *Law and Human Behavior, 28*, 157–176.

Olson, E. A., & Wells, G. L. (2012). The alibi-generation effect: Alibi-generation experience influences alibi evaluation. *Legal and Criminological Psychology, 17*, 151–164.

Pozzulo, J. D., Pettalia, J. L., Dempsey, J. L., & Gooden, A. (2015). Juvenile offenders on trial: Does alibi corroboration evidence and defendant age interact to influence jurors' perceptions and verdicts? *Psychiatry, Psychology and Law, 22*, 224–234. https://doi.org/10.1080/13218719.2014.937518

Redlich, A. D., Walsh, D., Oxburgh, G. E., & Myklebust, T. (2016). Introduction: International developments in practice for suspects of crime. In D. Walsh, G. E. Oxburgh, A. D. Redlich, & T. Myklebust (Eds.), *International developments and practices in investigative interviewing and interrogation* (Vol. 2, pp. 1–5). Routledge.

Sauerland, M., Mehlkopf, S., Krix, A. C., & Sagana, A. (2016). Deceiving suspects about the content of their alibis: Consequences for truthful and untruthful suspects. *Journal of Forensic Practice, 18*, 143–154.

Sinha-Roy, P. (2012). *Masseur drops sexual assault claim against John Travolta*. Reuters. Retrieved from http://www.reuters.com/article/2012/05/15/entertainment-usjohntravolta-idUSBRE84E13020120515

Sommers, S. R., & Douglass, A. B. (2007). Context matters: Alibi strength varies according to evaluator perspective. *Legal and Criminological Psychology, 12*, 41–54. https://doi.org/10.1348/135532506x114301

Thompson-Cannino, J., Cotton, R., & Torneo, E. (2009). *Picking cotton*. St. Martin's Press.

Van den Wyngaert, C., & De Smet, B. (2014). *Strafrecht en strafprocesrecht in hoofdlijnen [Criminal law and criminal procedure law in general lines]*. Maklu.

Van Koppen, M. V., & Nieuwkamp, R. (2017). Alibi's [alibis]. In P. J. van Koppen, J. W. de Keijser, R. Horselenberg, & M. Jelicic (Eds.), *Routes van het Recht. Over rechtspsychologie. [Routes of the law: About legal psychology]* (pp. 249–260). Boom Juridisch.

Van Koppen, P. J., & Penrod, S. D. (2003a). Adversarial or inquisitorial: Comparing systems. In P. J. van Koppen & S. D. Penrod (Eds.), *Adversarial versus inquisitorial justice: Psychological perspectives on criminal justice systems* (pp. 2–20). Plenum.

Van Koppen, P. J., & Penrod, S. D. (2003b). The John Wayne and Judge Dee versions of justice. In P. J. van Koppen & S. D. Penrod (Eds.), *Adversarial versus inquisitorial justice: Psychological perspectives on criminal justice systems* (pp. 347–368). Plenum.

Verschuere, B., Bogaard, G., & Meijer, E. (2021). Discriminating deceptive from truthful statements using the verifiability approach: A meta-analysis. *Applied Cognitive Psychology, 35*(2), 374–384. https://doi.org/10.1002/acp.3775

Vredeveldt, A., & van der Zee, S. (2017). De betekenis van consistentie in verklaringen [The Meaning of Consistency in Statements]. In P. J. van Koppen, J. W. de Keijser, R. Horselenberg & M. Jelicic (Eds.), *Routes van het Recht: Over de Rechtspsychologie [Routes of the Law: About Legal Psychology]*, (p. 669–685). Den Haag: Boom Juridisch.

Walsh, D., King, M., & Griffiths, A. (2017). Evaluating interviews which search for the truth with suspects: But are investigators' self-assessments of their own skills truthful ones? *Psychology, Crime & Law, 23*, 647–665. https://doi.org/10.1080/1068316x.2017.1296149

Chapter 7
Child Alibi Corroborators

Heather L. Price, Andre Kehn, Mariah Sorby, Madison B. Harvey, Mary Cops, and Nikola Klassen

On October 24, 2011, Shanna-Kay Hillary was only 14 years old. That afternoon was like any other: after soccer practice, she returned home from Potsdam High School, took a shower, and discussed dinner options with her father, Oral "Nick" Hillary. Little did she know, her account of the afternoon's events would be consequential in determining whether her father was convicted of murdering 12-year-old Garrett Phillips. Shanna-Kay claimed that she was at home with her father at the time the murder was said to be committed, and her alibi testimony was crucial in her father's defense. Over the next 5 years, Shanna-Kay would be asked to describe the timeline of that afternoon's events several times. The prosecutor questioned the credibility of her alibi testimony. Some of her statements were said to be too consistent, and she was accused of being coached or reminded of what she had said in prior statements. Other statements were not consistent enough (e.g., she could not remember the precise time she got home from school or ate dinner that evening; McKinley, 2016; Shapiro, 2016).

Adults who are parents of school-aged children are often alone with children. Thus, children are likely to be the only alibi corroborators for many adults, as was the case with Nick Hillary. There are, of course, other instances in which adults and children may spend time alone, but do not involve routine caregiving relationships. For example, a child may assist a neighbor with chores, volunteer at their church, or

H. L. Price (✉)
Thompson Rivers University, Kamloops, BC, Canada
e-mail: hprice@tru.ca

A. Kehn · M. Sorby · M. Cops
University of North Dakota, Grand Forks, ND, USA
e-mail: Andre.kehn@UND.edu; mariah.l.sorby@und.edu; mary.cops@und.edu

M. B. Harvey · N. Klassen
Simon Fraser University, Burnaby, BC, Canada
e-mail: madisonh@sfu.ca; nikola_klassen@sfu.ca

J. D. Behl, M. R. Kienzle (eds.), *Alibis and Corroborators*,
https://doi.org/10.1007/978-3-030-95663-9_7

help a coach with after-practice clean-up. In all of these circumstances, the adult may require a child's recollection of their time together to provide evidence of their innocence. However, there may also be instances in which naivety and the malleability of a child's memory are manipulated to provide evidence of innocence when the adult is actually guilty. In contrast to adults for whom motivation is often a salient consideration in alibi corroboration (Olson & Wells, 2004), children are sometimes perceived as inherently honest, and their mistaken recall is attributed to cognitive errors or a desire to please authority figures (e.g., Ross et al., 2003). For instance, Robin Mendez of Minocqua Wisconsin avoided the charges of murdering his wife in 1982 due to the alibi statements provided by his two daughters, Dawn and Christy, who were 13 and 11 years old at the time. Over three decades later, the women allege that their father manipulated and coached them into providing alibis for him. They now claim to be unsure if their memories of the events from all those years ago were accurate or fabricated (Adler, 2019).

Cognitive Abilities Involved in Alibi Corroboration

To corroborate an alibi, one must accurately recollect the time and place of interest to investigators. Further, one must confirm that the suspect was present during a sufficient duration of time that verifies the suspect could not have been involved in the crime. Difficulties in recalling the time, place, and duration of past experiences and activities are well-documented for all ages, particularly if the event is not significant or rehearsed (see Friedman, 1993 for review of adult temporal estimations; see Chap. 3). It is clear from past literature that adults do not directly put time stamps on memories, but instead rely on contextual cues to reconstruct the event and make estimations (Friedman, 1987, 1993; Koriat et al., 2000). For example, to determine the time of year, a person might recall the presence of snow on the ground and conclude that the event took place in the winter. The extant literature on adults' ability to make time estimates reveals some common patterns of inaccuracies. First, events that are remembered more vividly or in more detail tend to be perceived as temporally closer to the present (e.g., Friedman, 1993). This observation is based on distance theories of time estimation that suggest stronger memory traces are more recent (Friedman, 2004). Second, recollection of past experiences is often accompanied by "telescoping" errors, especially after long delays (Friedman, 1993; Koriat et al., 2000; Thompson et al., 1988). Telescoping occurs when a person perceives memories in the past as closer to the present than they actually are (Koriat et al., 2000; Thompson et al., 1988; Wang & Peterson, 2014). Both of these inaccuracies cause the person to close the distance between the actual event and the present in their mental timelines. Third, adults evince superior recall for finer time scales (e.g., day of the week) than larger time scales (e.g., specific date in the month; Friedman, 1987, 1993; Friedman & Wilkins, 1985; Koriat et al., 2000). Finally, there is longstanding evidence that adults tend to underestimate the duration of a task (Roy et al., 2005). These inaccuracies in time estimations can be particularly problematic for alibi corroborators who must search their memory for details about time, place, and duration for a day that was likely insignificant when experienced and may be in the distant past.

It is clear that recalling the time and place of past experiences and activities is difficult for adults. Though specific research on children has not been conducted regarding all of the above patterns (for an exception, see Wang & Peterson, 2014, on children's telescoping errors), it is reasonable to anticipate that this challenge is even more considerable for children. There are many relevant cognitive processes that are not fully mature in children (Luna et al., 2004; Pathman & Ghetti, 2014), which might limit their ability to perform to an adult-like level in recalling time and place. Yet, despite the need for advanced cognitive processes to pinpoint specific times, there is strong evidence that this ability begins to develop quite early and improves with age (e.g., Goodman & Melinder, 2007). Children as young as 4 years old can report events from specific time points in the past (Fivush, 1984; Friedman, 1991). Further, 6-year-olds can recall the day of the week from an event that took place 3 months ago (Pathman et al., 2013, but see Friedman, 1991) and the month and season of an event from several months ago (e.g., Friedman, 1991; Friedman & Lyon, 2005). Further, in one study, 8-to-12-year-olds were able to accurately judge the time of day and the month of salient life events that had occurred 4 years prior (Friedman et al., 2011). Finally, Jack et al. (2016) examined recall of five different time scales (time of day, day of week, month, season, year) for a lab-based event after 8 months in a study of 128 children (9–11 years), adolescents (14–16 years), and adults (25–60 years). Jack et al. (2016) found that children were only less accurate on some time scales (day of week, month) than adults and that adolescents were equally accurate to adults on all measured time scales. The authors, like others (Friedman, 1991; Friedman & Lyon, 2005; Jack et al., 2016; Pathman et al., 2013), concluded that all age groups relied on reconstruction to estimate most time scales.

Of course, tagging an event to its past temporal location is an important first step in alibi corroboration. However, knowledge of the event's duration can also be critical. A child might recall going to the park with her father last Wednesday after school, but if the crime was committed at 4:30 pm, the child must determine if they were at the park long enough to cover the time period of interest. Children's ability to estimate durations of past autobiographical events has received little empirical attention. However, in one creative study, Friedman et al. (2010) asked 6–12-year-old children to estimate the duration of a pediatric examination (actually 5–45 minutes) either 1 week or 1 month after the exam. Children erred by an average of 13 minutes in their estimations, and estimation accuracy was unaffected by delay. Importantly, the largest estimate error was off by 38 minutes, indicating that children's estimations were within a reasonably restricted range. The larger body of research on children's duration estimates using laboratory-based tasks (e.g., estimating the duration of an auditory tone) indicates that there is developmental improvement in duration estimation, which has been attributed to developmental increases in sensitivity to duration (see McCormack, 2015).

Along with the ability to recall the time, place, and duration of events, the order in which events occur is also a crucial aspect of memory recall. Temporal order memory refers to the ability to recall a sequence of actions within an event (Bauer & Leventon, 2013). The two processes involved in temporal order memory are reconstruction and distance-based processes. Recall that reconstruction involves being able to retrieve contextual details about a particular event to make inferences and judgments about when it occurred, whereas distanced-based processes allow an individual to determine the order of events by assessing the strength of a memory. The temporal distance effect occurs when an individual is more accurate in judging the order of two past events if the events took place temporally distant from, rather than temporally proximal to, each other (Deker & Pathman, 2021). Pathman et al. (2013) observed this effect in 8- to 10-year-olds, but the presence of this common phenomenon is less clear for younger children. A recent study examined 4- to 10-year-old children's recall of the timing of events over a 5-day trip to a zoo (Deker & Pathman, 2021; see also Friedman & Lyon, 2005; Friedman et al., 1995). At the end of the trip, the children were shown pictures of two different animals they had seen and asked which they saw first. Children were asked about both animals seen on different days and animals seen on the same day. The authors again reported a temporal distance effect in 8- to 10-year-olds (but not 4- to 5-year-olds or 6- to 7-year-olds), with higher accuracy observed when the two events were temporally distanced. However, when asked about two events which occurred on the same day, even 8- to 10-year-olds did not perform better than chance. These findings are particularly relevant to child alibi corroborators, as accurate recall of the temporal order of events is necessary to position a particular past event in relation to other past events to assist with temporal marking.

Estimates of time and duration are difficult if one is recalling a unique event, but the preceding discussion does not take into account the enhanced complexity in recalling such details if the day of note is part of a routine event. For instance, if a child comes home after school every day and remains home until retiring to bed, each day will have a similar structure, and the elements will be highly predictable. Recalling a particular day from this series of very similar days is likely to result in confusion between days (e.g., Woiwod et al., 2019). However, even if the activities during the event are novel – and thus, more distinctive in memory – temporally placing those events accurately and with confidence is difficult. Thus, temporal marking of individual instances of repeated events is likely to be challenging to do accurately.

Given all of these reviewed challenges, recalling temporal details would be difficult even if it took place shortly after an event. Of course, the reality in the legal system is that investigative resources are often scarce, investigations take time to do well, and there are countless sticking points in the legal system that can result in long delays. The problems associated with obtaining memory reports after a long delay are covered thoroughly elsewhere (e.g., Rubin & Wenzel, 1996; see also Chap. 3), but it is important to note that these difficulties, too, may be exacerbated for children relative to adults, who already struggle with some of the underlying cognitive processes involved in recounting past events.

The extant literature leads us to the conclusion that many of the circumstances in which children might be asked to provide alibi corroboration will have inherently difficult recall conditions. The result of such challenging conditions has predictable outcomes. Weaker event memory is linked to difficulty in retrieving precise event details (e.g., Pezdek & Roe, 1995). If an event is not highly distinct, the likelihood that details from other events will intrude on the event memory is heightened. For many reasons, the events about which children will often be asked to provide alibi corroboration (e.g., home in the evening with a parent) present the perfect conditions for inconsistent recall, even if the event took place as the suspect described. A child's confusion and inconsistency in reporting their and the suspect's actions may be independent of the accuracy of the suspect's alibi (see Fisher et al., 2009 for other instances in which inconsistencies present legal difficulties). Despite the likelihood of such errors, the sympathy for inconsistencies in recalling temporal details is likely to be low among investigators and others who judge the believability of an alibi corroborator.

Motivation

In addition to the cognitive abilities required to corroborate an alibi, there are also concerns of motivation. As Olson and Wells (2004) laid out in their seminal alibi taxonomy paper that delineated primary influences on perceptions of alibi corroborators, the relationship between the suspect and the alibi corroborator is critical because it speaks to the potential motivations of the corroborator. A deliberately deceptive statement that claims the suspect was with the corroborator at the time of the crime is considered more likely when the corroborator has reason to want the suspect to be free from suspicion. Such circumstances may be particularly relevant for child alibi corroborators because if a child is left alone with an adult, it will typically be an adult with whom they have an existing relationship. Thus, in the vast majority of cases, it is likely that children will be corroborating alibis for people with whom they are in regular contact. This familiarity may lead to conflicting motivations of wanting to be honest, but also wanting to protect people they believe – or want to believe – are good people.

Children can begin to tell deliberate lies as young as 3 years of age (e.g., Talwar & Lee, 2002). At this age, however, children may not be effective liars when probed about their account of the event, as they struggle to maintain their deception. It is not until children have developed further skills, at around age 8, that children may be able to effectively lie under additional questioning (Talwar & Lee, 2002). Children's deception skills then continue to increase with age (Lee, 2013).

As one might anticipate, children are often more willing to lie for a loved one than a stranger. Tye et al. (1999) demonstrated that over half of children lied to a person they believed was a police officer by falsely accusing a researcher of stealing a book, when they had actually witnessed their parent commit the theft. Similarly, Lyon et al. (2010) found both maltreated and non-maltreated children were more supportive of disclosures regarding a stranger's transgression compared to a parent's transgression in vignettes. However, Talwar et al. (2004) demonstrated children's willingness to tell the truth after being asked to conceal a parent's transgression, suggesting children are not always prepared to lie on behalf of a loved one. A child may be trying to protect their loved one, they may fear for their own or their loved one's safety, or they may fear the negative consequences of revealing a transgression (Bottoms et al., 2002; Last & Aharoni-Etzioni, 1995; Paine & Hansen, 2002; Tye et al., 1999). As demonstrated by Bottoms et al. (2002), children may also withhold disclosure of a transgression simply because they were asked to do so by a parent or loved one. Thus, it appears that children are not immune to the influences of loved ones on truth-telling.

Competing motivations when there is an opportunity to lie to protect a loved one are also detected by those who judge the believability of child alibi corroborators. In the relatively limited literature assessing perceptions of children's alibi corroboration in different relationship types, an alibi corroborated by the son of the suspect has been perceived as less credible – and may even be more harmful than no alibi corroboration – relative to an alibi corroborated by a less motivated other (neighbor, stranger; Dahl & Price, 2012; Snow & Eastwood, 2020). The reason for this skepticism likely mirrors concerns seen in the adult alibi literature: Eastwood et al. (2016) reported that their sample of undergraduate and police college students (the US equivalent to the police academy) perceived child alibi corroborators as vulnerable to outside influences, particularly when they had a pre-existing relationship with the suspect.

Perceptions of Children as Alibi Corroborators

Given the considerable cognitive and memory challenges involved in alibi corroboration, it is clear that it can be difficult for a child corroborator to provide a sufficiently detailed account that supports a suspect's accurate claim of innocence. Critically, however, it is not the child's *actual* accuracy, but instead the *perceptions* of the child's statement that will determine if the corroborative statement assists the suspect's plight.

The most well-known model that has been developed for predicting evaluations of children's credibility is the two-factor model of credibility that proposes children's credibility comprises assessments of a child's cognitive competence and honesty (Ross et al., 2003). Cognitive competence refers to beliefs about the child's overall cognitive abilities and ability to accurately recount a past event. Honesty assesses the child's motivation and capacity to deceive. The bulk of research on children's perceived credibility has reported that compared to adults, children are perceived as less cognitively competent, but more honest. Children may be seen as less cognitively competent because it may be believed that they are still developing and therefore do not have the capacity to accurately report details of an event (Leippe & Romanczyk, 1989). It is also frequently assumed that children are too naïve, particularly about sexual matters, to lie convincingly. Adults evaluating the child may believe the child would not be able to describe such details without actually having experienced them, leading to higher ratings of perceived honesty in comparison to adults (Bottoms & Goodman, 1994). More recently, researchers have begun to explore a third possible factor in assessing children's credibility: suggestibility or the degree to which a child might be influenced by external sources such as an adult's questioning (Kehn et al., 2016). There is already evidence that children's vulnerability to external influences is a concern in child alibi corroborators who have a relationship with the suspect (Eastwood et al., 2016). But which of these factors carries the most weight in any particular credibility judgment depends, at least in part, on the context of the decision at hand, including characteristics of the child and the suspect and the details of the crime.

In the adult witness literature, the consistency of a witness' statements is one of the most powerful influences on perceptions of witness credibility (Brewer et al., 1999; Myers et al., 1999; Potter & Brewer, 1999). Though it would be intuitive to predict a similar pattern for children, there has been limited research on perceptions of the consistency of children's alibi corroborations. Price and Dahl (2017) examined how the consistency of alibi statements and the age of the corroborator influenced how participants perceived the guilt of the suspect. Undergraduate students were instructed to act as mock investigators and evaluate an alibi presented by either a child (ages 6, 8, or 11 years) or an adult in interviews recorded both 1 week and again 5 years after the incident. Mock investigators were most skeptical about statements including major inconsistencies, but also showed some concern about minor inconsistencies, relative to consistent statements. However, this effect did not differ between child alibi corroborators of any age or compared to adult alibi corroborators. The lack of age differences implies that children are not given additional leeway for the challenging cognitive tasks associated with alibi corroboration.

However, another study suggests that children might be given the benefit of the doubt when another witness contradicts their alibi corroboration. Bruer et al. (2017; Study 2 and 3) explored how contradicting eyewitness evidence impacts the believability of an alibi corroboration given by a child or an adult. Undergraduate mock investigators were asked to judge if the suspect should be arrested or if more physical evidence was needed before an arrest could be made based on evidence from an alibi corroborator and an eyewitness. Bruer et al. found that when an adult eyewitness contradicted a child alibi corroborator, mock investigators required more physical evidence to arrest the suspect, compared to when no contradictory evidence was presented. When an adult eyewitness contradicted an adult alibi corroborator, no such effect was present. Thus, the child's alibi corroboration appeared more persuasive than the adult's corroboration.

The observation that child alibi corroborators may be advantaged, relative to adults, under certain circumstances is not new, but the effect is fickle and more complex than simply an age advantage. In the first study to explore children as alibi corroborators, Dahl and Price (2012) asked adults to assess a child or adult alibi corroborator who provided evidence to support the claim of innocence for a person suspected of committing a robbery. Participants rated the 6-year-old child as significantly more credible than a 25-year-old man (Dahl & Price, 2012; see also Price & Dahl, 2014). In these studies, child alibi corroborators claimed they were with the adult for a long period of time, thus making pinning down specific time frames less of a concern. As a result, children's cognitive competence was relatively less salient than children's honesty. In contrast, when the time frame was much narrower and thus required precise recall of temporal details (and thus cognitive competence was relatively more salient), as in Eastwood et al. (2016), adult alibi corroborators were more believable than child alibi corroborators. In other studies in which the interaction was relatively brief (seeing the suspect in a park, Study 1; father and son going for a walk, Study 2), Snow and Eastwood (2020) found no age differences between an 8- and a 25-year-old on the perceived credibility, honesty, or believability of alibi corroborators (Study 1). However, they did find that evaluators rated 8-year-olds as more honest than 25-year-olds (Study 2). Though we can conclude that circumstances that make honesty a salient child characteristic are likely to result in benefits to children's credibility, it is also the case that most methodological issues have not been sufficiently explored to assess any potential interactions between children's age, perceptions of honesty relative to cognitive competence, and other factors that might play a role in assessing their believability (e.g., relationships between the child and the suspect, the nature of the interaction).

In the limited studies that have examined children of different ages, few differences are seen between different ages of child alibi corroborators. Examining solely child alibi corroborators, Fawcett and Winstanley (2018) investigated the impact of corroborator age (8, 12, and 16 years) on perceived honesty and accuracy but found no significant differences across the three age groups. Price and Dahl (2017) similarly examined a range of young alibi corroborators (6, 8, and 11 years) after a delay of 5 years and also found no differences across ages in overall credibility, honesty, or accuracy. The only study we were able to locate that showed age differences between children of different ages was Snow and Eastwood (2020; Study 2) in which they observed a difference between a 4- and 8-year-old child alibi corroborator, with the latter being seen as more credible. The youngest age group in the Snow and Eastwood study was quite young (4 years) which might help to explain this result, as preschoolers are consistently rated as less cognitively competent than school-aged children in other domains (Ross et al., 1990). Additionally, data from Nunez et al. (2011) suggests that 8 years of age is perceived as the most credible age of a child witness.

There is evidence that other child characteristics, and the associated expectations adults have about these characteristics, can influence the believability of child witnesses, which may have implications for alibi corroborators. For example, Talwar and colleagues (2006; see also Talwar & Lee, 2002) found that adults rated girls as more truthful and capable than boys when describing true or false personal experiences (e.g., attending a wedding). Nunez et al. (2011) found a similar pattern in the context of child sexual abuse (CSA) cases, such that girls were perceived as more honest and as having greater cognitive abilities than boys. It has been suggested that the superior perceived credibility of girls in CSA cases may be due to the perception that girls are more likely to be victims of CSA and, thus, their description is consistent with an expected victim type (Haegerich & Bottoms, 2000).

Judges, jurors, and investigators who evaluate witness evidence will also have pre-existing expectations about the emotions a victim or witness should express while testifying, which can influence perceptions of credibility (van Doorn &

Koster, 2019; see Jussim et al., 1987 about expectancy violation theory). For child witnesses, the extant literature indicates that adults expect a display of negative emotions (e.g., sadness, fear; Bederian-Gardner & Goldfarb, 2014). For example, when children are appraised as highly emotional, they are more likely to be perceived as believable than children that are appraised as less emotional (Cooper et al., 2014; but see Golding et al., 2003), especially when the adult perceiver is high in empathy (Bederian-Gardner et al., 2017). A systematic review of victim emotionality and credibility suggests that sad, teary child victims are perceived as more credible than children showing other emotions (van Doorn & Koster, 2019). Along with the emotion a child presents, the speech style of a child witness has also been suggested to affect perceptions of credibility (Goodman et al., 1984). Powerless speech is characterized by hesitations, uncertainty, and a questioning tone when making statements, while powerful speech contains less of these traits (Nigro et al., 1989). And while children are expected to have more powerless speech than adults overall (Goodman et al., 1984), children with powerful speech are judged as more credible than children with powerless speech (Ruva & Bryant, 2004). Though most of this research has been conducted on child victims, these patterns and speculations suggest that child alibi corroborators may be more believable if their role in the alibi is stereotype-consistent. To our knowledge, this possibility has not yet been explored.

Finally, the perceived – and real – difficulty of the cognitive task of remembering may influence the credibility of a child alibi corroborator. As discussed earlier, children are likely to have relatively more difficulty remembering an event after a long delay (Flin et al., 1992), especially peripheral details (Peterson, 2011). The resulting expected impoverished recall has led some scholars to posit that children would be perceived as less credible corroborators for a delayed event compared to a more recent event (e.g., see Snow & Eastwood, 2020, who ultimately did not observe an interaction between age and delay). Though this relatively weaker recall after a delay is not unique to children, the effect may be exacerbated in children which could ultimately prove problematic, as delays from an event to an investigation of alibis, and then to court, are often measured in years. Further, adult evaluators appear to be insensitive to children's cognitive abilities relating to time and date, and children's uncertainty in reporting such detail may be seen as indicative of lower general reliability as witnesses (Cleveland & Quas, 2016).

Implications for Investigations

Children's cognitive skills will allow them to provide detailed alibi corroboration under particular circumstances, but it is critical to note that errors and inconsistencies do not necessarily mean the child is lying or that the suspect was not with the child during the time frame under investigation. Jurors have unrealistic expectations for alibi corroborators' consistency and accuracy (Crozier et al., 2017). However, as with all memory recall, a person's ability to provide precise information about a past experience will be affected by the strength of the memory for the event, the delay between the event and recall, and any events that took place in the delay period (e.g., rehearsal, exposure to new information). As the research described earlier makes clear, the particular circumstances of the event being recalled by a child alibi corroborator must be taken into account when evaluating the accuracy of the alibi. For instance, if a child is recounting a unique, special occurrence that takes place over an extended period of time (e.g., a Friday movie night with a rarely-seen uncle), the accuracy of their recollection a few days later is likely to be high. In contrast, if a child is recalling if their parent was present in a busy house for a half-hour period one weekday after school, as they often are, accurate recall is likely to be more difficult.

Over-valuing or de-valuing alibi corroborator evidence can have a substantial impact on achieving justice. For instance, Crozier et al. (2017) explain how one memory error in an alibi can lead to effects throughout the investigation, potentially resulting in a wrongful conviction. Despite evidence to the contrary (e.g., Fisher et al., 2009), commonly trained interrogation strategies, like the Reid technique, maintain the assumption that inconsistency in recall or detail of events is indicative of deception (Crozier et al., 2017; Inbau et al., 2013). As a result of this assumption, investigators may change how they conduct an interview, asking more guilt-presumptive questions. Subsequently, this single memory error can influence how the alibi corroborator is perceived by jurors and prosecutors; a defendant offering inconsistent testimony is often perceived as less credible and more likely to be guilty (Allison & Brimacombe, 2010; Brewer & Burke, 2002; Olson & Wells, 2004). As a result of this cascading effect, what began as a simple memory retrieval error in an investigation can result in diminished credibility at trial (see also Kassin et al., 2013 for a related discussion on the forensic confirmation bias).

Future Directions

The last decade has seen considerable gains in knowledge about children's role as alibi corroborators. However, there remains vast gaps in our understanding of how and when children are called on to provide this information, the types of cases in which children are likely to be relied upon, and when children are and are not believed. We can speculate about the impact of particular circumstances on children's believability based on the larger child witness literature, but alibis carry a unique set of assumptions, motivations, and considerations. We see the need for future research to extend in several key directions.

Perhaps most critically, the range of ages captured in the studies reviewed in this chapter is limited. There are few studies of preschoolers and adolescents, and comparisons between children of multiple ages within a single study are rare. This gap must be filled. Further, in a chapter on age differences in alibi corroboration, we would have ideally been able to take a lifespan approach. However, there is no research that we are aware of that addresses corroborators older than young adults.

As with the growing body of work that takes a lifespan perspective on eyewitness evidence (e.g., Fitzgerald & Price, 2015), alibi corroboration researchers must begin to consider studying participants across the full lifespan to be more informative to the justice system.

Relatedly, though the age of the child alibi corroborator is important, so too is the age of the person requiring the corroboration. As children age, they spend more time with peers. These social relationships, and the heavy emphasis youth are known to place on them, likely further complicate evaluations of child alibi corroborators. Yet we are unaware of any research that has examined how peer alibi corroborators are evaluated. Such complications might also play a role when the victim has a relationship with the alibi corroborator (e.g., the father is accused of killing the corroborator's mother).

Though we have made the case that children will often be the sole source of alibi corroboration for many adults, this may be even more likely to be the case for children with developmental disabilities who require additional support and supervision. As in the broader child witness literature (e.g., Hershkowitz et al., 2007), the child alibi corroborator literature must begin to attend to evidence from children with developmental disabilities. There are, of course, many other individual and demographic characteristics that have not been sufficiently explored, including sex, socioeconomic status, and cultural differences.

Finally, growing public and investigator interest in the resolution of cold cases has important implications for delays from the event of interest to recall of that event. Delay can introduce unique elements to child alibi corroborators. For instance, if the alibi corroborator is a child at the time the event took place, but when asked to recall that event later, the corroborator is an adult, what role will age play in the evaluation of the statement? As we have demonstrated, age can clearly influence the believability of a corroborator's statement. But in such circumstances, which age drives the evaluation of credibility: time of encoding (child) or time of retrieval (adult)?

Conclusion

Recalling details of an event with the precision required to concretely corroborate an alibi poses considerable difficulty for alibi corroborators. This difficulty is likely compounded for children who lack some of the requisite cognitive abilities and who lack the world experience to anchor their experiences. Yet, it is clear that children have the ability to provide accurate alibi corroboration under particular circumstances and their evidence should not be discounted simply due to their age. Irrespective of their abilities, it will ultimately be the investigators, jurors, and judges' beliefs about what a child alibi corroborator is able to recall that will determine legal outcomes. Alibi research may be in its childhood; however research on the impact of the age of the alibi corroborator credibility and ability is still in its infancy. We hope this chapter ignites new research ideas, further delineation of past findings, and a path toward better understanding how to obtain and evaluate information from child alibi corroborators.

References

Adler, L. C. (2019, April 12). Mendez trial begins with opening statements, daughters' testimonies. *Northwoods Star Journal*. https://starjournalnow.com/2019/04/12/mendez-trial-begins-with-opening-statements-daughters-testimonies/

Allison, M., & Brimacombe, C. A. E. (2010). Alibi believability: The effect of prior convictions and judicial instructions. *Journal of Applied Social Psychology, 40*(5), 1054–1084. https://doi.org/10.1111/j.1559-1816.2010.00610.x

Bauer, P. J., & Leventon, J. S. (2013). Memory for one-time experiences in the second year of life: Implications for the status of episodic memory. *Infancy, 18*(5), 755–781. https://doi.org/10.1111/infa.12005

Bederian-Gardner, D., & Goldfarb, D. (2014). Expectations of emotions during testimony: The role of communicator and perceiver characteristics. *Behavioral Sciences & the Law, 32*(6), 829–845. https://doi.org/10.1002/bsl.2146

Bederian-Gardner, D., Goldfarb, D., & Goodman, G. S. (2017). Empathy's relation to appraisal of the emotional child witness. *Applied Cognitive Psychology, 31*(5), 488–499. https://doi.org/10.1002/acp.3345

Bottoms, B. L., & Goodman, G. S. (1994). Perceptions of children's credibility in sexual assault cases. *Journal of Applied Social Psychology, 24*, 702–732. https://doi.org/10.1111/j.1559-1816.1994.tb00608.x

Bottoms, B. L., Goodman, G. S., Schwartz-Jenney, B. M., & Thomas, S. N. (2002). Understanding children's use of secrecy in the context of eyewitness reports. *Law and Human Behavior, 26*, 285–313. https://doi.org/10.1023/A:1015324304975

Brewer, N., Potter, R., Fisher, R. P., Bond, N., & Luszcz, M. A. (1999). Beliefs and data on the relationship between consistency and accuracy of eyewitness testimony. Applied Cognitive Psychology: The Official Journal of the Society for Applied Research in Memory and Cognition, 13(4), 297–313.

Brewer, N., & Burke, A. (2002). Effects of testimonial inconsistences and eyewitness confidence on mock-juror judgements. *Law and Human Behavior, 26*(3), 353–364. https://doi.org/10.1023/A:1015380522722

Bruer, K. C., Price, H. L., & Dahl, L. C. (2017). When an alibi is not enough: Judgments of evidence needed to lay charges in a burglary case. *Journal of Police and Criminal Psychology, 32*(2), 94–104. https://doi.org/10.1007/s11896-016-9209-6

Cleveland, K. C., & Quas, J. A. (2016). Adults' insensitivity to developmental changes in children's ability to report when and how many times abuse occurred. *Behavioral Sciences & the Law, 34*, 126–138.

Cooper, A., Quas, J. A., & Cleveland, K. C. (2014). The emotional child witness: Effects on juror decision-making. *Behavioral Sciences & the Law, 32*(6), 813–828. https://doi.org/10.1002/bsl.2153

Crozier, W. E., Strange, D., & Loftus, E. F. (2017). Memory errors in alibi generation: How an alibi can turn against us. *Behavioral Sciences & the Law, 35*, 6–17. https://doi.org/10.1002/bsl.2273

Dahl, L. C., & Price, H. L. (2012). "He couldn't have done it, he was with me!": The impact of alibi witness age and relationship. *Applied Cognitive Psychology, 26*, 475–481. https://doi.org/10.1002/acp.2821

Deker, L., & Pathman, T. (2021). Did I visit the polar bear before the giraffe? Examining memory for temporal order and the temporal distance effect in early to middle childhood. *Applied Cognitive Psychology*. https://doi.org/10.1002/acp.3804

Eastwood, J., Snook, B., & Au, D. (2016). Safety in numbers: A policy-capturing study of the alibi assessment process. *Applied Cognitive Psychology, 30*(2), 260–269.

Fawcett, H., & Winstanley, K. (2018). Children as alibi witnesses: The effect of age and confidence on mock-juror decision making. *Psychiatry, Psychology and Law, 25*, 957–971. https://doi.org/10.1080/13218719.2018.1482573

Fisher, R. P., Brewer, N., & Mitchell, G. (2009). The relation between consistency and accuracy of eyewitness testimony: Legal versus cognitive explanations. In R. Bull, T. Valentine, T. Williamson, R. Bull, T. Valentine, & T. Williamson (Eds.), *Handbook of psychology of investigative interviewing: Current developments and future directions* (pp. 121–136). Wiley-Blackwell.

Fitzgerald, R. J., & Price, H. L. (2015). Eyewitness identification across the life span: A meta-analysis of age differences. *Psychological Bulletin, 141*(6), 1228–1265. https://doi.org/10.1037/bul0000013

Fivush, R. (1984). Learning about school: The development of kindergartners' school scripts. *Child Development, 55*, 1697–1709.

Friedman, W. J. (1991). The development of children's memory for the time of past events. *Child Development, 62*, 139–155. https://doi.org/10.1111/j.1467-8#nelson5624.1991.tb01520.x

Friedman, W. J., Gardner, A. C., & Zubin, N. R. (1995). Children's comparisons of the recency of two events from the past year. *Child Development, 66*, 970–983. https://doi.org/10.1111/j.1467-8624.1995.tb00916.x

Friedman, W. J., & Lyon, T. D. (2005). Development of temporal reconstructive abilities. *Child Development, 76*, 1202–1216. https://doi.org/10.1111/j.1467-8624.2005.00844.x-i1

Friedman, W. J., Reese, E., & Dai, X. (2011). Children's memory for the times of events from the past years. *Applied Cognitive Psychology, 25*, 156-165. https://doi.org/10.1002/acp.1656

Flin, R., Boon, J., Knox, A., & Bull, R. (1992). The effect of a five-month delay on children's and adults' eyewitness memory. *British Journal of Psychology, 83*(3), 323–336. https://doi.org/10.1111/j.2044-8295.1992.tb02444.x

Friedman, W. J. (1987). A follow-up to "Scale effects in memory for the time of events": The earthquake study. *Memory & Cognition, 15*(6), 518–520. https://doi.org/10.3758/BF03198386

Friedman, W. J. (1993). Memory for the time of past events. *Psychological Bulletin, 113*(1), 44–66. https://doi.org/10.1037/0033-2909.113.1.44

Friedman, W. J. (2004). Time in autobiographical memory. *Social Cognition, 22*(5), 591–605. https://doi.org/10.1521/soco.22.5.591.50766

Friedman, W. J., Cederborg, A.-C., Hultman, E., Nghagen, O., & Magnussen, K. (2010). Children's memory for the duration of a paediatric consultation. *Applied Cognitive Psychology, 24*, 545–556. https://doi.org/10.1002/acp.157124

Friedman, W. J., & Wilkins, A. J. (1985). Scale effects in memory for the time of events. *Memory & Cognition, 13*(2), 168–175. https://doi.org/10.3758/BF03197009

Golding, J. M., Fryman, H. M., Marsil, D. F., & Yozwiak, J. A. (2003). Big girls don't cry: The effect of child witness demeanor on juror decisions in a child asexual abuse trial. *Child Abuse & Neglect, 27*, 1311–1321. https://doi.org/10.1016/j.chiabu.2003.03.001

Goodman, G. S., Golding, J. M., & Haith, M. M. (1984). Jurors' reactions to child witnesses. *Journal of Social Issues, 40*(2), 139–156. https://doi.org/10.1111/j.1540-4560.1984.tb01098.x

Goodman, G. S., & Melinder, A. (2007). Child witness research and forensic interview of young children: A review. *Legal and Criminological Psychology, 12*, 1–19. https://doi.org/10.1348/135532506X156620

Haegerich, T. M., & Bottoms, B. L. (2000). Empathy and jurors' decisions in patricide trials involving child sexual assault allegations. *Law and Human Behavior, 24*(4), 421–447. https://doi.org/10.1023/A:1005592213294

Hershkowitz, I., Lamb, M. E., & Horowitz, D. (2007). Victimization of children with disabilities. *American Journal of Orthopsychiatry, 77*, 629–635. https://doi.org/10.1037/0002-9432.77.4.629

Inbau, F. E., Reid, J. E., Buckley, J. P., & Jayne, B. C. (2013). *Criminal interrogations and confessions* (5th ed.). Jones & Bartlett Learning.

Jack, F., Friedman, W. J., Reese, E., & Zajac, R. (2016). Age-related differences in memory for time, temporal reconstruction, and the availability and use of temporal landmarks. *Cognitive Development, 37*, 53–66. https://doi.org/10.1016/j.cogdev.2015.12.003

Jussim, L., Coleman, L. M., & Lerch, L. (1987). The nature of stereotypes: A comparison and integration of three theories. *Journal of Personality and Social Psychology, 52*(3), 536–546.

Kassin, S. M., Dror, I. E., & Kukucka, J. (2013). The forensic confirmation bias: Problems, perspectives, and proposed solutions. *Journal of Applied Research in Memory and Cognition, 2*, 42–52. https://doi.org/10.1016/j.jarmac.2013.01.001

Kehn, A., Haugen, A., Warren, A., Schweitzer, K, & Nunez, N. L. (2016). *The child credibility assessment scale: Validity and predictability in child sexual and non-sexual abuse cases*. Paper presented at the annual American Psychology and Law Conference, Atlanta, Georgia, USA.

Koriat, A., Goldsmith, M., & Pansky, A. (2000). Toward a psychology of memory accuracy. *Annual Review of Psychology, 51*(1), 481–537.

Last, U., & Aharoni-Etzioni, A. (1995). Secrets and reasons for secrecy among school-aged children: Developmental trends and gender differences. *The Journal of Genetic Psychology, 156*(2), 191–203.

Lee, K. (2013). Little liars: Development of verbal deception in children. *Child Development Perspectives, 7*, 91–96. https://doi.org/10.1111/cdep.12023

Leippe, M. R., & Romanczyk, A. (1989). Reactions to child (versus adult) eyewitnesses: The influence of jurors' preconceptions and witness behavior. *Law and Human Behavior, 13*, 103–132. https://doi.org/10.1007/bf01055919

Luna, B., Garver, K. E., Urban, T. A., Lazar, N. A., & Sweeney, J. A. (2004). Maturation of cognitive processes from late childhood to adulthood. *Child Development, 75*(5), 1357–1372. https://doi.org/10.1111/j.1467-8624.2004.00745.x

Lyon, T. D., Ahern, E. C., Malloy, L. C., & Quas, J. A. (2010). Children's reasoning about disclosing adult transgressions: Effects of maltreatment, child age, and adult identity. *Child Development, 81*, 1741–1728. https://doi.org/10.1111/j.1467-8624.2010.01505.x

McCormack, T. (2015). The development of temporal cognition. In L. S. Liben, U. Muller, & R. M. Lerner (Eds.), *Handbook of child psychology and developmental science: Cognitive processes* (Vol. 2, 7th ed., pp. 624–670). John Wiley & Sons, Inc.; US.

McKinley, J. (2016, September 21). *Defendant's daughter testifies in Potsdam murder trial*. The New York Times. https://www.nytimes.com/2016/09/22/nyregion/potsdam-murder-trial-garrett-phillips-oral-nicholas-hillary.html

Myers, J. E. B., Redlich, A. D., Goodman, G. S., Prizmich, L. P., & Imwinkelreid, E. (1999). Jurors' perceptions of hearsay in child sexual abuse cases. *Psychology, Public Policy and Law, 5*, 388–419. https://doi.org/10.1037/1076-8971.5.2.388

Nigro G. N., Buckley M. A., Hill D. E., Nelson J. (1989) When Juries "Hear" Children Testify: The Effects of Eyewitness Age and Speech Style on Jurors' Perceptions of Testimony. In: Ceci S.J., Ross D.F., Toglia M.P. (eds) Perspectives on Children's Testimony. Springer, New York, NY. https://doi.org/10.1007/978-1-4613-8832-6_4

Nunez, N., Kehn, A., & Wright, D. B. (2011). When children are witnesses: The effects of context, age and gender on adults' perceptions of cognitive ability and honesty. *Applied Cognitive Psychology, 25*(3), 460–468. https://doi.org/10.1002/acp.1713

Olson, E. A., & Wells, G. L. (2004). Wat makes a good alibi? A proposed taxonomy. *Law and Human Behavior, 28*(2), 157–176. https://doi.org/10.1023/B:LAHU.0000022320.47112.d3

Paine, M. L., & Hansen, D. J. (2002). Factors influencing children to self-disclose sexual abuse. *Clinical Psychology Review, 22*, 271–295. https://doi.org/10.1016/s0272-7358(01)00091-5

Pathman, T., & Ghetti, S. (2014). The eyes know time: A novel paradigm to reveal the development of temporal memory. *Child Development, 85*, 792–807. https://doi.org/10.1111/cdev.12152

Pathman, T., Larkina, M., Burch, M. M., & Bauer, P. J. (2013). Young children's memory for the times of personal past events. *Journal of Cognition and Development, 14*(1), 120–140. https://doi.org/10.1080/15248372.2011.641185

Peterson, C. (2011). Children's memory reports over time: Getting both better and worse. *Journal of Experimental Child Psychology, 109*(3), 275–293.

Pezdek, K., & Roe, C. (1995). The effect of memory trace strength on suggestibility. *Journal of Experimental Child Psychology, 60*(1), 116–128. https://doi.org/10.1006/jecp.1995.1034

Potter, R., & Brewer, N. (1999). Perceptions of witness behaviour-accuracy relationships held by police, lawyers, and mock-jurors. *Psychiatry, Psychology, and Law, 6*, 97–103. https://doi.org/10.1080/13218719909524952

Price, H. L., & Dahl, L. C. (2014). Order and strength matter for evaluation of alibi and eyewitness evidence. *Applied Cognitive Psychology, 28*, 143–150. https://doi.org/10.1002/acp.2983

Price, H. L., & Dahl, L. C. (2017). Investigator sensitivity to alibi witness inconsistency after a long delay. *Behavioral Sciences & the Law, 35*, 60–74. https://doi.org/10.1002/bsl.2276

Ross, D. F., Dunning, D., Toglia, M. P., & Ceci, S. J. (1990). The child in the eyes of the jury: Assessing mock jurors' perceptions of the child witness. *Law and Human Behavior, 14*(1), 5–23. https://doi.org/10.1007/BF01055786

Ross, D. R., Jurden, F. H., Lindsay, R. C. L., & Keeney, J. M. (2003). Replications and limitations of a two-factor model of child witness credibility. *Journal of Applied Social Psychology, 33*, 418–431. https://doi.org/10.1111/j.1559-1816.2003.tb01903.x

Roy, M. M., Christenfeld, N. J., & McKenzie, C. R. M. (2005). Bias in memory predicts bias in estimation of future task duration. *Psychological Bulletin, 131*, 738–756. https://doi.org/10.1037/0033-2909.131.5.738

Rubin, D. C., & Wenzel, A. E. (1996). One hundred years of forgetting: A quantitative description of retention. *Psychological Review, 103*, 734–760. https://doi.org/10.1037/0033-295X.103.4.734

Ruva, C. L., & Bryant, J. B. (2004). The impact of age, speech style, and question form on perceptions of witness credibility and trial outcome. *Journal of Applied Social Psychology, 34*(9), 1919–1944. https://doi.org/10.1111/j.1559-1816.2004.tb02593.x

Shapiro, E. (2016, September 21). Nick Hillary's daughter and alibi witness testifies at his murder trial. *ABC News*. https://abcnews.go.com/US/nick-hillarys-daughter-alibi-witness-testifies-murder-trial/story?id=42243893

Snow, M. D., & Eastwood, J. (2020). Assessing the credibility of child alibi corroborators. *Journal of Forensic Psychology Research and Practice*, 1–21. https://doi.org/10.1080/24732850.2020.1840000

Talwar, V., & Lee, K. (2002). Development of lying to conceal a transgression: Children's control of expressive behaviour during verbal deception. *International Journal of Behavioral Development, 26*, 436–444. https://doi.org/10.1080/01650250143000373

Talwar, V., Lee, K., Bala, N., & Lindsay, R. C. L. (2004). Children's lie-telling to conceal a parent's transgression: Legal implications. *Law and Human Behavior, 28*(4), 411–435.

Talwar, V., Lee, K., Bala, N., & Lindsay, R. C. L. (2006). Adults' judgments of children's coached reports. *Law and Human Behavior, 30*(5), 561–570. https://doi.org/10.1007/s10979-006-9038-8

Thompson, C. P., Skowronski, J. J., & Lee, D. J. (1988). Telescoping in dating naturally occurring events. *Memory & Cognition, 16*(5), 461–468. https://doi.org/10.3758/BF03214227

Tye, M. C., Amato, S. L., Honts, C. R., Devitt, M. K., & Peters, D. (1999). The willingness of children to lie and the assessment of credibility in an ecologically relevant laboratory setting. *Applied Developmental Science, 3*, 92–109. https://doi.org/10.1207/s1532480xads0302_4

van Doorn, J., & Koster, N. N. (2019). Emotional victims and the impact on credibility: A systematic review. *Aggression and Violent Behavior, 47*, 74–89. https://doi.org/10.1016/j.avb.2019.03.007

Wang, Q., & Peterson, C. (2014). Your earliest memory may be earlier than you think: Prospective studies of children's dating of earliest childhood memories. *Developmental Psychology, 50*(6), 1680–1686. https://doi.org/10.1037/a0036001

Woiwod, D. M., Fitzgerald, R. J., Sheahan, C. L., Price, H. L., & Connolly, D. A. (2019). A meta-analysis of differences in children's reports of single and repeated events. *Law and Human Behavior, 43*(1), 99–116.

Chapter 8
The Strategic Use of Alibi Defenses

Kay L. Levine and Colin Miller

Introduction

In the spring of 2006, a young woman named Crystal Mangum accused three members of the Duke University lacrosse team of sexually assaulting her in a bathroom (Cohan, 2016). The indictments alleged that the players committed rape, kidnapping, and robbery during a team party at which Ms. Mangum had been hired to work as a stripper. When these allegations became public, a media firestorm erupted, fueled not just by the salaciousness of the charges but also by the confluence of race (the players are white, while Ms. Mangum is black) and class (Duke is an elite school, and many of the lacrosse players come from wealthy families, while Ms. Mangum resided in the surrounding city of Durham, attended North Carolina Central University, and worked to support herself and her child). The elected prosecutor, Mike Nifong, also spoke publicly about the case on numerous occasions, all but assuring the public that this was an open-and-shut case and vilifying the entire lacrosse team culture as well as the three identified players.

But once the narrative provided by Ms. Mangum was closely compared to the evidence, the case fell apart. The unraveling began when one of the accused players, Reade Seligmann, produced tangible proof that he was not at the house at the time of the alleged attack; he had an alibi. There was (1) a receipt and security camera footage from an ATM machine showing Mr. Seligmann's withdrawal of cash at the time Ms. Mangum said he was attacking her; (2) a cab driver's affidavit attesting to pick up and drop off times and locations for Mr. Seligmann; (3) a dorm security card

K. L. Levine (✉)
Emory University School of Law, Atlanta, GA, USA
e-mail: klevin2@emory.edu

C. Miller
University of South Carolina School of Law, Columbia, SC, USA
e-mail: Mille933@law.sc.edu

J. D. Behl, M. R. Kienzle (eds.), *Alibis and Corroborators*,
https://doi.org/10.1007/978-3-030-95663-9_8

swipe showing Mr. Seligmann's entry into the dorm long before Ms. Mangum was found by police; and (4) cell phone records showing numerous brief calls to Mr. Seligmann's girlfriend during the period when the attack was alleged to have occurred. Considered together, this collection of evidence established an alibi for Mr. Seligmann, and it was enough to challenge the narrative about what might have happened at the lacrosse party that night.

But the existence of this alibi evidence did more than just establish Mr. Seligmann's lack of involvement in a crime. It called into question everything Ms. Mangum had reported, and those questions only multiplied once DNA tests eventually revealed that none of the lacrosse players was the source of DNA found on her body that night. The elected prosecutor eventually recused himself, and the state Attorney General – after conducting his own investigation – not only dismissed the charges but declared all three players innocent. Such is the power that alibi evidence can hold.

As the Duke lacrosse case lays bare, and as a survey of defense attorneys that will be discussed throughout this chapter also suggests, alibi evidence has the capacity to force a fundamental re-thinking of the prosecution's story of the crime. It can upend the timeline that the prosecution posits based on witnesses' recollections of when and where things happened. It can poke holes in the prosecution's burden of proof by damaging the credibility of prosecution witnesses and can even establish the defendant's actual innocence (Steele, 2020). While a strong alibi might not lead to the conclusion that no crime occurred, it shows a jury that the defendant could not have been the perpetrator.

Viewed through this lens, an alibi appears to be the holy grail for defendants, and for that reason it is frequently featured in crime fiction and Hollywood blockbusters. But in reality, alibi evidence shelters only a relative handful of defendants who face charges in our criminal courts. True alibi evidence is hard to come by, and convincing a jury of its trustworthiness is a further challenge still (see discussion in Chap. 4 of this volume about believability). Moreover, alibi notice rules in every jurisdiction (see Appendix A at the end of this chapter) require the defense to share key facts of the alibi with the prosecutor up front, thereby allowing the prosecutor to re-craft the suggested timeline or to marshal rebuttal evidence to refute the claims of alibi witnesses well before trial. The Duke lacrosse case thus offers up a colorful example of what alibi evidence can do when the planets align, but its successful use is a rare cosmic event in a defense attorney's career.

In this chapter we illuminate the strategic use of the alibi defense in US criminal courtrooms. Our discussion unfolds in three parts. We first explain the nuts and bolts of how alibis work in criminal cases, paying particular attention to the influence of time: the precision with which police and prosecutors articulate the timeline for the alleged crime; the defense attorney's assessment of the right time to present alibi evidence to law enforcement, the prosecutor, or the tribunal; the defendant's ability to positively establish their alternate location at the time the crime allegedly occurred; and the amount of time that passes between the crime and the arrest of the defendant. We next provide a guide to alibi notice rules in federal court as well as in the 50 state jurisdictions in the United States. We examine the history and variety of rules about when notice must be provided, the constitutionality of those rules, and the impact of a defendant changing their mind after previously notifying the court and prosecution of their intention to rely on an alibi defense. In the final section of the chapter, we discuss two specific risks that defense attorneys face when considering whether to litigate an alibi defense at trial: procuring a false alibi and failing to present an alibi defense when there is evidence to support it. Throughout the essay, we offer evidence from an original survey of practicing and retired defense attorneys about how they investigate and deploy alibi defenses on behalf of their clients. Our survey respondents, who hail from all parts of the country and have differential levels of practice (84% have practiced for 11+ years) and client experience (46% had majority indigent clients), document the concerns and challenges they face when considering whether, when, and how to present an alibi at trial.

Part One: What Do We Mean by Alibi?

The alibi defense rests on the assertion that the police have arrested the wrong person for the crime. But an alibi requires something more than merely questioning police judgment: to successfully challenge the case against them, the defendant must argue that they *could not be* the right person, based on their confirmed presence somewhere else at the time of the crime (Nolan & Nolan-Haley, 1991). An alibi is not technically an affirmative defense; it is instead a challenge to the prosecutor's proof on the issue of whether the defendant is the person who committed the crime. For that reason, it violates Due Process to require the defendant to prove their alibi; the burden of proof on the issue of identity remains with the prosecution (Johnson v. Bennett, 1968). But beyond merely questioning the government's ability to prove the identity of the perpetrator, the defense provides a substitute narrative about where the defendant actually was during the period in question. This explicit alternative narrative, when conveyed correctly, is more persuasive than a simple assertion of "I wasn't there" or "it wasn't me" because it is buttressed by readily observable facts and/or independent witnesses.

There are several audiences for alibi evidence, each of which operates at a different phase of the criminal case and makes use of the alibi information differently. A suspect might first attempt to share alibi information with the police during the investigation phase. If their story checks out they could be released, but because police manuals instruct that a defective alibi can help the interrogator ultimately get the suspect to confess, there is a risk in sharing it early (Inbau et al., 2013; Drizen & Leo, 2004). If the police are not responsive, the defendant, through their attorney, might present alibi evidence to the prosecutor, aiming to have charges dismissed before trial. Lastly, defense counsel can ask the factfinder at trial (judge or jury) to acquit the defendant because the alibi evidence raises a reasonable doubt as to the defendant's presence at the scene of the crime.

Defense attorneys must decide when is the opportune time to show their cards, in order to make best use of what they have. Reveal alibi evidence shortly after charging and the prosecutor has a chance to undercut this defense by shifting the timeline or digging up dirt on the alibi witnesses (Steele, 2020). Raise it for the first time right before trial, and an innocent client might be sitting in jail unnecessarily for months or even years waiting for their turn to speak, due to delays in the court schedule. What is more, some jurors inherently assume that if a case makes it to trial, investigators must have considered the alibi unbelievable, causing them to reject it (Steele; Sommers & Douglass, 2007). Our survey respondents said, in addition to jurisdictional rules about notice, their decision to go to the prosecutor in advance of trial usually depends on the strength of the alibi evidence (21% of our respondents pointed to personal witnesses and 20% pointed to physical corroborating evidence as important), the facts of the case (17%), the prosecutor's reputation for fairness (12%), and a pre-existing professional relationship with the prosecutor (12%). Factors perceived as less influential were the seriousness of the charged crime (5%), defendant's criminal history (4%), and the lawyer's professional relationship with judge (3%). One of our respondents described the timing dilemma principally as one of how to best provide support for her witnesses:

> If an alibi is solid and it can be proven by independent and outside sources, then I always favor presenting it to the DA before trial. However, if the alibi depends on testimony from a witness that the DA's office can find and lean on with threats of VOP's [violations of probation] or calling DFACS to their children, then I tend to play those cards a little closer to the vest. I may spring that alibi on the state 10 days before trial and see if my witness(es) can hang in there long enough to testify at trial.

Whatever the relevant audience or timing of the revelation, when a defendant presents an alibi, they makes three related assertions about their whereabouts at the time the crime occurred: (1) they were not at the location where the crime occurred (location X), (2) they were instead at some other specific location (location A), and (3) location X and location A are not the same place and not reachable within a reasonable timeframe. To maintain an alibi, it is thus not sufficient merely to claim absence from location X at the time the crime occurred; a successful alibi rests on the defendant's ability to establish affirmatively that they were at location A – a separate and independent location – during the crime period. In fact, the word "alibi" itself means "in another place" (Culhane & Hosch, 2012, p. 958).

The defendant bears the burden of raising the alibi, although the prosecution must ultimately disprove it beyond a reasonable doubt at trial in order to prove that the defendant is the person who committed the crime (Johnson v. Bennett, 1968). There is no formal legal proof standard required at the police investigation or prosecutorial charging stage, but neither police nor prosecutors are inclined to resist formal processing just because the suspect or defendant says they were somewhere else. Social science evidence suggests police officers and prosecutors often lack enthusiasm for conducting a good faith investigation into the defendant's alibi. For example, one survey of police officers found that fewer than half of respondents indicated that they always thoroughly investigated an alibi before making an arrest, although an additional 38% said it was often investigated (Dysart & Strange, 2012, see also Chap. 9 of this text). In this same study, four officers asserted that they had never heard a believable alibi story (Dysart & Strange, 2012). Prosecutors might be no better than police at having the courage to act on truthful information. One author writing in 1964 reported the results of his survey of prosecutors, in which 75% said they would proceed with a case even though an investigated alibi was perceived to be true (Epstein, 1964). Even when presented with strong corroborating evidence, some police and prosecutors will look for reasons to discount or discredit the alibi, guided by tunnel vision and other forms of confirmation bias that further bind them to an already-established image of the defendant's guilt (Burke & Marion, 2012). They might even try to intimidate (or discourage) the potential alibi corroborators with reminders about perjury or the potential for filing a violation of probation, to get them to back off their story.

Proof standard and timing issues aside, alibis depend on specific claims about both time and location. And for this reason, defense attorneys require, first and foremost, a clear statement from the police or prosecutor about when and where the alleged crime occurred. In some investigations, the police report these facts with precision (e.g., "at 6:09 am on June 12, 2019, at Zukes Jewelry Mart located on the corner of 5th and Elm in Center City, the rear entrance store alarm sounded"). In others, the time cannot be precisely identified because it derives from live witness recollection rather than from technology sensors or time-stamped surveillance footage; in those instances, the police construct the time using phrases like "shortly after midnight" or "between the hours of 2 and 4 pm." Time frames become diffuse when live witnesses use behavioral clues to jog their memories, such as recalling what TV show they were watching when they heard the gunshot or estimating how long after they dropped their children off at school they saw a hooded figure running in the neighborhood. The fuzzier the time frame, the harder it is for defendants to establish a full alibi, because defendants must account for their whereabouts during the entire period. Any unaccounted-for blocks of time allow the police and prosecution to assert that the defendant could have committed the crime during one of these periods.

Time and location play a role in the quality of defense evidence, as well; 87.5% of our survey respondents said that the client's ability to be specific about their location was "heavily" or "moderately" influential in their decision to investigate and present an alibi defense.

For example, defense attorneys first need to distinguish between true alibis and soft alibis. With a true alibi, the defendant can pinpoint their location (location A) at the exact time the crime is alleged to have occurred, a location that is some distance away from the site of the crime (location X). They argue, in essence, that the laws of physics make it impossible for them to have been in two distinct places on the planet at the same time (Sullivan, 1971). With a soft alibi, the defendant is able to establish that they were a certain distance away from the crime scene at time A and that such distance is too great to have permitted them to travel to or from the crime scene by time X – the time the crime occurred. They argue, in other words, that the laws of physics make it impossible for them to have been in location A at time A and also in location X at time X. As the breadth of the time frame for when the crime occurred increases, defendants may have a harder time advancing either true alibis or soft alibis, as police and prosecutors may get increasingly creative about what the laws of physics might enable the defendant to do. An aggressive prosecutor convinced of the defendant's guilt might argue, for instance, that the defendant could have reached location X at time X from location A at time A by driving 100 miles per hour on mountain roads. We can also identify partial alibis – instances where the defendant can account for their whereabouts during part of the time in question, but not for the whole period. A defendant's inability to document their movements during certain periods allows the police and prosecutor to argue that they could have committed the crime during one of these open periods. Notably, 75% of our survey respondents believe that police and/or prosecutors "sometimes" or "frequently" blur or extend the crime timeline just to make it harder for defendants to establish an alibi. The remainder believed that this happens "rarely" – but not a single respondent said it "never" happens.

For both true and soft alibis, the defendant's ability to establish their presence at location A during time A hinges on the availability of live witnesses and tangible evidence; rarely is the defendant's word about their presence sufficient to convince police, prosecutors, or jurors (or defense attorneys) of this fact. Live witnesses, who might be friends, family members, co-workers, acquaintances, or strangers, are needed to attest that they saw the defendant at time A in location A. When a defendant's personal testimony about an alternate location is not corroborated by other witnesses, particularly if witnesses were listed in the notice document but do not appear in court, a prosecutor can argue that the alibi is weak and not worthy of belief (e.g., People v. Holland, 1989). But even when they appear in court, live witnesses do not all manifest the same level of persuasiveness or credibility as physical evidence; consequently, defense attorneys must take care to thoroughly interview potential alibi witnesses before presenting their testimony to the tribunal.

Social science evidence has confirmed that the "relational distance" between the defendant and the live witness affects perception of the witness' credibility (Nieuwkamp et al., 2019, p. 903). The closer the witness is to the defendant in terms of personal relationship, the more likely it seems that the witness has a motive to lie to help the defendant (Culhane & Hosch, 2004; Lindsay et al., 1986; Burke & Turtle, 2003; Marion & Burke, 2013). Social psychologists Olson and Wells (2004) identified this as the difference between "motivated" and "unmotivated" corroborators. Having a stranger or co-worker (an unmotivated corroborator) swear that they saw the defendant at time A, in location A, will therefore carry more weight than having one's mother or close friend (a motivated corroborator) make the same statement. Defense attorneys are painfully aware of this fact, as evidenced by this statement from one of our survey respondents: "If it's mom or girlfriend, I don't use it: they always lie."

More problematic still is the alibi witness whose cover story implicates the defendant in another crime. One of our survey respondents described a client whose trial counsel had refused to call the client's illicit drug customers as alibi witnesses: his defense to charges of shooting one rival drug dealer was to claim that they were on the other side of town selling to their customers at the time the shots were fired. Our survey respondent commented: "[It's] probably true, but confessing to felony drug sales wasn't going to be a major improvement over the assault charge at issue."

Ironically, the greater the relational distance between the defendant and the witness, the less likely it is that the defendant's presence at location A at time A will be noted, let alone remembered, by the witness (Steele, 2020; Charman et al., 2017). This means that the witness whose testimony has the greatest persuasive potential is also the witness who is least likely to be found by the defense team or to provide helpful testimony if they are found. This irony heightens the impact of time on the defense's ability to present a successful alibi for yet another reason. The more time that passes between the commission of the crime and the defense's opportunity to investigate, the harder it will be for the defendant to find independent witnesses who can corroborate their presence at location A at time A (Charman et al., 2017). Lisa Steele (p. 1092) explains the challenge like this:

> Unlike an eyewitness to a crime, an alibi witness has no reason to realize when they interact with the defendant that they will be asked to recall him or her later. The alibi witness may have interacted with dozens of people during the critical time, and may not recall which customers were there at that time.

As this description makes clear, by the time the defense attorney receives the police report and is able to interview their client, potential unmotivated alibi witnesses might have moved, or taken another job, or lost their ability to recall any details of the day in question. These are likely normal, non-memorable, everyday-type interactions with low potential for strong memory traces in the first place, and they occur between people who do not know each other currently or plan to see each other in the future. Moreover, social psychologists suspect that alibi evaluators might be suspicious of someone who is readily able to provide an alibi for a distant past event "when there seems to have been no reason for an innocent person to be able to recall what he or she was doing that day" (Olson & Wells, 2004, p. 175). For all of these reasons, 62.5% of our survey respondents indicated that the amount of time elapsed between the date of the alleged crime and the client's arrest was "heavily" or "moderately" influential in their decision to investigate and present an alibi; only 17% expressed that this factor had zero weight in their decision calculus.

Because live witness testimony is vulnerable to credibility attacks and memory loss, defense attorneys much prefer to establish the location of the defendant using physical evidence – this aligns with social science research suggesting triers of fact are more persuaded by physical evidence than by witness testimony (Steele, 2020; Olson & Wells, 2004). This category includes store surveillance footage, receipts, social media posts, GPS records, and the like. While 91% of our survey respondents said access to such evidence was "heavily" or "moderately" influential in their decision-making about whether to present an alibi, such evidence is far from common in criminal cases. Dysart and Strange (2012) report that suspects provide leads or references to physical alibi evidence in fewer than 25% of investigations; Turtle and Burke (2003) observed in their survey of American and Canadian cases that only 14% of alibis were supported by physical evidence. Two of our respondents specifically lamented that clients never or rarely have receipts, but another suggested that GPS tracking through ankle monitors can be helpful.

Physical evidence can also prove an alibi false, as occurred in the storied murder/kidnapping case of Nathan Leopold and Richard Loeb. Leopold and Loeb were accused of kidnapping and killing a third boy, Bobby Franks, in Chicago in 1924. While Leopold and Loeb claimed to have been driving around on the afternoon Franks was kidnapped, Leopold's distinctive eyeglasses were found near Franks' deceased body. This discovery effectively dismantled their alibi (Linder, 1997).

Physical evidence that cannot easily be manipulated by the defendant is regarded as the gold standard, such as when the defendant is captured on film in an official record made by a third party for its own purposes (Olson & Wells, 2004). Such was the case documented in the movie Long Shot (2017), where a defendant who was accused of a murder happened to be caught on camera at a professional baseball game on the afternoon in question. Likewise, Mr. Seligmann's ATM receipt, time-stamped surveillance video, and cell phone records helped unravel Ms. Mangum's claims of being attacked by him between midnight and 1 am near Duke's campus.

Sustainability is an issue here as much as with live witnesses, because the passage of time sometimes interferes with the defendant's ability to find physical evidence. Receipts get thrown in the trash; store surveillance videotapes get re-used; workplace records get destroyed in accidental fires. For this reason, the defendant has a great interest in learning the details of the prosecution's timeline as soon as possible, so that whatever independent physical evidence exists can be requested and studied. Closeness in time between crime and investigation of an alibi has also been shown to be important to law enforcement: the sooner an alibi can be investigated, the greater the likelihood that the alibi story will be useful in determining whether the suspect had any involvement in the crime (Dysart & Strange, 2012). For instance, one officer reported that he had been able to find a time-stamped cash register receipt in the wastebasket of the motel room the defendant had recently vacated; this corroborated his alibi and led to his release.

In short, successful alibis depend on the preservation, discovery, and presentation of physical evidence and credible live witnesses. But many defendants will be disadvantaged in their ability to find and produce such evidence, at least in the quantity and quality that factfinders seem to require. In our survey, 83% of respondents believed that the defense must present "extremely convincing" or "moderately convincing" alibi evidence in order to prevail, despite the fact that the prosecution has the burden of persuasion on this issue. This finding is consistent with a concern raised by one of our respondents that defense attorneys "far too often … reject the use of alibi defenses out of a concern that it will cause a jury to flip the burden of proof."

While most people use cell phones these days (and thus may be able to produce cell phone records to document their approximate location by tower pings), other kinds of independent evidence are more contingent. Defendants with steady jobs are more likely than the unemployed or underemployed to have work records to document their whereabouts during a shift or to know the full names of the people with whom they worked in the past. Defendants who work, shop, and travel in the aboveground economy are more likely than those who traverse the underground economy to have friends and co-workers with stable addresses and without criminal records, rendering those friends and co-workers more likely to agree to testify and less likely to be impeached if they do testify. One of our survey respondents commented on the difference between retained and appointed cases when it comes to the ease of evidence-gathering to support an alibi:

> My retained clients tend to be employed and thus have a work schedule that helps establish timelines, locations and possible witnesses. Also, my paid clients also generally live a lifestyle that lends itself to providing more possible witnesses that are willing to come forward and involve themselves in the criminal justice process. Many of my appointed cases have possible witnesses that may be helpful to an alibi defense but those witnesses want nothing to do with the police, any investigators, the DA's Office or the court. For many of these people, nothing good comes from them getting involved, even if it helps out a person that may be falsely accused.

Putting these observations together, the de facto requirements of a successful alibi are likely to magnify the set of disadvantages already faced by the poor – which means this defense might be largely out of reach for many defendants being processed through the criminal courts, even if they are innocent. This socioeconomic disparity challenges a core, often unstated assumption on which the legal system rests, that innocent people should be able to produce relatively strong and accurate alibis regardless of circumstance (Olson & Charman, 2012). The frequency of disregarded alibis in cases that led to wrongful conviction suggests that this assumption ought to be re-examined; more than 25 percent of the first 157 exonerations involved an alibi that was not believed (Burke et al., 2007). In fact, weak alibi evidence (such as the alibi witness' inability to positively identify the defendant) is not merely less effective; it can be exploited by the prosecutor or police as a form of incriminating evidence (Garrett, 2011; Olson & Wells, 2004; McAllister & Bregman, 1989: Sullivan, 1971). For that reason, "[t]here is nothing as dangerous as a poorly investigated alibi. An attorney who is not thoroughly prepared does a disservice to his client and runs the risk of having his client convicted even [when] the prosecution's case is weak" (Skakel v. Commissioner, 2018, p. 64).

Having thus examined the uneven socio-legal terrain that defense attorneys must navigate when considering whether and how to raise an alibi defense, we next consider the formal legal rules that govern the strategic presentation of such defenses at trial. Part Two addresses statutory notice rules defense attorneys must follow, while Part Three concerns false alibis and post-trial ineffective assistance of counsel claims for failure to investigate or raise an alibi.

Part Two: Alibi Notice Rules

In this section, we turn our attention to the statutory schemes that require the defense to give the prosecution notice of its intent to raise an alibi defense at trial. Notice schemes arose to address the ease with which a defendant could fabricate an alibi, particularly mid-way through a trial. We offer the reader a quick tour through three issues – the history of these notice rules, the constitutionality of these rules, and the impact on a defendant of changing their mind about relying on a particular alibi at trial.

The History of Alibi Notice Statutes

Alibi notice rules developed in state jurisdictions in the decade following World War I, after a handful of commentators lamented that an alibi is "one of the main avenues of escape of the guilty" and declared (without evidence) that a significant amount of perjury occurs each year in connection with the alibi defense (Millar, 1920, p. 350; Burdick, 1925). Following these warnings, the first states to adopt notice of alibi statutes were Michigan in 1927, Ohio in 1929, and New York in 1935; by 1942 12 other jurisdictions had followed suit (Epstein, 1964). The purpose of these statutes was "to prevent the sudden 'popping-up' of … 'phoney [sic] alibi' witnesses at the eleventh hour and at a time which, in practice, affords the prosecutor no opportunity to check either the credibility of the witnesses or the accuracy of their statements" (People v. Schade, 1936, p. 617). At the time of this writing, 44 states have alibi notice statutes or rules on the books, as we document in the Appendix to this chapter. The six states that have declined to follow this trend are Alabama, Arkansas, California, Delaware, Kentucky, and Texas.

Development of notice rules in the federal courts was considerably slower than in the states. The Supreme Court Advisory Committee on Rules of Criminal Procedure unsuccessfully proposed a federal notice of alibi rule in 1943–1944 and again in 1962. The following decade, in 1971, the Advisory Committee again proposed a federal notice of alibi rule as well as an amendment to the prosecutorial discovery rule that would have required prosecutors to disclose, inter alia, "a list of the names and addresses, plus record of prior felony convictions, of all witnesses the prosecution intend[ed] to call during its case-in-chief" (Lietz III, 2009, p. 40). In 1975, the notice of alibi rule, Federal Rule of Criminal Procedure 12.1, became law, but the proposed amendment to prosecutorial discovery was stricken.

The content of jurisdictional notice schemes is fairly consistent across the country: defendants must generally inform the court and the prosecutor of (1) any intended alibi defense; (2) the place(s) where the defendant claimed to be at the time of the crime; and (3) the name, address, and telephone number of each alibi witness. Statutory schemes also require reciprocal disclosure by the prosecution, if it intends to introduce rebuttal witnesses on the issue of the defendant's alibi. The aim is to prevent unfair surprise by either side, but these rules likely also foster plea deals once the defendant is made aware of how the prosecution will respond.

While the core elements of alibi notice provisions are fairly standard, there are some notable variations in the timing of the defendant's mandatory disclosure. For example, Federal Rule 12.1 requires that in federal prosecutions, such notice must be provided *upon request by the prosecutor*. A number of states follow this rule as well; for example, in Idaho, a "defendant shall serve alibi notice within 10 days of the prosecutor's request unless judge rules otherwise" (Idaho Statutes Section 19-519(1) and in Rhode Island, a "defendant shall serve alibi notice within 21 days of the prosecutor's request" (Rhode Island Superior Court Rule of Criminal Procedure 16(c)). Other state statutes and rules require the defendant to serve the alibi notice within a certain number of days before trial, even without a prosecutor request. In Florida, for instance, the "defendant shall file and serve the alibi notice not less than 10 days before trial or such other time as the court may direct" (Florida Rule of Criminal Procedure 3.200), while the state of Oregon simply requires notice "not less than 5 days before trial" (Oregon Revised Statutes Section 135.455(1)). Finally, some state statutes and rules require the defendant to serve the alibi notice within a certain number of days after the arraignment. For example, a defendant in Montana "shall serve the alibi notice within 30 days after the arraignment or at a later date as the court may permit for good cause" (Montana Code Annotated Section 46-15-323(2)).

At the foundation of all notice schemes is the belief that failure to provide timely notice will unfairly limit the prosecutor's ability to respond to the defense, which might result in the acquittal of a factually guilty person. For that reason, noncompliance will bar a defendant from raising the defense. We consider the constitutionality of notice rules in the subsequent section.

The Constitutionality of Alibi Notice Statutes

The first constitutional concern raised by alibi notice statutes is self-incrimination: because these statutes force the defendant to give a preview of their case to the state, the statutes arguably compel the defendant to speak in violation of their self-incrimination privilege, as granted by the 5th Amendment. In Williams v. Florida (1970), the Supreme Court rejected this argument and held that notice statutes do not violate the Fifth Amendment privilege against self-incrimination. According to the Court, such statutes do not impact the defendant's decision about *whether to call* alibi witnesses but instead merely compel the defendant to *accelerate the timing* of their disclosure. In other words, because the defendant would have willingly revealed the alibi information at trial, there is no self-incrimination problem with requiring them to reveal this information sooner. Because notice statutes do not violate the self-incrimination clause, a noncompliant defendant cannot complain when the trial court prevents them from introducing evidence of an alibi at trial

But the reach of the notice violation penalty is limited to the production of outside evidence; some state and federal courts have affirmatively held that alibi notice statutes cannot curtail a defendant's right to testify personally about their presence at an alternate location during the time the crime was allegedly committed (see Baxter v. Duckworth, 1989). In these jurisdictions, a defendant who failed to file proper notice still would be able to testify that they were at an alternate location although they could not present any outside testimony or evidence to corroborate their claim. Whether the jury would believe such testimony is another matter entirely.

The second issue raised by notice statutes is reciprocity. Assume that an alibi notice statute required the defense to give notice of an alibi defense but did not place a reciprocal obligation on the State to provide notice of rebuttal witnesses it planned to call to discredit the defendant's alibi. This would be unconstitutional. In *Wardius v. Oregon* (1973, p. 475–476), the Supreme Court held that "[a]lthough the Due

Process Clause has little to say regarding the amount of discovery which the parties must be afforded … it does speak to the balance of forces between the accused and his accuser." A state whose alibi notice statute does not place reciprocal notice obligations on the State regarding rebuttal witness violates the Due Process Clause. Moreover, even in the absence of such a unilateral alibi notice statute, a judge's order requiring the defense but not the State to give notice of alibi evidence would violate Due Process (see, e.g., United States ex rel. Veal v. DeRobertis, 1982).

Changing One's Mind About Relying on an Alibi

While an alibi notice statement is not itself evidence, what happens when a defendant decides to rely on a different defense at trial and never mentions the alibi? Does the law support impeachment use of the notice statement as a prior inconsistent statement by the defendant? It does not. If it is a federal prosecution, Federal Rule of Criminal Procedure 12.1(f) prohibits the prosecution's use of the statement: "Evidence of an intention to rely on an alibi defense, later withdrawn, or of a statement made in connection with that intention, is not, in any civil or criminal proceeding, admissible against the person who gave notice of the intention." Several states also have statutes or precedent stating that "evidence related to an alibi notice is inadmissible if the defendant withdraws or abandons that defense before trial" (State v. Greene, 2014, p. 455-56). Finally, four states – Maine, Maryland, New Mexico, and North Carolina – always deem evidence connected to alibi notices inadmissible, regardless of whether the notice was withdrawn (State v. Simms, 2011; see also N.C. Stat. Ann. § 15A-905(c)(1)).

Will the defendant be disadvantaged if they provide notice of one alibi but then testify to a different alibi at trial? Some courts allow for the prosecution to impeach a defendant on this basis (Mosteller, 1986). For example, assume that a defendant charged with murder withdraws their initial alibi notice saying "I was at a birthday party at the time of the murder" and replaces it with an amended alibi notice saying, "I was at my mother's house at the time of the murder." In an impeachment jurisdiction, the prosecutor could question the credibility of the defendant's trial testimony (that they were at their mother's house) by asking them about the birthday party alibi they had previously advanced (State v. Gay, 1957). The potential for impeachment use is important because studies have shown that many people are inclined to change alibis over time – not necessarily to completely shift the story, but to make modifications as their memories sort through relevant details. Research on memory has shown that people often provide general details first, but have a harder time recalling specific details – those tend to come later (Culhane et al., 2013). Yet both lay persons and law enforcement regard stable stories as inherently more trustworthy than changed stories, which means a lapse in memory could prove detrimental even to an innocent suspect who tries to correct for it later on (Culhane & Hosch, 2012). As Steele (2020, p. 1091) notes, "even changes that genuinely strengthen the alibi … tend to weaken how factfinders perceive it."

For these reasons, many defense attorneys believe it is ill-advised to file a notice of alibi too early. Two-thirds of our survey respondents said they only file the notice when they have solid evidence of the alibi, in contrast to just 25% who indicated they file the notice whenever a client brings up the issue.

Part Three: Trial Litigation Issues

In this final section, we examine two risks faced by defense attorneys whose clients raise the issue of an alibi. The first concerns an alibi the defense attorney knows, or suspects, is false. The second concerns an alibi the defense attorney knows, or suspects, is weak. In both circumstances, defense counsel must consider the ethical and practical implications of choosing to present or to forego the alibi as a part of their defense strategy.

Procuring a False Alibi

Alibi witnesses do not just vary in their degree of persuasiveness to a factfinder; like witnesses generally, they also vary in their degree of truthfulness. Ethical canons instruct attorneys how to behave with untruthful witnesses. Most importantly, if an attorney knows that an alibi witness is going to perjure themselves, the attorney cannot call them as a witness (e.g., Tibbs v. United States, 1993, p. 639–41). To do so would constitute a form of fraud on the tribunal.

Model Rule of Professional Conduct 3.3(a)(3) states that:

> A lawyer shall not knowingly…offer evidence that the lawyer knows to be false. If a lawyer, the lawyer's client, or a witness called by the lawyer, has offered material evidence and the lawyer comes to know of its falsity, the lawyer shall take reasonable remedial measures, including, if necessary, disclosure to the tribunal. A lawyer may refuse to offer evidence, other than the testimony of a defendant in a criminal matter, that the lawyer reasonably believes is false.

But if defense counsel calls an alibi witness in good faith and later learns during trial that the witness has perjured themselves (i.e., the witness admits to defense counsel after-the-fact that they lied on the stand), what should the attorney do? The comment to Model Rule 3.3 states that the proper course for defense counsel in this circumstance "is to remonstrate with the client confidentially, advise the client of the lawyer's duty of candor to the tribunal and seek the client's cooperation with respect to the withdrawal or correction of the false statements or evidence." If that effort fails and the client refuses to allow their attorney to correct the record, defense counsel must take further remedial action, which could have a drastic impact on the defense. Counsel should seek first to withdraw from representation, but "[i]f withdrawal … is not permitted or will not undo the effect of the false evidence, the advocate must make such disclosure to the tribunal as is reasonably necessary to remedy the situation."

As the last sentence of Rule 3.3(a)(3) notes, defense counsel cannot prevent their client from testifying, even if the client indicates that they plan to give perjured testimony about an alibi (see McCoy v. Louisiana, 2018, noting that the decision about whether to testify is reserved for the client). But the attorney must not knowingly participate in eliciting perjured testimony. While the ABA has discouraged the practice, eliciting testimony in narrative form (rather than the standard question-and-answer form) "continues to be a commonly accepted method of dealing with client perjury" (Shockley v. State, 1989, p. 1379–80). Thus, if a client refuses counsel's advice that they not perjure themselves regarding an alibi, defense counsel could call the client, ask them a broad question such as "What do you wish to tell these jurors," and allow the client to testify without any additional questions (see Commonwealth v. Mitchell, 2003).

Finally, what if the prosecutor has evidence that the defendant asked a friend or neighbor to lie on their behalf? Proof of the solicited false alibi corroboration will do more than render the defendant's defense ineffective; prosecutors can argue that procurement of a false alibi is affirmative evidence of the defendant's consciousness of guilt (e.g., Henry v. Poole, 2005; Commonwealth v. Young, 1999). In other words, the prosecutor will explain to the jury that a defendant who needs a friend to lie on their behalf signals that they must be guilty.

For all of these reasons, our survey respondents emphasized that the defense attorney (or their investigator) must interview a proposed alibi witness right up front, to see if the story is credible. One of our respondents remarked that a successful interview "is the single most influential factor" in his decision to present an alibi defense. He then observed, "Usually, the witness caves – [admits] my client put them up to it." Another said she was always alert for jail calls from the defendant to the alibi witnesses "trying to mold their testimony to fit" the alibi. A third said he pro-actively explains to each witness the law of perjury and previews how the prosecution team will treat him on the witness stand. After this advisement, "9 times out of 10," our respondent reports, "the witness tells me my client put them up to it and it's all made up." Successful alibi witnesses are rare, but they are "crystal clear about their facts – unshakeable," one of our respondents says. These narratives serve as a cautious reminder of the attorney's duty to investigate the witnesses before calling them to testify, lest they commit perjury on the client's behalf and sink the case.

Neglecting to Investigate or Present a Potential Alibi

When the client raises the issue of an alibi, "it is up to defense counsel to make a judgment as to whether or not an alibi defense should go forward" (Sullivan, 1971, p. 160). This judgment becomes critical when the defense attorney believes the alibi is weak, but the client disagrees.

A defense attorney who fails to investigate and/or present an alibi defense might be accused of providing ineffective assistance to their client, in violation of the 6th Amendment. To prove such a claim, the client must show two things: (1) the attorney committed an error so serious it fell below the standard of competent practice (judged by prevailing professional norms), and (2) such an error was prejudicial to the client, meaning if it had not been made, there was a reasonable probability that the defendant would not have been convicted or would have received a lighter sentence (Strickland v. Washington, 1984).

Considering first the error prong of the *Strickland* test, ineffective assistance claims might stem from an attorney's failure to investigate potential alibi witnesses that the client mentions (Towns v. Smith, 2005; Bryant v. Scott, 1994; Blackmon v. Williams, 2016). This type of error received notoriety recently in the criminal appeal of Adnan Syed, whose case was profiled on the podcasts *Serial* and *Undisclosed*. Syed's attorney failed to locate a local teenager whom Syed had told her could conclusively place him at the local library at the time of the alleged murder. An attorney cannot disregard witnesses because they assumed that they know what they would say (United States v. Moore, 1976). Moreover, the attorney has an affirmative duty to investigate beyond the facts told to them by their client. An attorney's failure to conduct an independent investigation falls outside professional norms of client defense and cannot be excused by excessive caseload pressures or lack of funds; likewise, omissions that stem from "oversight, carelessness, ineptitude, or laziness" fall short of constitutionally sound representation (*Wilson v. Mazzuca*, 2009, p. 502).

Attorneys are, however, permitted to make strategic decisions in their representation of clients, and those strategic decisions include channeling energy into the most persuasive defenses (those that stand the greatest chance of leading to an acquittal). Defense attorneys, after all, want to secure victory for their clients, and they are aware that all defense narratives are not created equal. An attorney might decide not to pursue an alibi because it is weak – where, for example, the witness cannot provide sufficient detail, will say more harmful than positive things about the defendant's behavior, or will directly contradict the physical evidence. In any of these circumstances, introduction of the alibi witness might well lead to aggressive prosecutorial cross-examination that will ultimately make things worse for the defendant, a prediction that is fully consistent with much of the social science evidence reported herein. Sometimes an attorney will choose not to present the alibi because they worry that jurors will automatically discredit the defendant's witnesses as having a motive to lie for them, which would create a risk to the defendant's entire case (Spearman v. Commissioner, 2016). This too is consistent with the social science evidence presented here. Forgoing an alibi defense in this circumstance would not count as a transgression of professional norms, even if the client is unhappy about it. The challenge is thus for the appellate court to distinguish between the explicit strategic decision to let go of a potentially weak alibi claim and the unprofessional error of negligently failing to try.

Turning to the prejudice prong, appellate courts need to assess the impact of the attorney's failure to pursue an alibi on the case's eventual outcome. Only those errors that might have affected the outcome will merit a reversal of the criminal conviction. From the Supreme Court of Connecticut (Skakel v. Commissioner, 2018), we have a particularly clear articulation of a four-part test courts should use to gauge this impact: (a) how important was this alibi to the defendant's defense?

For a case in which alibi is the primary or only defense, prejudice from the attorney's failure to raise it is easier to show; (b) how significantly would this witness have contributed to the alibi defense? If this witness' testimony would have merely been cumulative of testimony provided by others, the attorney's failure to find or call them to the stand would be considered unimportant. But if there were no other alibi witnesses, or if this witness would have been the only unmotivated corroborator, the failure to find or call them would be regarded as significant (Montgomery v. Petersen, 1988; *Carter v. Duncan*, 2016); (c) how easily could the defense attorney have found this witness if they tried? Courts are reluctant to excuse attorneys who fail to locate witnesses who were readily available at the time of trial; and (d) was the defendant faced with serious charges, and did they face a significant sentence if convicted? This last point is not so much about judging the effect of the attorney error on the outcome but rather is calculated to assess just how much was at stake for the defendant if they lost (a stake that would have been known to the attorney at the time and should have motivated them to work harder).

Ideally, counsel should make the decision about whether to present the alibi in consultation with their client. While decisions about which witnesses to call are within trial counsel's discretion, if the client insists on testifying, the attorney cannot prevent it. Aside from client testimony, lawyers often insist that "the client should have some input on the decision of whether or not to present an alibi defense" (Steele, 2020, p. 1101). Many of our survey respondents suggested that disputes between the attorney and the client on this issue should be talked through, because the client might have priorities that would otherwise remain unknown to the attorney. For instance, "it may be important to the client that his or her family testify and demonstrate the client's innocence, even if that risks weakening the case" (Steele, p. 1101). One of our survey respondents made the point like this: "If the attorney has done their research into the issue, the client trusts the attorney. If you tell the client his proposed alibi witness will cave under cross-examination, the client reconsiders his defense at trial."

Conclusion

In this chapter, we have tried to de-mystify the alibi as a tool of defense strategy in courtrooms across the United States. Although fictional media tends to portray the alibi defense as a showstopper frequently invoked by suspects, the reality is far more sobering. Governed by strict notice rules and subjecting defendants to the risk of impeachment if their story changes, the alibi defense provides very little cover for most defendants seeking protection.

Aside from complying with the doctrinal rules about notice and hedging against the risk of a changing story, a defense attorney must carefully consider whether presenting an alibi defense in the first place serves the best interest of their client. As we have discussed, social science evidence suggests that strong alibis are hard to construct. The strength of an alibi will depend heavily on the defendant's ability to put forth unmotivated witnesses and/or tangible physical evidence to establish their presence at the alternative location at the time in question. Such witnesses and evidence are not always easy to find, particularly for defendants who work and live outside of middle class culture. Defense attorneys faced with presenting a weak alibi or invoking some other defense sometimes choose to avoid the risk altogether, as they are concerned that the prosecutor will transform a weak alibi into evidence of guilt.

A defense attorney must also steer clear of presenting false evidence of an alibi, for both tactical and ethical reasons. First, they must warn their client about the tactical risk posed by introducing false evidence: a prosecutor who has proven an alibi to be false is likely to use this fabrication against the defendant, arguing to the jury that it manifests a guilty conscience. Second, in the event the client insists on testifying to something the attorney knows to be false, the attorney puts their professional reputation at risk by validating such testimony through direct examination or closing argument. But a defense attorney who fails to investigate or raise an alibi defense might find themselves in hot water if the client gets convicted, forced to explain to a subsequent tribunal why the failure was a strategy call, rather than an instance of neglect.

For all of these reasons, the decision to present an alibi is far from straightforward, and attorneys must develop intuition over time about the best way to proceed. The terrain is fraught with uncertainty about jurors' reactions to the evidence and laced with hidden land mines in the prosecutor's impeachment strategy. Hemmed in by notice rules and dependent on witnesses or evidence that might not be found or believed, the alibi defense thus resembles a mirage in the desert for most defendants in American criminal courts.

Appendix: Alibi Notice Statutes/Rules

Alabama No alibi notice statute/rule.

Alaska Alaska Rule of Criminal Procedure 16(c)(5) ("Unless a different date is set by the court, no later than 10 days prior to trial").

Arizona Rule 15.2(b)(1) ("Unless the court orders otherwise, the defendant must disclose the material…no later than…in superior court, 40 days after arraignment, or 10 days after the State's disclosure").

Arkansas No alibi notice statute/rule.

California No alibi notice statute/rule.

Colorado Colorado Code of Criminal Procedure Section 16-7-102 ("as soon as practicable, but not later than thirty-five days before trial").

Connecticut Connecticut Rule 40-21 ("within twenty days, or at such other time as the judicial authority may direct").

Delaware No alibi notice statute/rule.

Florida Florida Rule of Criminal Procedure 3.200 ("not less than 10 days before trial or such other time as the court may direct").

Georgia Georgia Code Annotated Section 17-16-5 ("within ten days of the demand of the prosecuting attorney or ten days prior to trial, whichever is later, or as otherwise ordered by the court").

Hawai'i Hawai'i Rule of Penal Procedure 12.1 ("within the time provided for the filing of pretrial motions or at such later time as the court may direct").

Idaho Idaho Statutes Section 19-519 ("within ten (10) days or at such different time as the court may direct").

Illinois Illinois Supreme Court Rule 413(d)(iii) ("Subject to constitutional limitations and within a reasonable time after the filing of a written motion by the State").

Indiana Indiana Code of Criminal Law and Procedure 35-36-4 ("no later than: (1) twenty (20) days prior to the omnibus date if the defendant is charged with a felony; or (2) ten (10) days prior to the omnibus date if the defendant is charged only with one (1) or more misdemeanors").

Iowa Iowa Rule of Criminal Procedure 2.11(11)(a) ("within the time provided for the making of pretrial motions or at such later time as the court shall direct").

Kansas Kansas Statutes Annotated Section 22-3218 ("at least seven days before the commencement of the trial").

Kentucky No alibi notice statute/rule.

Louisiana Louisiana Code of Criminal Procedure Article 727 ("Upon written demand of the district attorney...the defendant shall serve within ten days, or at such different time as the court may direct").

Maine Maine Rule of Criminal Procedure 16A(b)(3) ("not more than 7 days after service of such demand").

Maryland Maryland Rule 4-263(e)(4) (no time specified).

Massachusetts Massachusetts Rule of Criminal Procedure 14(b)(1) (no time specified).

Michigan Michigan Compiled Laws Section 768.20 ("at the time of arraignment on the information or within 15 days after that arraignment but not less than 10 days before the trial of the case, or at such other time as the court directs").

Minnesota Minnesota Rule of Criminal Procedure 9.02(5)(e) ("before the Rule 11 Omnibus Hearing").

Mississippi Mississippi Rule of Criminal Procedure 17.4(a) ("Upon the written demand of the prosecuting attorney…, the defendant shall serve within ten (10) days, or at such other time as the court may direct").

Missouri Missouri Rule of Criminal Procedure 25.05(a)(5) (no time specified).

Montana Montana Code Annotated Section 46-15-323(2) ("Within 30 days after the arraignment or at a later time as the court may for good cause permit").

Nebraska Nebraska Revised Statute Section 29-1927 ("at least thirty days before trial, except that such notice shall be waived by the presiding judge if necessary in the interests of justice").

Nevada Nevada Revised Statutes Section 174.233 ("not less than 10 days before trial or at such other time as the court may direct").

New Hampshire New Hampshire Rule of Criminal Procedure 14(b)(2)(C) ("within sixty calendar days if the case originated in superior court, or thirty calendar days if the case originated in circuit court-district division, after the entry of a plea of not guilty, or within such further time as the court may order for good cause shown").

New Jersey New Jersey Court Rule 3:12-1 ("within 10 days after a written demand by the prosecutor").

New Mexico New Mexico Rule of Criminal Procedure 5-508 ("not less than ten (10) days before trial or such other time as the district court may direct").

New York New York Consolidated Laws Section 250.20 ("within eight days of service of such demand").

North Carolina North Carolina General Statutes Section 15A-905(c)(1) ("within 20 working days after the date the case is set for trial pursuant to G.S. 7A-49.4, or such other later time as set by the court.").

North Dakota North Dakota Rule of Criminal Procedure 12.1(a) ("within the time provided for the making of pretrial motions or afterward as the court directs").

Ohio Ohio Revised Code Section 2945.58 ("not less than seven days before the trial").

Oklahoma 22 Okl.St.Ann. Section 585 ("at or before five (5) days prior to the trial").

Oregon Oregon Revised Statutes Section 135.455 ("not less than five days before the trial").

Pennsylvania Pennsylvania Rule of Criminal Procedure 567 ("not later than the time required for filing the omnibus pretrial motion provided in Rule 579").

Rhode Island Rhode Island Superior Court Rule of Criminal Procedure 16(c) ("within twenty-one (21) days after receipt of such demand and particulars").

South Carolina South Carolina Criminal Rule 5(e) ("Upon written request of the prosecution…, the defendant shall serve within ten days, or at such time as the court may direct").

South Dakota South Dakota Codified Laws Section 23A-9-1/Rule 12.1(a) ("within ten days, or at such different time as the court may direct").

Tennessee Tennessee Rule of Criminal Procedure 12.1 ("Unless the court directs otherwise, the defendant shall serve such notice within ten days of the state's request").

Texas No alibi notice statute/rule.

Utah Utah Code of Criminal Procedure Section 77-14-2 ("not less than 10 days before trial or at such other time as the court may allow").

Vermont Vermont Rule of Criminal Procedure 12.1(a) ("on the date of the status conference, or at least 28 days prior to trial, whichever is sooner").

Virginia Virginia Supreme Court Rule 3A:11(d)(2) (no time specified).

Washington Washington Superior Court Criminal Rule 4.7(b)(2)(xii) (no time specified).

West Virginia West Virginia Rule of Criminal Procedure 12.1(a) ("within 10 days, or at such different time as the court may direct").

Wisconsin Wis. Stat. Section 971.23(8) ("at the arraignment or at least 30 days before trial").

Wyoming Wyoming Rule of Practice & Procedure 12.1(a) ("Upon written demand of the attorney for the state…, the defendant shall serve within 10 days, or at such different time as the court may direct").

References

Baxter v. Duckworth (1989). 761 F. Supp. 576 (N.D. Ind.).

Blackmon v. Williams (2016). 823 F.3d 1088 (7th Cir.).

Bryant v. Scott (1994). 28 F.3d 1411 (5th Cir.).

Burdick, C. K. (1925). Possibility of improvement by statutory changes and constitutional amendments affecting procedure. *ABA Journal, 11*, 510–514.

Burke, T. M., & Marion, S. B. (2012). Alibi witnesses. In B. L. Culter (Ed.), *Conviction of the innocent* (pp. 239–256). American Psychological Association.

Burke, T. M., & Turtle, J. W. (2003). Alibi evidence in criminal investigations and trials: Psychological and legal factors. *The Canadian Journal of Police and Security Services, 1*, 286–294.

Burke, T. M., Turtle, J. W., & Olson, E. A. (2007). Alibis in criminal investigations. In M. P. Toglia, J. D. Read, D. F. Ross, & R. C. L. Lindsay (Eds.), *The handbook of eyewitness psychology* (Vol. 1, pp. 157–174). Lawrence Erlbaum Associates.

Carter v. Duncan (2016). 819 F.3d 931 (7th Cir).

Charman, S. D., Reyes, A., Villalba, D. K., & Evans, J. R. (2017). The (Un)reliability of alibi corroborators: Failure to recognize faces of briefly encountered strangers puts innocent suspects at risk. *Behavioral Science And Law, 35*(1), 18.

Commonwealth v. Mitchell (2003). 781 N.E.2d 1237 (Mass.).

Commonwealth v. Young (1999). 748 A.2d 166 (Penn.).

Cohan, W. D. (2016). *Remembering (and misremembering) the Duke Lacrosse case*. Vanity Fair (Mar 10, 2016).

Culhane, S. E., & Hosch, H. M. (2004). An alibi witness' influence on juror's decision- making. *Journal of Applied Social Psychology, 34*, 1604–1616.

Culhane, S. E., & Hosch, H. M. (2012). Changed alibis: Current law enforcement, future law enforcement, and layperson reactions. *Criminal Justice and Behavior, 39*(7), 958–977.

Culhane, S. E., et al. (2013). Generation and detection of true and false alibi statements. *Psychiatry, Psychology and Law, 20*(4), 619.

Drizen, S., & Leo, R. (2004). The problem of false confessions in the post-DNA world. *North Carolina Law Review, 82*, 891.

Dysart, J., & Strange, D. (2012). Beliefs about alibis and alibi investigations: A survey of law enforcement. *Psychology, Crime and Law, 18*(1), 11–25.

Epstein, D. M. (1964). Advance notice of alibi. *Journal of Criminal Law and Criminology, 55*(1), 29–38.

Federal Rules of Criminal Procedure, Rule 12(f), 12.1.

Garrett, B. L. (2011). *Convicting the innocent: Where criminal prosecutions go wrong*. Harvard Univ. Press.

Henry v. Poole (2005). 409 F.3d 48 (2nd Cir.).

Inbau, F. E., Reid, J. E., Buckley, J. P., & Jayne, B. C. (2013). *Criminal interrogation and confessions* (5th ed.). Jones & Bartlett Learning.

Johnson v. Bennett (1968). 393 U.S. 253.

Lietz, W. C., III. (2009). Trial by Ambush should be a two-way street: The federal notice of alibi rule and mandatory disclosure of defense witnesses. *The Champion (July)*, 38–45.

Linder, D. O. (1997). *The Leopold and Loeb trial: A brief account*. http://law2.umkc.edu/faculty/projects/ftrials/leoploeb/Accountoftrial.html

Lindsay, R. C. L., Lim, R., Marando, L., & Cully, D. (1986). Mock-Juror evaluations of eyewitness testimony: A test of metamemory hypothesis. *Journal of Applied Social Psychology, 15*, 447–459.

Long Shot (2017). https://www.netflix.com/title/80182115

McAllister, H. A., & Bregman, N. J. (1989). Juror underutilization of eyewitness nonidentifications: A test of the disconfirmed expectancy explanation. *Journal of Applied Social Psychology, 19*, 20–29.

McCoy v. Louisiana (2018). 138 S. Ct. 1500.

Marion, S., & Burke, T. M. (2013). False alibi corroboration: Witnesses lie for suspects who seem innocent, whether they like them or not. *Law and Human Behavior, 37*(2), 136.

Millar, R. (1920). The modernization of criminal procedure. *Journal of Criminal Law and Criminology, 11*, 344.

Montgomery v. Petersen (1988). 846 F.2d 407 (7th Cir).

Mosteller, R. P. (1986). Discovery against the defense: Tilting the adversarial balance. *California Law Review, 4*, 1567.

N.C. Stat. Ann. § 15A-905(c)(1).

Nieuwkamp, R., Horselenberg, R., & van Koppen, P. (2019). True and false alibis among prisoners and their detection by police detectives. *Psychiatry, Psychology and Law, 25*(6), 902–921.

Nolan, J. R., & Nolan-Haley, J. M. (1991). *Black's law dictionary, abridged* (6th ed.). West Publishing.

Olson, E. A., & Charman, S. D. (2012). "But can you prove it?" Examining the quality of innocent suspect alibis. *Psychology, Crime and Law, 18*, 453–741.

Olson, E. A., & Wells, G. L. (2004). What makes a good alibi? A proposed taxonomy. *Law and Human Behavior, 28*(2), 157–176.

People v. Holland (1989). 445 NW2d 206 (Mich.).

People v. Schade (1936). 292 N.Y.S. 612, 616 (Queens County Ct.).

Shockley v. State (1989). 565 A.2d 1373 (Del.).

Skakel v. Commissioner (2018). 329 Conn. 1.

Sommers, S. R., & Douglass, A. B. (2007). Context matters: Alibi strength varies according to evaluator perspective. *Legal and Criminological Psychology, 12*, 41–54.

Spearman v. Commissioner (2016). 164 Conn. App. 530.

State v. Gay (1957). 307 P.2d 885 (Utah).

State v. Greene (2014). 329 P.3d 450 (Kan.).

State v. Simms (2011). 25 A.3d 144 (Md.).

Steele, L. J. (2020). Investigating and presenting an alibi defense. *Criminal Law Bulletin, 56*(6), 1084–1111.

Strickland v. Washington (1984). 466 U.S. 668.

Sullivan, T. (1971). Presentation of the defense. *Journal of Criminal Law and Criminology, 62*, 153–172.

Tibbs v. United States (1993). 628 A.2d 638 (D.C.).

Towns v. Smith (2005). 395 F.3d 251 (6th Cir.)

Turtle, J., & Burke, T. M. (2003). Alibi evidence in criminal investigations and trials: An archival analysis of Canadian and U.S. cases. Paper presented at the International Psychology-Law Conference, Edinburgh, Scotland, cited in Tara M. Burke and Stephanie B. Marion (2012). Alibi witnesses. In B. L. Culter (Ed.), *Conviction of the innocent* (pp. 239–256). Washington, DC: American Psychological Association.

United States v. Moore (1976). 554 F.2d 1086 (D.C. Cir.).

United States ex rel. Veal v. DeRobertis (1982). 693 F.2d 642 (7th Cir.).

Wardius v. Oregon (1973). 412 U.S. 470.

Williams v. Florida (1970). 399 U.S. 78.

Wilson v. Mazzuca (2009). 570 F.3d 490 (2d Cir.).

Chapter 9
The Effect of Erroneous Alibis

Stephanie A. Cardenas, William E. Crozier, and Deryn Strange

Introduction

On January 24, 1992, Willie Veasy clocked in to work at 5:59 p.m. as a dishwasher at Houlihan's Restaurant in Jenkintown, Pennsylvania (Chaudry et al., 2017). Veasy worked the busy Friday night shift along with three other dishwashers until he clocked out at 1:52 or 1:54 am. At around 10:00 p.m. that same day, John Lewis, a man many colloquially referred to as "The Jamaican," was shot and killed on a dimly lit street in North Philadelphia just 7 miles south of Houlihan's. Several months later, eyewitness to the shooting, Denise Mitchell, picked 26-year-old Willie Veasy out of a photo array. Nearly a decade later, she would go on to sign an affidavit recanting this identification due to her being "virtually legally blind" at the time of the event (Chaudry et al., 2017, *Episode 4*, 8:59).

Four and a half months after the 1992 shooting, on June 9 at 6:35 a.m., Detectives Worrell and Devlin brought a sleep-deprived and likely hung-over Veasy in for questioning. According to Jim Trainum, a retired homicide detective who interviewed Veasy, the detectives "yelled at him, threatened him," and "banged their fists on the table" throughout the course of an unrecorded interrogation (Chaudry et al., 2017, *Episode 2*, 24:53). Eventually, the pressure of the detectives' intimidation tactics would lead Veasy to provide a false confession to his involvement in the

S. A. Cardenas (✉)
Department of Psychology, Williams College, Wachenheim Science Center, Williamstown, MA, USA
e-mail: sac1@williams.edu

W. E. Crozier
Duke University School of Law, Duham, NC, USA

D. Strange
Department of Psychology, John Jay College of Criminal Justice, CUNY, New York, NY, USA

J. D. Behl, M. R. Kienzle (eds.), *Alibis and Corroborators*,
https://doi.org/10.1007/978-3-030-95663-9_9

murder – a confession he would almost immediately recant. In a statement drafted by Detective Devlin, Veasy unsurprisingly struggled to account for a specific Friday night over 4 months prior and incorrectly claimed to have been playing basketball with several friends near his home that night when a friend, Lyndell, drove up in a car with other friends and told Veasy to get inside. Veasy confessed that once in the car, Lyndell asked him if he wanted to exact revenge on some men who had recently robbed Lyndell. Though Veasy admitted some involvement, he claimed it was Lyndell and another man who did the actual shooting. According to Trainum, Veasy believed the confession would bring an end to the interrogation, but no conviction. Like many others before him, Veasy had faith that the lack of evidence would show the detectives had the wrong person, and they would set him free (Kassin, 2005; Santos, 2006).

According to the record of Veasy's interrogation, he made no mention of working at Houlihan's that night. Unbeknownst to him at the time, true alibi was significantly stronger than the incorrect alibi he provided. A few days later, on June 20, Detective Mangoni uncovered an official record of Veasy having been at work on the night of the shooting: a machine-stamped timecard with handwritten corrections from his shift manager, Susan Meyers. Critically, Meyers had crossed out 5:59 p.m. and replaced it with 6:00 p.m. since employees were not allowed to punch in early and also crossed out 1:52 or 1:54 a.m. and replaced it with 1:50 a.m. since employees were also not allowed to punch out after changing their clothes. At trial, Meyers did not recall making these specific corrections, but categorically denied the prosecutions' claims that Veasy had tampered with the time clock. The clock, as it turns out, was very difficult to adjust and could only be altered by managers. Neither she nor the kitchen manager could recall a single time Veasy had not shown up for a scheduled shift. Further, Veasy could not have left his station unnoticed on the busy night shift when records show over 848 customers were served. A missing dishwasher would have raised some alarms. In short, Veasy had a strong alibi, but one that was difficult for both him and his manager to recall and further verify.

Veasy had the kind of powerful alibi evidence that, if regarded objectively, *should* have exculpated him and altered the course of the investigation away from him. Yet in the report where Detective Mangoni documented Veasy's presence at work, Mangoni seemed to put little stock in the alibi, adding: "It is noted that Willie Veasy did give a post Miranda admission of participating in the shooting" (*Commonwealth v. Veasy*, 2017, p. 63). The confession trumped an alibi that represented the gold standard of alibi evidence (Olson & Wells, 2004),—i.e., difficult-to-fabricate physical evidence, and familiar persons (the restaurant and kitchen managers who would be unlikely to risk perjury to lie for Veasy. Despite the presence of newly compelling evidence, the process of "cumulative disadvantage" all too common in wrongful conviction cases was already in motion (Scherr et al., 2020, p. 353). The process began when Mitchell misidentified Veasy as the shooter and was exacerbated when he could not recall his actual whereabouts during his interrogation. Veasy's initial erroneous alibi precluded consideration of an otherwise strong alibi and lay a presumption of guilt so powerful that it irrevocably poisoned an otherwise highly credible alibi defense.

In 1993, after 4 days of deliberation, a jury convicted Veasy of second-degree murder and sentenced him to life in prison without parole. He served 27 years before finally being exonerated in 2019 with the help of the Pennsylvania Innocence Project. Veasy's case, discussed at length over several episodes in the *Undisclosed* podcast, strikingly demonstrates how criminal injustice can result from an erroneous alibi, even one subsequently amended to be correct (Chaudry et al., 2017).

The Problem of Erroneous Alibis

In this chapter, we explore what an erroneous alibi is and how it can undermine the fair administration of justice. We begin by defining erroneous alibis and corroborations. Next, we examine the individual- and system-level factors that contribute to these errors at the various stages of the criminal justice system. We consider the process and implications of intentionally and unintentionally erroneous alibi evidence as a matter of both individual human psychology and structural factors. Throughout this chapter, we explore how such erroneous alibis and corroborators have directly and indirectly contributed to wrongful convictions weaving in the stories of exonerees Ronald Cotton, Sean Ennis, Glen Nickerson, Dwight Love, and Luis Rojas. Like Willie Veasy, each exoneree had alibi evidence that, for reasons we will explore here, failed to prevent their wrongful convictions. Finally, we close the chapter with a discussion of avenues for future research and recommendations for policy reform to mitigate the damage of erroneous alibis.

What Does Erroneous Alibi Evidence Look Like?

An alibi is a plea of having been at a different place during the commission of the crime (Olson & Wells, 2004). On its face, an erroneous alibi is self-descriptive: an alibi that is not accurate. However, what makes an alibi inaccurate is a bit more complicated. Alibis that contain minor inaccuracies (such as being off by 15 minutes or offering some inconsequential detail like what was on TV) may not be fatally flawed, but major errors, such as who you were with or where you were, are highly problematic. Because an erroneous alibi is unlikely to have strong supporting evidence – if it has any evidence at all – it becomes a challenge to investigate and identify corroborating evidence supporting it.

A further challenge when evaluating the accuracy of an alibi is the entangling of believability and accuracy. After all, an accurate alibi should have some supporting evidence, and we might expect it to be inherently more believable than an erroneous one. For example, an accurate alibi likely has a combination of both strong and weak corroborating evidence, but an erroneous one may have only weak evidence. Yet the type of evidence that supports an alibi, and by extension perceptions of its believability, is not a perfectly diagnostic cue to accuracy.

The extent to which legal decision-makers, including police officers, detectives, prosecutors, judges, and juries, regard the accused's alibi evidence as believable is critical to the viability of the accused's alibi defense. Thus, a "bad" alibi is one that lacks believability because it cannot be used to locate supporting evidence or because the supporting evidence buckles under the weight of investigative or judicial scrutiny. It is worth noting then that the accuracy of an alibi, while related to believability, is nonetheless an independent quality of the alibi. That is, while we would likely consider an alibi that we know is inaccurate to be non-believable, one can also imagine a believable, yet inaccurate, alibi or, conversely, a non-believable, yet accurate, alibi. But because alibis often contain many details, some of which can be accurate and some of which can be inaccurate, alibi "accuracy" can be difficult to define. The perception of an alibi as functionally accurate or inaccurate is therefore often in the eye of the beholder.

Further, alibis are not necessarily always either entirely correct or incorrect. The reconstructive nature of memory means that alibis often contain details that are a mixture of both correct and incorrect statements. Our prior work used a diary-study technique to assess the generation of alibis for varied naturalistic events (Cardenas et al., 2020). The results of over 507 verified alibi statements across two studies suggest that alibis frequently contain errors that vary across and within person, setting, and location details. For example, alibi providers had greater difficulty correctly recalling *what* they were doing at the to-be-recalled time period than *where* they were or with *whom*. Still, an alibi with an incorrect account of *what* the person was doing may still be regarded as accurate so long as it puts the accused at a different location from where the crime occurred during the commission of the crime.

Because alibi claims can be either wholly or partially inaccurate, the underlying corroborating evidence should be considered piece-meal rather than holistically diagnostic of accuracy as well. Suspects who search for evidence to confirm or disconfirm the memories they reported to form an alibi may find this approach helpful, but only to an extent. Evidence (or the lack thereof) that indicates an inaccurate detail in an alibi (e.g., another person saying, "You weren't at the basketball court, you were at work") can signal that the provider is on the wrong path and should reexamine their memory. However, evidence that, at least superficially, seems to support an incorrect alibi (such as your roommate saying, "You weren't home, maybe you were playing basketball") can further mislead the provider into thinking their alibi is accurate. Thus, one piece of corroborating evidence is likely insufficient to confirm an alibi's accuracy or inaccuracy on its own. In sum, even after triangulating all these varied characteristics of the alibi, there is no guarantee that triangulation will be diagnostic of an alibi's accuracy.

The Base Rate of Inaccurate Alibi Evidence

Since 1989, DNA testing and the discovery of other types of evidence have led to the exoneration of more than 3133 innocent persons wrongfully convicted in the United States for crimes they did not commit (Innocence Project, 2021; NRE,

2021). Though undoubtedly the presence or absence of an alibi played a role in many documented wrongful conviction cases, the number of exoneree cases involving erroneous alibi evidence is unknown. The magnitude of the alibi's role in wrongful conviction cases is typically overshadowed by other factors incorrectly tying a defendant to the crime. The currently recognized leading causes of wrongful convictions are not weak, missing, or even incorrect alibis, but rather mistaken eyewitness identifications, false confessions, unvalidated and improper forensic evidence, and misconduct by prosecutors and law enforcement (Innocence Project, 2021; Gross et al., 2020).

Unlike other causes of wrongful conviction, alibi evidence is exculpatory evidence, the absence of which does not confirm the accused's involvement in a crime. It is undoubtedly a positive outcome when an incorrect alibi does *not* serve to incriminate an innocent suspect to the same extent as a false confession or mistaken eyewitness identification. While an alibi often falls on the defense to provide, inaccurate inculpatory evidence is in the hands of the prosecution and police, making it easier to seek out to support the investigators' theory of the crime and harder for the defense to contest. Not coincidentally, in a recent by the NRE, Gross and others (2020) discovered that of the various documented instances of police and prosecutorial misconduct, most involved concealing of exculpatory evidence, witness tampering, fabricating evidence, and misconduct in interrogations and at trial.

The attention to and affirmative nature of coercive interrogation and investigation tactics that facilitate false confessions and mistaken eyewitness identifications may explain why these factors have received so much empirical attention and alibis comparatively little. Even so, alibis can play a key role in wrongful convictions. The government's failure to investigate alibis denies a defendant access to a critical piece of exculpatory evidence. This evidence bolsters the claim that they are *not* culpable for the crime and that detectives should look elsewhere for the true culprit.

Despite the clear difficulty required to generate an accurate alibi, it is surprisingly difficult to determine how often real-world defendants' alibis are accurate or inaccurate. Investigators are not obligated to verify a defendant's alibi. Indeed, by the time the police have charged a suspect, they may have other (ostensibly) inculpatory evidence, logically dictating that the defendant's alibi is false. Given that courts (e.g., *People v. Riggs*, 2008 44 Cal. 4th 248) held the prosecution was obligated to turn over to the defense witnesses that supported the defendant's alibi as a matter of *Brady*, why continue the investigation of the alibi? Instead, it probably falls to the defense to verify an alibi. Outside of Chap. 8 in this text, we know of no research that asks defense attorneys about their views and approaches to alibis. But, it stands to reason that verifying an alibi is a time-consuming and labor-intensive task, one which an overworked public defender may deem an ineffective way to represent their client. It is easy to see how a defense attorney may want to invest their time in questioning a forensic report or getting a false confession excluded, rather than tracking down a defendant's acquaintance to support a (possibly weak) alibi. Thus, many alibis are likely not fully investigated, and so we have no way of knowing how often alibis are accurately or inaccurately offered by innocent people.

Base Rates from Experiments

We do have some evidence, however, from empirical studies that suggest inaccurate alibis may not be all that uncommon. To illustrate, laboratory studies in which participants have been asked to generate alibis for events which occurred several days prior suggest that though people are highly willing to provide alibis, such alibis contain inaccuracies between 22% and 53% of the time (Leins & Charman, 2016; Olson & Charman, 2012; Strange et al., 2014). For example, in two studies by the current authors, when recalling events from their own lives, participants reported completely incorrect information about who they were with (person details), where they were (setting details), *and* what they were doing (action details) around 22% of the time (Cardenas et al., 2020). For nearly half of the alibis, participants recalled alibis that contained at least one major inaccuracy (e.g., about action details). Rarely did participants recall alibis that could be considered perfectly accurate across person, setting, and action details.

Several studies have examined the innocent provider's ability to generate corroborating evidence finding that innocent providers consistently overestimate the ease of verifying their alibis (Cardenas et al., 2020; Matuku & Charman, 2020; Olson & Charman, 2012; Strange et al., 2014; Culhane et al., 2013) – in some cases, estimating being able to generate corroborating evidence for 92.4% and 96.49% of their alibis, respectively (Cardenas et al., 2020; Nieuwkamp et al., 2016b). Yet this estimation turns out to be overly optimistic. Participants in Cardenas and colleagues' (2020) studies provided corroborating evidence they found after an entire week's search. Despite grandiose predictions that they would be able to generate 895 pieces of supporting evidence, participants submitted only 96 pieces of evidence – just 10%.

Though other studies have found higher rates for the ability to generate evidence – in as many as 52.9% and 70.4% of alibis – one consistent finding is that providers are wrong about the quantity and type of evidence they can provide (Strange et al., 2014; Olson & Charman, 2012). Olson and Charman (2012) found that 25% of participants changed the evidence they initially thought of to support their alibis, most commonly to a weaker form of evidence. Extensive errors in initial alibis lead to changes in alibi statements over time, which in turn necessitate a revision to providers' original corroboration plans (Olson & Charman, 2012). Yet no research has examined whether such overestimations adversely impact providers' credibility in criminal contexts. Would legal decision-makers fault providers more for failing to provide the testimony of a motivated other (e.g., a family member) than for some difficult-to-fabricate physical evidence? Ironically, one reason for why difficult-to-fabricate evidence is more believable is also what makes it so difficult to access. Security camera footage documenting your presence at a location away from the scene of the crime is compelling evidence, but the barrier to accessing such footage may be high or even insurmountable. Barriers may include not knowing that such footage exists and not having permission or the means to access the footage. Such compelling footage may not even exist – after all, how often are we in places where being recorded is the norm? Understanding the difficulty of accessing corroborating evidence may lead to more lenient evaluations. In support of this proposition, preliminary work by Olson and Wells (2012) found evidence of an 'alibi-generation effect'—namely, that the experience of generating an alibi can make people empathetic about the difficulties associated with producing accurate alibis and therefore, more likely to rate alibis as stronger than they might have otherwise. Perhaps a similar alibi corroboration effect could be found to temper expectations of corroborating evidence. Further, no published studies to date have assessed attorneys' perceptions of whether the weak evidence participants do generate is even capable of bolstering an alibi defense (however, see Chap. 8 for a summary of defense attorney's views).

Because alibis commonly contain inaccuracies, it is natural that attempts to corroborate such alibis should often be unsuccessful. Given the paucity of research examining alibis verified for accuracy, fewer studies still have been able to examine whether more accurate alibis lead to greater quantitatively and qualitatively corroborating evidence. We know of only two such studies. The first, by Matuku and Charman (2020), found no relation between accuracy and quantity of person or physical corroborating evidence generated. An exploratory analysis of Study 2 of Cardenas et al.'s (2020) openly available data similarly found similar results.

Major Causes of Erroneous Alibi Evidence

Beyond the detection of inaccurate alibis, it is even more important to identify the factors that underlie such inaccuracies. There may be many potential reasons why alibi evidence presented in defense of an innocent person may contain inaccuracies. Yet few empirical studies have investigated alibi generation by innocent persons, let alone the source of such alibi errors. Over the past several years, this growing area of research has focused primarily on memory-based errors resulting from the type of event (Cardenas et al., 2020; Leins & Charman, 2016), the delay in questioning (Culhane et al., 2008, 2013; Nieuwkamp et al., 2016b; Olson & Charman, 2012), the alibi elicitation technique (Cardenas et al., 2020; Leins & Charman, 2016; Matuku & Charman, 2020), the investigators' presumption of the providers' guilt (Portnoy et al., 2019), and the providers' actual guilt (Sauerland et al., 2019; Deeb et al., 2018; Nahari et al., 2014; Vernham et al., 2020) and ethnicity (Culhane et al., 2008).

The majority of alibi generation research examines how unintentional sources of errors can cause inaccurate alibis. Still, alibis may contain inaccuracies for intentional reasons. Here we consider alternative paths, both unintentional and intentional, that can lead to erroneous alibi evidence. We also note the important overlap between affirmatively erroneous alibis and instances where an alibi is absent – a situation in which a defendant may have an alibi, but, for either intentional or unintentional reasons, is unable to present it at trial.

Unintentionally Erroneous Alibi Evidence

Fallibility of Memory

Perhaps the most common reason for an alibi error is also the most mundane; producing an alibi is a very difficult memory test (see Crozier et al., 2017). Whether it is forgetting where you put your keys, the name of a new acquaintance, or what you did last weekend, everyone is familiar with being unable to recall a piece of information no matter how hard you try. Despite the higher stakes, alibis are no different (Kassam et al., 2009). In fact, because a person's alibi is likely a common activity, such as being at work, recalling that specific event from memory to provide an alibi is particularly challenging. Rather than a unique, stand-out, or special event, the alibi memory is likely mundane, unimportant, and forgettable. As such, the memory may be poorly encoded and lack easy retrieval cues. Here, we explain several memorial processes that lead to people providing inaccurate alibis that they believe are accurate.

Reliance on Schemas

Studies show that innocent people take a heuristic approach to reporting their alibis (Cardenas et al., 2020; Leins & Charman, 2016). When confronted with the difficult task of recalling an event for which they may not have formed a solid memory, participants tend to ask themselves "What would I normally have been doing?" at the time during which the crime occurred. When providing an alibi, a participant considers where they would have been during that time period, and these expectations may form the basis of their alibi. That is, they may use schemas to fill in the gaps for their memories rather than continuing the memorial search.

Research supports evidence for schematic processing in two ways. First, participants are better able to report accurate alibis for schema-consistent events than schema-inconsistent events. For example, in Cardenas et al. (2020), 39.92% of schema-consistent alibis were completely accurate across setting, action, and location categories compared to just 24.41% of schema-inconsistent alibis. Second, when participants make errors in their reporting of schema-*in*consistent events, those errors are often substitutions of schema-consistent events. In other words, participants' alibi statements hold true to their schemas even in situations where participants deviate from their routines. Studies show that for schema-inconsistent alibis, participant errors tended to include details that were consistent with their schemas between 54% and 60% of the time (Cardenas et al., 2020; Leins & Charman, 2016).

The evidence is less clear on whether reliance on schemas adversely impacts the generation of corroborating evidence. Preliminary results suggest, through an exploratory analysis of the corroborating evidence generated by participants in Cardenas et al. (2020), that greater event schema-consistency, but not alibi accuracy, predicted a greater amount of corroborating (person or physical) evidence generated. That is, events that conformed with participants' daily routines led to significantly greater pieces of corroborating evidence than events that did not conform with participants routines.

Source Monitoring Errors

Another problem for selecting a specific, accurate memory is the fact that people are notoriously bad at remembering where a memory is from. This process of attributing information in memory to the correct source, first outlined by Johnson et al. (1993) as the source monitoring framework, can lead to a variety of accurate information mixed in with inaccurate information. For example, you could accurately remember that you were at work, but mistake which Friday, or even which day of the week, the event in question occurred; similarly, you could remember that someone greeted you when you got to work, but attribute that greeting to the wrong coworker. Higher stakes do not preclude such errors. Ronald Cotton, who was wrongfully convicted for the rape of Jennifer Thompson-Cannino, committed such an error (Thompson-Cannino et al., 2009). When questioned by police, Cotton initially accidentally reported having been with friends at the time of the crime and even provided their names only to have his friends disconfirm this evidence. He had based his alibi on a memory for an event that had occurred at a different time period.

The potential for source confusion in alibi details is conceivably endless; an alibi provider could misattribute days, locations, people, activities, and so on. These errors can be avoided when other cues are present (such as remembering that you could not have been at work on July 4, because it was a holiday, so it must have been a different Friday, or realize that it could not have been Rebecca that greeted you, because she is always in the back storeroom). However, as the source of the information becomes more similar, so too are the errors more likely to occur. For example, if you are asked about last Friday, you may only need to go through one Friday's worth of memories to provide an alibi – but if the Friday in question was 3 months ago, you will have to sort through any number of possible Fridays to choose the correct one. What is even more difficult is that while an accurate detail may provide a cue to other accurate details, source monitoring errors can occur independently. A person may remember a single Friday extremely accurately – but if it is not the right Friday, the whole alibi is erroneous. A person could also pick the right Friday and correctly recall their location and activity, but misattribute who they were working with – a single detail error that could lead to doubt being cast on the whole alibi when no one can corroborate the story.

Phenomenology of Innocence

Aside from cognitive, memorial factors that lead to erroneous alibis, we posit that social factors can lead a person to provide an alibi without carefully considering its accuracy, which may turn out later to be erroneous. Kassin (2005) proposed that innocence itself could put innocent defendants at risk. Since then, research has demonstrated that innocent suspects are more likely to waive Miranda rights (e.g., Kassin & Norwick, 2004; Scherr & Franks, 2015), experience diminished physiological stress response in interrogation settings (Guyll et al., 2013), and confess expecting to be later exonerated (Perillo & Kassin, 2011). But are innocent suspects also more likely to readily provide alibis than guilty suspects? Preliminary evidence based on a sample of social science laboratory participants suggests a high willingness to provide alibis between 88% and 99.5% of the time even when participants are barred from using external resources such as calendars (Cardenas et al., 2020; Culhane et al., 2008; Nieuwkamp et al., 2016b; Olson & Charman, 2012).

One key element missing from these studies is that participants did not provide alibi evidence within the context of a true criminal investigation. Given law enforcements' and legal decision-makers' negative perceptions of inaccurate and changed alibis (Culhane & Hosch, 2012), innocent suspects may or may not be more reluctant to disclose an alibi except under circumstances of absolute confidence. On the one hand, a wealth of research suggests that innocent defendants, confident in the exonerating power of their innocence, consistently make choices that put them at risk of conviction, such as waiving their right to silence (Kassin & Norwick, 2004; Moore & Gagnier, 2008; Scherr & Franks, 2015) and confessing under interrogative pressures, expecting later to be exonerated (Perillo & Kassin, 2011). On the other hand, it is possible that knowledge of the potential adverse repercussions resulting from claims about incorrect alibi evidence could lead to lower base rates of generated alibis. To examine this possibility, future work could examine whether informing participants of the consequences of providing erroneous alibi evidence improves their accuracy or at least inhibits their proclivity to provide an alibi they are unsure of.

Perhaps suspects and defendants are equally as insensitive to the inaccuracies of their alibi statements and ability to locate corroborating evidence as research participants. Participants typically self-report moderate to high confidence in the accuracy of their alibi recall ability suggesting that they are not sensitive to their own faulty memories (Cardenas et al., 2020). Further work could then examine whether warning real providers of the adverse consequences to their credibility would decrease base rates of inaccurate alibis. However, even if providers appreciate the consequences of unintentionally providing erroneous alibis, they may still weigh the risk of damage to their credibility from *not* providing an alibi at the time of questioning to be greater than the risk of providing an incorrect alibi.

Coercive Interrogation Tactics

The context in which the innocent person is questioned about their alibi may lead to more or less accurate alibis. Consider an innocent person who is given ample notice to generate their alibi, to probe it for inaccuracies, and to investigate it prior to giving an official statement to the police. Though this person may be no more likely to generate an error free alibi from the onset, they do have the opportunity to correct their errors privately without arousing police suspicion. In contrast, the individual who is facing the immediate demands of a detective in an interrogation room may be less likely to have the opportunity to correct any such errors. They may lack the means to verify their alibis (say, by calling a friend or colleague) or search for other forms of physical evidence that might support their alibi.

Suspects asked to generate alibis within the interrogation room may be most disadvantaged by these contextual differences, but the research on these social motivators for providing an alibi is scant. How often do suspects provide alibis merely to appease their interrogators' demands or to defend themselves against a stated presumption of guilt? Do detectives pause an interrogation to verify a suspect's alibi? Interrogators likely continue the interrogation taking the approach of tracking down information not immediately verifiable at a later time. What might have happened if detectives had halted Veasy's interrogation while they awaited confirmation of the truthfulness of his statements?

Intentionally Erroneous Alibis

False Alibis Evidence

False alibis are, by definition, erroneous because they are inaccurate, but they are in a somewhat unique category. We discuss them here for completeness. Though we do not with what frequency, guilty people may fabricate alibis with fake physical evidence, lying family, or threatened witnesses. Indeed, people providing knowingly false alibis report feeling confident that they could get a motivated alibi witness to corroborate their alibis (Culhane et al., 2013). The chances of identifying such false alibis during an interview are slim; people, including supposedly trained law enforcement personnel, tend to be at about chance level for detecting a lie (Hartwig & Bond Jr., 2011), if they can at all (Luke, 2019). Instead, these alibis are likely best identified through more traditional detective work, thereby underscoring the importance that all alibis be thoroughly investigated with the goal of verification *and* falsification. Promisingly, a recent study by Vernham et al. (2020) compared the characteristics of truth-telling pairs against liar-pairs in which one person completed a mission while another completed a mock theft. Liar-pairs provided more unverifiable details (such as leaves were falling in the park) than truth-telling pairs who included more verifiable details (such as bumping into a friend, George). Briefly trained alibi evaluators were then able to discriminate between truthful and deceitful statements by considering the extent to which statement details could or could not be verified. Because participants were all tasked with generating alibis, and there were no adverse consequences for lying, this study cannot tell us if guilty participants would generate false alibis or not – but it does give us some insight into the features of false alibis that detectives can hone in on.

There are of course several reasons an alibi corroborator might assist in the fabrication of an erroneous alibi, such as a lack of trust in the police and the criminal justice system, fear or pressure from the suspect and/or their associates, the promise of incentives (e.g., money, group inclusion), or sympathy toward the suspect (Dysart & Strange, 2012). It is worth noting that an alibi corroborator could provide a factually incorrect account of the defendants' whereabouts for any of the above reasons regardless of the suspect's guilt or innocence. This suggests that the motivations behind these intentionally fabricated alibis, if uncovered, should not be interpreted as diagnostic of the defendants' culpability.

Desire to Conceal the Ugly (But Not Necessarily Illicit) Truth

In some cases, a suspect may also provide intentionally erroneous alibis when wishing to conceal their true alibis. Suspects may weigh the advantages and disadvantages of disclosing their alibi to an investigator during initial questioning without fully appreciating the stakes. An innocent alibi provider may reason that hiding their salacious or otherwise embarrassing activities, or even other criminal involvement, may be a good option. For example, in the 2001 film *Legally Blonde*, the defendant on trial for the murder of her husband refuses to provide her lawyers with her extremely strong alibi, because admittance that she was getting liposuction would harm her exercise health business (Luketic, 2001). Given the difficulties previously discussed associated with corroborating erroneous alibis, a provider may change their mind once the need for a stronger alibi defense becomes apparent, choosing to disclose their true alibi. A change from the initial alibi to the more salacious alibi may then damage their credibility, though these findings to date are mixed (Allison et al., 2012; Keeping et al., 2017; Jung et al., 2013; Nieuwkamp et al., 2016a).

Absent Alibis

Finally, we note absent alibis. Absent alibis are those which for whatever reason are not considered during the course of an investigation, trial, or post-conviction relief motions. Simply put, absent alibis fail to exculpate the accused, not because they were deemed insufficient, but rather because they were denied proper consideration. An absent, but *accurate*, alibi is of course different from a present, but *inaccurate*, alibi. Though absent alibis do not fit with the traditional idea of inaccurate alibis, we discuss them here as they contribute to an inaccurate and incomplete alibi defense. In many cases, the absent alibi is not the fault of the suspect, but the result of a failure to fully investigate—either on the part of detectives or defense attorneys—that results in an incomplete or absent alibi defense.

In the summer of 2020, the National Registry of Exonerations (NRE) along with Gross and others (2020) released a report documenting the role of misconduct by prosecutors and law enforcement in the conviction of 2400 innocent and exonerated persons. Among the most common and egregious forms of misconduct, they discovered, is the failure to disclose exculpatory evidence to the defense. In 19 cases, the they found that authorities had concealed alibi evidence including interviews and video evidence. In one such 1987 case, authorities concealed the time of the crime by failing to disclose testimony from a man who had driven the victim to the police station shortly after the crime occurred. Though the accused, Sean Ennis, actually had a strong alibi for the time period during which the crime took place, it was deemed irrelevant as it did not correspond with the time the prosecution claimed the crime had occurred. Ultimately, not knowing the correct time of the crime kept Ennis from mounting a proper alibi defense (although see Chap. 8 for defense attorney considerations in trial strategy), which could have helped him secure his freedom. Ennis who was wrongfully convicted for the rape and kidnapping in 1990 was exonerated 4 years later.

Further, there have been documented cases of alibi corroborators who have also deliberately provided – or failed to provide – evidence corroborating a defendants' alibi. Corroborators disinclined to become involved in a criminal investigation may also decline to provide corroboration. Some may even be externally pressured not to get involved. For example, in the case of one exoneree, Glen Nickerson, law enforcement threatened to charge alibi witnesses as accomplices to the crime and lose child custody if they testified on Nickerson's behalf. Luckily, Nickerson's alibi witnesses testified anyway. Similarly, a police officer involved in the case of Dwight Love, another exoneree wrongfully convicted of murder, threatened to arrest Love's girlfriend if she corroborated his alibi of having been with her and hid earlier statements in which she had corroborated his alibi. It is not difficult to imagine how corroborators, particularly those unknown to the defendant or less than completely certain in their memory, may buckle under the pressure of threats of prosecution and thus fail to corroborate an alibi for a defendant. If this happens with any frequency, it would be difficult to detect because such corroborators may vanish without a trace.

Impact of Erroneous Alibis

While the causes of erroneous alibis are clear from both real-life cases and psychology research, their impact is still somewhat unexplored territory. As previously discussed, erroneous alibis are rarely the focal point of a criminal case. And yet, as we discuss here, erroneous alibis may subtly influence the entire course of the case from the start of the investigation through prosecution to trial.

On the Magnitude of the Errors

As previously discussed, alibis can vary greatly in the extent to which they are incorrectly reported. But at what point are the errors large enough to deem the whole alibi unreliable or even be taken as evidence of deceit? Surveys of law enforcement suggest that the bar is high for deeming an alibi believable, but low for deeming it non-believable (Dysart & Strange, 2012). Small recall errors are largely inconsequential for lay people. Not remembering that you arrived late to work a few weeks ago because you left your metro card at home and had to walk all the way back home to retrieve it is unlikely to impact your life. But the consequences of even small errors may become amplified in a criminal investigation. We often misremember or forget our own recent histories with impunity yet hold alibi providers to a higher standard. Lay beliefs about memory that equate it with video recordings (Simons & Chabris, 2011) as well as the role that motivations ought to play in effective retrieval of memories (Kassam et al., 2009) bolster this unreasonably high standard for alibi providers in criminal contexts.

The majority of alibi research has concentrated on investigating what happens when an individual's alibi undergoes a dramatic change – from moving out of an apartment to being at a hotel with a mistress, from being in regularly scheduled class to participating in a research study (Nieuwkamp et al., 2016a; Leins & Charman, 2016). Whereas such transformations in a suspects' alibi are reminiscent of notable real-world cases, small errors may also subtly alter the course of an investigation. For example, imagine a suspect's claim of having watched a particular television show at a friend's home contradicted by that same friend's account of having watched a movie instead. The suspect may be correct about their whereabouts, the company they kept, and to some extent the activity they were engaged in. Yet a detective seeking confirmatory evidence of their guilt might attribute the slightly differing accounts to deliberate deceit, and therefore guilt, rather than to an innocent lapse in memory. Critically, in either case, whether the suspect was engrossed in a movie or a television show, they could not have committed the crime. Though small discrepancies may not substantively alter the central claim that the suspect was not at the time and place of commission of the crime, it may still carry an outsized influence on credibility evaluations by investigators and other triers of fact.

Larger errors in contrast can be more consequential if they deny the suspect the opportunity to present evidence establishing they could not have committed the crime. For example, whereas Veasy had been at work on the night of the murder, he claimed to have been playing basketball with friends. For obvious reasons, verifying an incorrect alibi presents a significantly greater challenge than verifying a correct alibi. Challenging need not mean impossible: Veasy's friends could have intentionally or unintentionally falsely corroborated his alibi. They could have, just as likely, also not corroborated his alibi. In contrast, finding strong evidence to corroborate the alibi would have been impossible. For example, had there been security footage, Veasy would not have appeared in it, nor could he have provided a sign-in if he had been playing at a gym with a membership. In short, chasing down an erroneous alibi would likely consume considerable energy and lead to a dead end.

In the absence of empirical work, we can only speculate that small errors are less impactful than larger errors. However, preliminarily, we know that lay people are unable to distinguish accurate and inaccurate alibis (Crozier et al., 2019). Even so, the relative impact and relevance of small errors compared to larger errors is unknown. The impact of a small error in an investigation may be more difficult to detect. Small errors may provide fuel for detectives' biases, particularly if they interview a suspect with a strong presumption of guilt. Nonetheless, it is not difficult to imagine that absent the mistaken eyewitness identification of Veasy, investigators might have forgiven Veasy a lapse in memory for an event occurring over 4 months prior.

No research has examined whether legal decision-makers and law enforcement are more or less sensitive to partial alibi changes when they pertain to a suspects' whereabouts versus who they were with or what they were doing during that time period. For example, alibi evaluators may be more forgiving of the inability to recall what one was doing inside one's home than whether one was home or not on a Sunday evening 2 weeks prior. If a person does learn that they have an error in an alibi, they are put in a precarious decision: Should they correct the alibi, thereby changing their story, or drop the alibi altogether? We may think a changed alibi is better than nothing – but that may not necessarily be the case.

Cascading Effects of Erroneous Alibi Evidence

A mistaken alibi or lack of alibi does not, in and of itself, lead to a wrongful conviction. Instead, it is the cascading effects of seeking evidence that confirms a person's guilt, to the exclusion of searching for evidence that confirms their innocence, that may lead to a wrongful conviction (Scherr et al., 2020; Crozier et al., 2017). Incorrect alibis provided early on can bias the course of a criminal investigation, from the custodial interrogation to the ensuing criminal investigation, and the subsequent plea negotiations and/or trial.

The cost of providing an incorrect alibi or corroboration may be doubly damaging since it not only denies the suspect a key piece of defense evidence, but if discovered as false, the error may become evidence of deceit and cast further suspicions. Even if an erroneous alibi is supplanted with a correct alibi later on, the credibility of any newly available corroborating evidence may be called into question. This is what happened to Veasy. Veasy's defense team provided strong evidence. Yet the context of the mistaken eyewitness identification, the false confession, and the initially erroneous alibi collectively rendered his evidence less credible. The prosecution was already convinced of Veasy's guilt. The prosecuting attorney would later argue that Willie had fabricated the timecard to construct an alibi for himself. This theory, the defense would later argue, made little sense. Why would Veasy go through the trouble of fabricating a false alibi months before being questioned only to then not use it when detectives questioned him? What benefit could saying he had been playing basketball with friends – a clearly inferior alibi – have for exculpating him from the murder?

Beyond disregarding the inconsistency of Veasy's alibi, the prosecution also attempted to bolster their theory of Veasy's involvement with other logically weak arguments at trial. For example, in closing arguments, the prosecution claimed that Houlihan's management team had attempted to hide the evidence suggesting Veasy could have left during his shift for a few hours without being noticed to avoid liability for his alleged crimes. Veasy's lawyers argued back the unlikeliness of this claim because Houlihan's could not, under the law, be held liable for the murder if Veasy had in fact committed it during his work shift. All of this reinforces the idea that an erroneous alibi can cause otherwise accurate corroboration to be regarded as inaccurate. Veasy's case demonstrates how providing an incorrect alibi at the investigative stage can set investigators on a path toward confirming their beliefs about the providers' guilt. Course correcting later, although possible, may occur too late or not at all.

There are clearly negative consequences to providing a good alibi once an error has been identified. However, the damage of an erroneous alibi can affect legal processes beyond believability assessments of the alibi itself. If the police grow suspicious because of an alibi error, a person of interest may become a suspect and end up in an interrogation room where they are subject to coercive interrogation tactics (Crozier et al., 2017). In turn, prosecutors could push for a plea deal more strongly, putting pressure on the defendant to take the deal despite their innocence (Redlich et al., 2017).

Future Directions and Suggested Police Reforms

Real-Life Versus Laboratory Study Differences

Numerous differences between real-life suspects and research participant suspects may lead to different alibi evidence generation outcomes, including the frequency and timing of alibi disclosure, the content of events being recalled, and the type of evidence that can be collected. Research has examined the impact of context on assessments of alibi believability, but rarely on alibi generation itself (cf. Portnoy et al., 2019).

Suspects and corroborators in laboratory studies typically are questioned within a few minutes, hours, or days after the to-be-remembered event. In criminal investigations, the time interval between when a crime occurs and when a suspect or corroborator is questioned may extend to several weeks or months. Does a delay between when the event occurred and when a provider is questioned matter? On the one hand, because memories tend to fade with time, field investigations of alibi generation might uncover evidence of even worse rates of alibi recall than those seen in laboratory studies (Olson & Charman, 2012). On the other hand, the nature of an innocent suspects' alibi might be so mundane and uneventful, a fixture of their daily routines, that the majority of the forgetting may happen soon after the event with few or no further changes attributable to the passage of time, as predicted by Ebbinghaus's early work on the "forgetting curve" (Ebbinghaus, 1885; Murre & Dros, 2015). Indeed, some work suggests no association between questioning delay and alibi accuracy (Cardenas et al., 2020; Culhane et al., 2013; for an exception, see Olson & Charman, 2012). Suspects' alibis were not any more likely to be accurate when reported a few days after the event than when reported several weeks after. This work suggests that delayed questioning alone is not associated with accuracy, and so suspects in criminal contexts may be no more disadvantaged by the delayed questioning than laboratory participants. However, this potential memorial equivalence does not account for any other factors that might interact with delayed questioning.

Though delayed questioning may not significantly decrease alibi accuracy, we should be careful not to assume that delays are equally unimportant for the generation of physical corroborating evidence. We argue elsewhere that suspects are likely unable to recall their alibis because they may lack a memory to retrieve or else the memory trace is too weak (Cardenas et al., 2020). If true, then the focus of generating believable alibis should shift from the internal search of one's memories to the external search of cues and physical- and person-based corroborating evidence. For example, an innocent provider might find numerous external mnemonic resources among their friends and colleagues. By asking networks of people, rather than individuals, to recall a prior event, the innocent individual might capitalize on the individual or collective memories of others to fill in the gaps for their memories. Similarly, those individuals and the suspect can benefit from earlier questioning when they are able to produce corroborating evidence that might otherwise have disappeared if questioning were delayed. Receipts, surveillance recordings, and other miscellaneous forms of evidence that might be destroyed, discarded, or forgotten when considered unimportant should benefit from being categorized as probative evidence. Yet prior research a systematic delay exists in some jurisdictions between initial interviews and follow-up interviews with alibi corroborators and the search for physical evidence. In one survey, law enforcement indicated that when it comes to investigation procedures, detectives were more likely than patrol officers to follow up on a suspect's alibi story (Dysart & Strange, 2012). Such delays may negatively impact the ability of providers to locate evidence.

Bringing Social Cognition to Alibi Research

We can learn more about how innocent suspects generate inaccurate alibis or about when accurate alibis are interpreted as erroneous by examining the interplay between social factors and memorial processes. Two recent examples include Portnoy et al.'s (2019) examination of the impact of a presumption of guilt on alibi generation and Rozman and Nahari's (2021) investigation of the influence of intergroup bias on alibi credibility assessments among Israeli-Jews and Israeli-Arabs. For example, there are clear limitations to suspects relying only on their own memories when there are vast social networks of knowledge they could be tapping into to generate more accurate alibis. How might the ability to tap into a social network depend on differences among population samples across demographic characteristics such as employment status, race, or socioeconomic status? For example, full-time employees and students are likely to have colleagues, classmates, and fixed schedules which might form a larger, more cohesive and accessible network that can lead to supporting evidence. Individuals living in communities where trust in police is high may have social networks that are more willing to speak to the police and provide testimony on a defendant's behalf than individuals living in communities with greater distrust of the police. If trust in the police is low within an individual's network, then finding individuals willing to become involved in the investigation may be more difficult.

Safeguards Against Erroneous Alibis

Certain procedural safeguards may prevent some of the sources of erroneous alibis. Among the most obvious proposals is the need to conduct more thorough alibi investigations. Because innocent suspects are highly likely to generate inaccurate alibis, they would clearly benefit from receiving help investigating their accounts or producing alibis that contain fewer inaccuracies from the start. Nonetheless, Dysart and Strange (2012) found that 77% of surveyed law enforcement had received no prior training on how to conduct alibi interviews. Addressing this glaring gap in investigators' skill set seems critical. Although we have little insight into how such interviews are currently conducted, there are also other interview techniques we could utilize, such as avoiding using suggestive questioning, verifying multiple pieces of evidence, emphasizing to suspects that it's okay if they can't remember (and conversely, not pressuring them into generating alibis), and giving them a chance to think about their account and come back once they have had an opportunity to independently verify their account. Further, we now know that mental reinstatement of context—a major component of the cognitive interview used to elicit more accurate details among eyewitnesses—is less effective among alibi providers (Cardenas et al., 2020). We also know of some promising research on the efficacy of chronological timelines for improving the generation of physical corroborating evidence (Matuku & Charman, 2020). Investigations on alibi elicitation techniques are likely to be an important asset to complement the study of estimator variables such as race, age, and event type.

In the event that an erroneous alibi is provided during the investigation, there are still stopgap processes that may prevent miscarriages of justices. Although both need more research, prosecutors and jurors could benefit from a better understanding of the natural limitations of erroneous alibis – and when an erroneous alibi is and is not indicative of a guilty perpetrator. Therefore, future research should examine the effect of judicial instructions on jury decision making in both cases where alibis are used as a legal defense, as well as cases where, though not an official defense, an alibi claim is presented or discussed throughout the trial.

Perhaps the most unstudied area of research on alibis is prosecutors. In nearly every jurisdiction in the United States, prosecutors at the district/county, state, and federal level weigh the evidence when deciding to bring charges. However, we do not know how prosecutors view alibis generally, let alone erroneous alibis, or how relevant alibis are in making charging decisions or on trial strategy. Further, we do not yet know whether prosecutors may fall back on the same bias against an erroneous or changed alibi as police and laypeople. On the most basic front, it is unknown how often prosecutors receive information about an alibi and whether or not it was fully investigated. Beyond that, future research should examine how alibis (both accurate and inaccurate) impact prosecutor decision-making for charging or dismissing a case, whether to offer a plea bargain, and their theory of the case and what witnesses to call.

If a case does go to trial, the jury is the last line of evaluators that determines whether an erroneous alibi is too flawed to prevent a conviction. As discussed previously, laypeople may not have the most accurate understanding of why alibi errors occur – much like eyewitness memory evidence (Chin & Crozier, 2018), their conceptions of how alibis are generated, and what can go wrong may be based on mistaken beliefs rather than the reality and limitations of human psychology. As such, legal procedures are likely necessary to sensitize jurors to when an alibi error is problematic and when it is not. The defense may consider calling an expert to discuss the cognitive and social factors we discuss here that could result in an erroneous alibi. Although eyewitness evidence experts are regularly employed in real cases (although research has questioned their efficacy; e.g., Martire & Kemp, 2009; Jones et al., 2017), we know of no existent research on the efficacy of an alibi expert. Another option could be jury instructions, by which a judge explains that erroneous alibis may not be indicative of guilt. To our knowledge, no research has investigated this possibility as a way to sensitize jurors to alibi issues (we note that Allison & Brimacombe, 2010, used jury instructions in a case with alibi evidence, but those instructions focused on the defendant's prior record and not the alibi itself).

Addressing the Failure to Investigate

In documented cases of wrongful convictions, the intentionality behind inaccurate alibis and corroboration cannot always be easily discerned. Does an investigator fail to investigate an alibi do so out of malice or because they are under-resourced? In their report, the Gross et al. (2020) conclude that among the main causes of why government police officers and prosecutors commit misconduct is a "lack of resources to train, supervise, and conduct high quality investigations and prosecutions" (p. 133). Consequently, officials may be tempted, "to close cases by cheating, lying, and concealing" which "makes suspects vulnerable to misconduct, because police don't look for evidence that clears them, and overworked defense lawyers can't fill the gap" (p. xxv). Consider the case of Luis Rojas who was convicted of murder in 1992 only to be exonerated 6 years later when novel alibi evidence demonstrating his innocence with absolute certainty emerged. As it turned out, a police sergeant had seen Rojas at a different location near the time of the crime. Further, an eyewitness to the shooting had seen Rojas handcuffed in a squad car and told the police that Rojas "was definitely the wrong man" (*People v. Rojas*, 1995; Gross et al., 2020). The police sergeant's testimony was not presented at trial, and the eyewitness was never asked to view a lineup. The government and Rojas's defense attorney were both responsible for two gross failures: First, the failure to initially interview a witness as believable and available as a police sergeant and, second, to further investigate the warnings of a believable eyewitness who provided a contradictory account to the government's case. In Rojas's case an alibi, which on its face appeared to be false and inaccurate, could have been proven true had it been properly investigated.

The high rate of errors in suspects' alibis suggests a need for more extensive investigations by detectives, prosecutors, or investigators hired by the defense. Defendants may find themselves unable to procure evidence for their own alibi defense because they are incarcerated or lack access to certain forms of evidence (e.g., surveillance footage, authority to interview witnesses) and thus must rely on the government or private defense for help.

The writers of the 2020 NRE report argue that these failures, which directly led to Rojas's wrongful conviction may be attributable to neglect that does not rise to the level of misconduct. They point to the workload police officers and attorneys were facing in the 1990s in New York City as one reason for the failure to conduct more thorough investigations. Similarly, in a recent survey assessing perspectives on prosecutorial misconduct, only a third of 355 state and federal judges agreed that 'failing to investigate or disclose a defendant's alibis' constituted behavior that ought to be investigated as possible misconduct (Cardenas et al., 2022). Determining whether an alibi and/or corroborator was intentionally or unintentionally incorrect is important to the extent that it informs the remedies that ought to be implemented in any given context. For example, defendants may have a right to effective assistance of counsel, to be free from physical abuse, and obstruction of justice, but they do not necessarily have the right to high-quality investigations (Gross et al., 2020). Attributing intentionality to what can more reasonably be characterized as reckless negligence serves to redirect the blame to bad actors rather than systemic structural issues within our criminal justice system.

Researchers proposed the Self-Administered Interview© (SAI) to facilitate the task of overburdened law enforcement needing to interview multiple eyewitnesses to a crime quickly (Gabbert et al., 2009; Horry et al., 2021). Briefly, eyewitnesses are provided with a booklet of questions relating to the incident and asked to use a self-administered version of the cognitive interview that would typically be administered by trained officers over a longer period of time. The SAI© had been found to lead to increased recall comparable to the cognitive interview and saves officers' time. A similar self-administered interview could be implemented for use in the alibi domain. Police could follow up on promising reports by alibi witnesses to gather additional information while saving time on interviewing less helpful witnesses.

In sum, we echo here the recommendations of practitioners who similarly recognize the need for policies for investigating alibis more thoroughly. The understanding that inaccurate alibis are the norm and not diagnostic of deceit coupled with measures to increase base accuracy levels should hopefully help diminish the wrongful conviction of innocent persons.

References

Allison, M., & Brimacombe, C. A. E. (2010). Alibi believability: The effect of prior convictions and judicial instructions. *Journal of Applied Social Psychology, 40*(5), 1054–1084. https://doi.org/10.1111/j.1559-1816.2010.00610.x

Allison, M., Mathews, K. R., & Michael, S. W. (2012). Alibi believability: The impact of salacious alibi activities. *Social Behavior and Personality: An International Journal, 40*(4), 605–612. https://doi.org/10.2224/sbp.2012.40.4.605

Cardenas, S. A., Crozier, W., & Strange, D. (2020). Right place, wrong time: The limitations of mental reinstatement of context on alibi-elicitation. *Psychology, Crime & Law, 27*(3), 201–230. https://doi.org/10.1080/1068316X.2020.1798424

Cardenas, S. A., Kassin, S. M., Meterko, V., & Barksdale, F. (2022). *Prosecutorial misconduct: Assessment of perspectives from the bench.* Poster presented at the annual conference of the American Psychology–Law Society, Denver, CO.

Chaudry, R., Miller, C., & Simpson, S. (Hosts). (2017, October 23). State v. Willie Veasy [Audio podcast episodes]. In *Undisclosed.* https://undisclosed-podcast.com/episodes/willie-veasy/

Chin, J. M., & Crozier, W. E. (2018). Rethinking the ken through the lens of psychological science. *Osgoode Hall Law Journal, 55*, 625. https://heinonline.org/HOL/P?h=hein.journals/ohlj55&i=610

Commonwealth v. Veasy (2017). PCRA Petition CP-51-CR-0641521-1992. https://undisclosed-podcast.com/docs/willie-veasy/PCRA%20Petition%20of%20Willie%20Veasy.pdf

Crozier, W. E., Cardenas, S.A., Merriwether, E., & Strange, D. (2019). *Beyond believability: Observer's credibility and memory quality ratings for mock crime alibis.* Paper presented at SARMAC, Cape Cod, MA.

Crozier, W. E., Strange, D., & Loftus, E. F. (2017). Memory errors in alibi generation: How an alibi can turn against us. *Behavioral Sciences & the Law, 35*(1), 6–17. https://doi.org/10.1002/bsl.2273

Culhane, S. E., & Hosch, H. M. (2012). Changed alibis: Current law enforcement, future law enforcement, and layperson reactions. *Criminal Justice and Behavior, 39*(7), 958–977. https://doi.org/10.1177/0093854812438185

Culhane, S. E., Hosch, H. M., & Kehn, A. (2008). Alibi generation: Data from U.S. Hispanics and U.S. non-Hispanic whites. *Journal of Ethnicity in Criminal Justice, 6*(3), 177–199. https://doi.org/10.1080/15377930802243395

Culhane, S. E., Kehn, A., Horgan, A. J., Meissner, C. A., Hosch, H. M., & Wodahl, E. J. (2013). Generation and detection of true and false alibi statements. *Psychiatry, Psychology and Law, 20*(4), 619–638. https://doi.org/10.1080/13218719.2012.729018

Deeb, H., Granhag, P. A., Vrij, A., Strömwall, L. A., Hope, L., & Mann, S. (2018). Visuospatial counter-interrogation strategies by liars familiar with the alibi setting. *Applied Cognitive Psychology, 32*(1), 105–116. https://doi.org/10.1002/acp.3383

Dysart, J. E., & Strange, D. (2012). Beliefs about alibis and alibi investigations: A survey of law enforcement. *Psychology, Crime and Law, 18*(6), 11–25. https://doi.org/10.1080/1068316X.2011.562867

Ebbinghaus, H. (1885). *Über das Gedächtnis.* Dunker.

Gabbert, F., Hope, L., & Fisher, R. P. (2009). Protecting eyewitness evidence: Examining the efficacy of a self-administered interview tool. *Law and Human Behavior, 33*(4), 298–307. https://doi.org/10.1007/s10979-008-9146-8

Gross, S. R., Possley, M. J., Roll, K. J. & Stephens, K. H. (2020). Government misconduct and convicting the innocent: The role of prosecutors, police, and other law enforcement. National Registry of Exonerations, September 1, 2020. https://www.law.umich.edu/special/exoneration/Documents/Government_Misconduct_and_Convicting_the_Innocent.pdf

Guyll, M., Madon, S., Yang, Y., Lannin, D. G., Scherr, K., & Greathouse, S. (2013). Innocence and resisting confession during interrogation: Effects on physiologic activity. *Law and Human Behavior, 37*(5), 366–375. https://doi.org/10.1037/lhb0000044

Hartwig, M., & Bond, C. F., Jr. (2011). Why do lie-catchers fail? A lens model meta-analysis of human lie judgments. *Psychological Bulletin, 137*(4), 643. https://doi.org/10.1037/a0023589

Horry, R., Hughes, C., Sharma, A., Gabbert, F., & Hope, L. (2021). A meta-analytic review of the Self-Administered Interview©: Quantity and accuracy of details reported on initial and subsequent retrieval attempts. *Applied Cognitive Psychology, 35*(2), 428–444. https://doi.org/10.1002/acp.3753

Innocence Project. (2021). *The cases*. https://www.innocenceproject.org/all-cases/

Johnson, M. K., Hashtroudi, S., & Lindsay, D. S. (1993). Source monitoring. *Psychological Bulletin, 114*(1), 3. https://doi.org/10.1037/0033-2909.114.1.3

Jones, A. M., Bergold, A. N., Dillon, M. K., & Penrod, S. D. (2017). Comparing the effectiveness of Henderson instructions and expert testimony: Which safeguard improves jurors' evaluations of eyewitness evidence? *Journal of Experimental Criminology, 13*(1), 29–52. https://doi.org/10.1007/s11292-016-9279-6

Jung, S., Allison, M., & Bohn, L. (2013). Legal decision-making on crimes involving an alibi. *Applied Psychology in Criminal Justice, 9*(1), 45–58. https://roam.macewan.ca/islandora/object/gm:768

Kassam, K. S., Gilbert, D. T., Swencionis, J. K., & Wilson, T. D. (2009). Misconceptions of memory: The Scooter Libby effect. *Psychological Science, 20*(5), 551–552. https://doi.org/10.1111/j.1467-9280.2009.02334.x

Kassin, S. M. (2005). On the psychology of confessions: Does innocence put innocents at risk? *American Psychologist, 60*(3), 215–228. https://doi.org/10.1037/0003-066X.60.3.215

Kassin, S. M., & Norwick, R. J. (2004). Why suspects waive their Miranda rights: The power of innocence. *Law and Human Behavior, 28*(2), 211–221. https://doi.org/10.1023/B:LAHU.0000022323.74584.f5

Keeping, Z., Eastwood, J., Lively, C. J., & Snook, B. (2017). Don't stop believing: The relative impact of internal alibi details on judgments of veracity. *Psychology, Crime & Law, 23*(9), 899–913. https://doi.org/10.1080/1068316X.2017.1338700

Leins, D. A., & Charman, S. D. (2016). Schema reliance and innocent alibi generation. *Legal and Criminological Psychology, 21*(1), 111–126. https://doi.org/10.1111/lcrp.12035

Luke, T. J. (2019). Lessons from Pinocchio: Cues to deception may be highly exaggerated. *Perspectives on Psychological Science, 14*(4), 646–671. https://doi.org/10.1177/1745691619838258

Luketic, R. (Director). (2001). *Legally blonde* [Film]. Type A Films, Marc Platt Productions, Metro-Goldwyn-Mayer.

Martire, K. A., & Kemp, R. I. (2009). The impact of eyewitness expert evidence and judicial instruction on juror ability to evaluate eyewitness testimony. *Law and Human Behavior, 33*(3), 225–236. https://doi.org/10.1007/s10979-008-9134-z

Matuku, K., & Charman, S. D. (2020). Enhancing innocent suspects' memories for corroborating alibi evidence. *Psychology, Public Policy, and Law, 26*(4), 442. https://doi.org/10.1037/law0000264

Moore, T. E., & Gagnier, K. (2008). "You can talk if you want to": Is the police caution on the right to silence comprehensible? *Criminal Reports, 51*, 233–249.

Murre, J. M., & Dros, J. (2015). Replication and analysis of Ebbinghaus' forgetting curve. *PLoS One, 10*(7), e0120644. https://doi.org/10.1371/journal.pone.0120644

Nahari, G., Vrij, A., & Fisher, R. P. (2014). Exploiting liars' verbal strategies by examining the verifiability of details. *Legal and Criminological Psychology, 19*(2), 227–239. https://doi.org/10.1111/j.2044-8333.2012.02069.x

National Registry of Exonerations. (2021). Exoneration detail list. https://www.law.umich.edu/special/exoneration/Pages/detaillist.aspx

Nieuwkamp, R., Horselenberg, R., & van Koppen, P. J. (2016a). A lie and a mistress: On increasing the believability of your alibi. *Psychiatry, Psychology and Law, 23*(5), 733–745. https://doi.org/10.1080/13218719.2016.1142934

Nieuwkamp, R., Horselenberg, R., & Van Koppen, P. J. (2016b). The illusion of the perfect alibi: Establishing the base rate of non-offenders' alibis. *Journal of Investigative Psychology and Offender Profiling, 14*(1), 23–42. https://doi.org/10.1002/jip.1470

Olson, E. A., & Charman, S. D. (2012). "But can you prove it?'—Examining the quality of innocent suspects" alibis. *Psychology, Crime and Law, 18*(5), 453–471. https://doi.org/10.1080/1068316X.2010.505567

Olson, E. A., & Wells, G. L. (2004). What makes a good alibi? A proposed taxonomy. *Law and Human Behavior, 28*(2), 157–176. https://doi.org/10.1023/B:LAHU.0000022320.47112.d3

Olson, E. A., & Wells, G. L. (2012). The alibi-generation effect: Alibi-generation experience influences alibi evaluation. *Legal and Criminological Psychology, 17*(1), 151–164. https://doi.org/10.1111/j.2044-8333.2010.02003.x

People v. Riggs. 44 Cal. 4th 248 (2008). https://casetext.com/case/people-v-riggs

People v. Rojas. 213 A.D.2d 56, 630 N.Y.S.2d 28 (1995). https://casetext.com/case/people-v-rojas-61

Perillo, J. T., & Kassin, S. M. (2011). Inside interrogation: The lie, the bluff, and false confessions. *Law and Human Behavior, 35*(4), 327–337. https://doi.org/10.1007/s10979-010-9244-2

Portnoy, S., Hope, L., Vrij, A., Granhag, P. A., Ask, K., Eddy, C., & Landström, S. (2019). "I think you did it!": Examining the effect of presuming guilt on the verbal output of innocent suspects during brief interviews. *Journal of Investigative Psychology and Offender Profiling, 16*(3), 236–250. https://doi-org.ez.lib.jjay.cuny.edu/10.1002/jip.1534

Redlich, A. D., Bibas, S., Edkins, V. A., & Madon, S. (2017). The psychology of defendant plea decision making. *American Psychologist, 72*(4), 339. https://doi.org/10.1037/a0040436

Rozmann, N., & Nahari, G. (2021). Credibility assessment in context: The influence of intergroup bias and the context of the crime. *Psychology, Crime & Law*. https://doi.org/10.1080/1068316X.2021.1909021

Santos, F. (2006, September 20). *DNA evidence frees a man imprisoned for half his life*. The New York Times. https://www.nytimes.com/2006/09/21/nyregion/21dna.html

Sauerland, M., Krix, A. C., & Sagana, A. (2019). Deceiving suspects about their alibi is equally harmful to the innocent and guilty. *Applied Cognitive Psychology, 33*(6), 1238–1246. https://doi.org/10.1002/acp.3577

Scherr, K. C., & Franks, A. S. (2015). The world is not fair: An examination of innocent and guilty suspects' waiver decisions. *Law and Human Behavior, 39*(2), 142–151. https://doi.org/10.1037/lhb0000121

Scherr, K. C., Redlich, A. D., & Kassin, S. M. (2020). Cumulative disadvantage: A psychological framework for understanding how innocence can lead to confession, wrongful conviction, and beyond. *Perspectives on Psychological Science, 15*(2), 353–383. https://doi.org/10.1177/1745691619896608

Simons, D. J., & Chabris, C. F. (2011). What people believe about how memory works: A representative survey of the US population. *PLoS One, 6*(8). https://doi.org/10.1371/journal/pone.0022757

Strange, D., Dysart, J., & Loftus, E. F. (2014). Why errors in alibis are not necessarily evidence of guilt. *Zeitschrift für Psychologie, 222*(2), 82–89. https://doi.org/10.1027/2151-2604/a000169

Thompson-Cannino, J., Cotton, R., & Torneo, E. (2009). *Picking cotton: Our memoir of injustice and redemption*. St Martin's Press.

Vernham, Z., Vrij, A., Nahari, G., Leal, S., Mann, S., Satchell, L., & Orthey, R. (2020). Applying the verifiability approach to deception detection in alibi witness situations. *Acta Psychologica, 204*, 103020. https://doi.org/10.1016/j.actpsy.2020.103020

Chapter 10
Future Directions in Alibi Research

Joshua D. Behl and Megan R. Kienzle

In her novel, *The Body in the Library*, Agatha Christie pens "no innocent person ever has an alibi." Of course, we know this to be false. Rather, it seems, a more accurate quote (albeit a lot wordier) may be "every innocent person has an alibi – but the claim may not be believed, easily generated, or able to be corroborated with either physical or person evidence." The goal of this text was to not only serve as a state of the science on alibis and corroborators but to also make recommendations on where the field could go from here.

As virtually all chapters stated, the current field of alibi research only began in 2004 when Olson and Wells published their taxonomy. Since then, there have been roughly 200 social scientific articles and chapters written on the topic. Contrast that with the hundreds of articles that have been written on such varying topics as eyewitness misidentification, interrogations, and false confessions, jury decision-making or, more recently, plea bargaining and scholars may be left wondering why the topic of alibis has been so neglected.

Why Study Alibis?

From our perspective, there could be three main reasons alibis, as a topic, are understudied. First, questions about alibis and corroborators are not that interesting to the field compared to other topics (however, readers of this book likely find this to be

J. D. Behl (✉)
Department of Behavioral Sciences, Flagler College, St. Augustine, FL, USA
e-mail: jbehl@flagler.edu

M. R. Kienzle
Department of Criminal Justice, Austin Peay State University, Clarksville, TN, USA
e-mail: kienzlem@apsu.edu

J. D. Behl, M. R. Kienzle (eds.), *Alibis and Corroborators*,
https://doi.org/10.1007/978-3-030-95663-9_10

untrue). Second, questions about alibis and corroborators have been answered (either by eyewitness or alibi paradigms). Third, other topics are viewed as more important to focus our research efforts. Perhaps readers will agree with any one of these reasons. However, we believe that alibis and those who corroborate alibi claims should be of great interest to the field. In Wells et al.'s (1998) examination of the first 40 cases of DNA exoneration, it was shown that 28% of those wrongful convictions were caused, at least in part, by weak or no alibi. However, every single innocent person has an alibi (see Chap. 3). Therefore, an unbelieved or uncorroborated alibi could be viewed as the single greatest cause of wrongful conviction in the United States – that certainly justifies expanded research. Another possible reason for the paucity of research on alibis is that some researchers may view the topic of alibis as interchangeable with eyewitnesses (as was suggested by feedback we received during this books creation) – after all, an alibi is simply an eyewitness that someone was at a different place at the time of the crime (Behl et al., 2012). However, we believe that alibis, as a topic of study, should be viewed as separate and apart from eyewitnesses. While there are some obvious similarities, the differences should not be ignored.

To begin, eyewitnesses are witnesses to a specific, often unique, and exciting event (a crime) that has taken place (Curci et al., 2020). Even if the witness does not get interviewed by law enforcement until days, weeks, or months later, it stands to reason that the witness has discussed the incident with friends and family or replayed the unusual and memorable event in their minds a time or two. This is not the case with alibis or corroborators, who are being asked to recall a potentially "normal" or routine event that happens with some semblance of regularity. Therefore, the potential for memory issues or a lack of confidence in one's memory for the event is understandable given the comparison. Since research suggests that jurors perceive confidence to be related to accuracy (Wells et al., 1979; Brewer & Wells, 2006; Semmler et al., 2011), what does this mean for a suspect's or corroborator's believability on a witness stand? Can a good defense attorney explain away a corroborator's lack of confidence due to the routine nature of when an alibi claim is made, or will the lack of confidence overshadow a potentially exonerating piece of evidence to triers of fact? How might a lack of confidence affect a corroborator's willingness to serve as such crucial corroborating evidence in the first place?

Similarly, especially as it relates to person evidence for support, an alibi differs from an eyewitness in that it is a two-step, multi-person memory test – first, the suspect has to accurately remember where they were and *who* they were with; second, the corroborator must also accurately remember where they were and who they were with. If these two details do not match up, the suspect's alibi is viewed with more skepticism (as shown in Chap. 9). Therefore, the two-part memory test, and potential for compounded memory issues, adds a layer of complication that is not present with an eyewitness – not to mention that both parties could have strong memories for an event, but a corroborator may not want to get involved in the investigation due to external or social pressures (discussed in more detail below).

Finally, an eyewitness is a piece of inculpatory evidence that police and prosecutors likely want to be admitted as evidence in support of the claim of guilt. An alibi is a type of defense that is brought by the accused in support of their innocence. Therefore, there is also a structural, power dynamic that cannot be ignored when comparing eyewitnesses to alibis. The State is willing to invest time, energy and resources into identifying, arresting, and convicting a guilty party. Is the state willing to exert that same time, energy, and resources into helping prove someone did not commit a crime? If not, is a defense attorney (typically appointed as opposed to hired) able to exert equal time, energy, and resources to even the playing field when searching to supplement their exculpatory case evidence as the State has put into seeking out inculpatory evidence?

Taken together, these reasons suggest that alibis should be viewed as not just an extension of the eyewitness literature, but as its own unique topic area – albeit related. To that end, the **Appendix** at the conclusion of this text is a preliminary list of unstudied research topics that can help form the foundation of research of which this book is a first step. This list of over 100 unique research ideas, compiled by all the contributors of this text, could be the starting point for graduate students and researchers to expand the nascent field of alibis and corroborators. The next few sections go through some of the most practically important topics, in our minds, that future researchers should concentrate their attention.

A Focus on Corroborators

One particular area that is ripe for future research is that of the alibi corroborator. Most of the research on alibis to date has focused more on the suspect and their ability to remember and obtain evidence in support of their alibi. Very little research has focused on the corroborator (see Kienzle & Levett, 2018; Marion & Burke, 2013; Marion et al., 2016 for exceptions to this trend) and examined factors that may influence their memories and their willingness to serve or offered theories to explain corroboration. What little research is done on corroborators tends to focus on how base characteristics (e.g., relationship to the suspect) may affect their believability (Olson & Wells, 2004; Olson & Charman, 2012).

Chapter 8 of this text offers some quite troubling insights into the world of the corroborator that researchers should pay attention to. Specifically, Levine and Miller mention that police may intimidate corroborators out of offering their corroboration in court by checking for active arrest warrants or sending the Department of Children and Family Services to their homes for visits – clear intimidation tactics that should be outlawed. However, these examples, while dramatic and questionably ethical, may not be the norm. Could police influence corroborators through other, more subtle means – like suggestive questioning (Behl et al., 2012)? What other factors may influence one's willingness to serve as a corroborator? The complexity of this suspect-corroborator relationship is in need of more focused research attention.

The Role of Defense Attorneys

A corroborator is not the only role that many assume will be willing to assist in an alibi claim. A defense attorney is similarly assumed to be dedicated to their client (the suspect) in a criminal case. Therefore, the role of the defense attorneys should be another major area of research in the study of alibis (prosecutors will be discussed in a later section). If a defense attorney does not believe their client, how much energy will they put into investigating the innocence claim? Factors that influence defense attorney's beliefs of the alibi claim should therefore be researched. However, this research should not stop there. Research should also examine different trial strategies that defense attorneys could use when presenting the alibi during the cycle of a trial. For example, is it a more effective strategy to introduce the alibi claim late so that law enforcement has less time to investigate and try to influence the alibi claim? Or, does doing so only get you over the hurdle of law enforcement pressure, but now a suspect is looked upon with more skepticism in the eyes of the judge and jury because of the delayed notice? These trial strategies could have a profound impact on the outcome of the case.

Race and Alibis

One area that has jumped out at us as being completely understudied is the intersection of race and alibi corroboration. In fact, to our knowledge, there are only a handful of studies that look at race (for examples, see Sargent & Bradfield, 2004; Culhane et al., 2008). When race has been studied, it has been done in basic ways that do not account for the complexity of cultural differences or the suspect-corroborator relationship. For example, Culhane et al. (2008) examined if Hispanic suspects relied on more motivated familiar others compared to white suspects. These differences in potential corroborators are important as there may be differential believability based on the cultural norms of different races. However, research should not stop there (and should certainly be expanded beyond just a White-Black-Hispanic framework).

Some other areas that could be explored are borrowed from eyewitness literature. Is there a cross-race effect in alibi corroboration such that a nonmotivated stranger will have a more difficult time remembering and identifying a suspect from a different race, and therefore be less willing to offer a corroboration, compared to a suspect of the same race? Will alibi evaluators view a suspect with a different race corroborator differently compared to a suspect with a same race corroborator? Are societal expectations on schema-consistent racial behaviors – or society's differential racial perceptions of stereotypical behaviors – differentially believed by evaluators compared to schema-inconsistent racial behaviors? Are members of certain races more hesitant to serve as corroborators due to distrust of law enforcement or a desire not to be scrutinized due to historical (and present day) wrongs? There is even the possibility that the taxonomy itself could be structured in a manner that is racially insensitive, specifically with what researchers define as "strong" physical evidence. Is this evidence only viewed as strong from a white experience that does not take into consideration the perspectives (or available opportunities for evidence) of different groups?

While race is of obvious importance, other, extra-legal demographic variables should not be ignored. For example, the impacts of age, socioeconomic status, education level, gender, and ethnicity should be of interest to researchers to get a broader picture of their effects on alibi generation and believability. Much like Kovera (2017) suggested that jury researchers adopt the estimator/system variable approach utilized in eyewitness research (Wells, 1978), we believe that this approach should be used in the alibi context as well (see Chap. 5 for a compelling argument for this). By examining the role of both estimator and system variables (including both legal and extra-legal variables), we would be able to expand the research into how the two types of variables may also interact with each other in ways that can have profound impacts on the consideration of alibi evidence specifically and the outcome of a criminal investigation and trial more broadly.

The Role of the Evaluator

One such system variable that needs more understanding is the role of the alibi evaluator. While some work has been done in this area (e.g., Sommers & Douglass, 2007; Olson & Wells, 2012; Olson, 2013; Culhane & Hosch, 2012), future research should explore not just evaluator believability of an alibi claim, but also how an evaluator, specifically law enforcement or attorneys, handles the claim. For example, what level of attention does law enforcement give to investigating the alibi claim over time spent investigating evidence of guilt? Do prosecutors structure their trial strategy around refuting the alibi claim if they believe it to be weak? Or, is the claim ignored as prosecutors believe that jurors will not consider the evidence? What is the effect of evidence order on alibi believability? Will police and prosecutors actively work to disprove an alibi that is offered after several pieces of evidence pointing toward guilt? When a case involves some evidence of guilt and some of innocence (as many likely do), where do detectives focus their energy first and/or most effectively?

A lot of these questions fit well within the current theoretical framework of tunnel vision and investigator bias (e.g., Meissner & Kassin, 2002; Kassin et al., 2003; Phillips et al., 1999; Narchet et al., 2011; Greathouse & Kovera, 2009). It is possible investigators and prosecutors may focus their attention on one possible suspect and ignore exculpatory evidence that they uncover. How tunnel vision and investigator bias affect alibi investigations is yet to be determined and could have deleterious effects on the evidence and ultimate outcome of the investigation. For example, will law enforcement and prosecutors disregard an alibi with strong supporting evidence if they believe the suspect to be guilty through other evidence? What is the effect of police/prosecutor tunnel vision on a legitimate alibi claim in court?

Another, related, area that has potential to be of profound importance is law enforcement's perception of material v. immaterial evidence (or evidence that law enforcement interprets as relevant to the case v. irrelevant to the case). Is there potential that law enforcement is internally categorizing any alibi evidence as immaterial and therefore do not feel the need to disclose it as required by Brady v. Maryland, 373 U.S. 83 (1963)? While there are legal definitions of "material" and "immaterial," do law enforcement and prosecutors define those terms the same way? Research on law enforcement and prosecutors' definitions and interpretations of the relevance of evidence, especially as it relates to alibis, is needed and has potential to make a large impact on policy prescriptions to try and shield innocents from unwarranted prosecution.

Policy Prescriptions for Alibis and Corroborators

Policy prescriptions should be a primary focus of innocence researchers. In fact, sweeping policy recommendations have been made for such topics as eyewitnesses (Wells et al., 2020), interrogations (Kassin et al., 2010), and plea-bargains (see the special issue in Psychology, Public Policy, and Law on pleas, edited by Wilford & Redlich, 2018). When attempting to complete this text, the editors reach out to over 50 researchers, attorneys, and innocence networks to solicit a chapter on this important topic. By this point in the text, you should realize that we were unsuccessful in obtaining such a chapter. We believe the reasons for this difficulty can be explained by the dearth of empirical research on which to base such alibi policy recommendations. Most we heard from were hesitant to offer policies that did not have an empirical backing. Therefore, to better understand the effectiveness of alibi policy, more research and a better understanding of the phenomenon are needed. Future policies surrounding alibis will allow legislators, practitioners, and researchers alike to gain more insight into this unique, understudied, and profoundly influential topic. We hope that this text, including the Appendix, will be a small step in bringing about this change.

References

Behl, J. D., Kienzle, M. R., & Levett, L. M. (2012, August 2–5). *Suggestive questioning affects likelihood of alibi corroboration* [Paper presentation]. American Psychological Association 120th Annual Convention. Orlando, FL, United States.

Brady v. Maryland, 373 U.S. 83 (1963).

Brewer, N., & Wells, G. L. (2006). The confidence-accuracy relationship in eyewitness identification: Effects of lineup instructions, foil similarity, and target-absent base rates. *Journal of Experimental Psychology: Applied, 12*(1), 11–30.

Culhane, S. E., & Hosch, H. M. (2012). Changed alibis: Current law enforcement, future law enforcement, and layperson reactions. *Criminal Justice and Behavior, 39*(7), 958–977.

Culhane, S. E., Hosch, H. M., & Kehn, A. (2008). Alibi generation: Data from US Hispanics and US non-Hispanic whites. *Journal of Ethnicity in Criminal Justice, 6*(3), 177–199.
Curci, A., Lanciano, T., Curtotti, D., & Sartori, G. (2020). Lessons for the courtroom from the study of flashbulb memory: An integrative review. *Memory, 28*(3), 441–449.
Greathouse, S. M., & Kovera, M. B. (2009). Instruction bias and lineup presentation moderate the effects of administrator knowledge on eyewitness identification. *Law and Human Behavior, 33*(1), 70–82.
Kassin, S. M., Goldstein, C. C., & Savitsky, K. (2003). Behavioral confirmation in the interrogation room: On the dangers of presuming guilt. *Law and Human Behavior, 27*(2), 187–203.
Kassin, S. M., Drizin, S. A., Grisso, T., Gudjonsson, G. H., Leo, R. A., & Redlich, A. D. (2010). Police-induced confessions: Risk factors and recommendations. *Law and Human Behavior, 34*(1), 3–38.
Kienzle, M. R., & Levett, L. M. (2018). A novel paradigm for examining alibi corroboration and evidence interaction: Does a confession affect the likelihood of alibi corroboration for friends and strangers? *Psychology, Public Policy, and Law, 24*(3), 353–364.
Kovera, M. B. (2017). Conclusion: The future of jury research. In M. B. Kovera (Ed.), *The psychology of juries* (pp. 287–297). American Psychological Association. https://doi.org/10.1037/0000026-013
Marion, S. B., & Burke, T. M. (2013). False alibi corroboration: Witnesses lie for suspects who seem innocent, whether they like them or not. *Law and Human Behavior, 37*(2), 136–143.
Marion, S. B., Kukucka, J., Collins, C., Kassin, S. M., & Burke, T. M. (2016). Lost proof of innocence: The impact of confessions on alibi witnesses. *Law and Human Behavior, 40*(1), 65–71.
Meissner, C. A., & Kassin, S. M. (2002). "He's guilty!": Investigator bias in judgments of truth and deception. *Law and Human Behavior, 26*(5), 469–480.
Narchet, F. M., Meissner, C. A., & Russano, M. B. (2011). Modeling the influence of investigator bias on the elicitation of true and false confessions. *Law and Human Behavior, 35*(6), 452–465.
Olson, E. A. (2013). "You don't expect me to believe that, do you?" Expectations influence recall and belief of alibi information. *Journal of Applied Social Psychology, 43*(6), 1238–1247.
Olson, E. A., & Charman, S. D. (2012). 'But can you prove it?'–Examining the quality of innocent suspects' alibis. *Psychology, Crime & Law, 18*(5), 453–471.
Olson, E. A., & Wells, G. L. (2004). What makes a good alibi? A proposed taxonomy. *Law and Human Behavior, 28*(2), 157–176.
Olson, E. A., & Wells, G. L. (2012). The alibi-generation effect: Alibi-generation experience influences alibi evaluation. *Legal and Criminological Psychology, 17*(1), 151–164.
Phillips, M. R., McAuliff, B. D., Kovera, M. B., & Cutler, B. L. (1999). Double-blind photoarray administration as a safeguard against investigator bias. *Journal of Applied Psychology, 84*(6), 940–951.
Sargent, M. J., & Bradfield, A. L. (2004). Race and information processing in criminal trials: Does the defendant's race affect how the facts are evaluated? *Personality and Social Psychology Bulletin, 30*(8), 995–1008.
Semmler, C., Brewer, N., & Douglass, A. B. (2011). Jurors believe eyewitnesses. In B. L. Cutler (Ed.), *Conviction of the innocent: Lessons from psychological research* (pp. 185–209). American Psychological Association.
Sommers, S. R., & Douglass, A. B. (2007). Context matters: Alibi strength varies according to evaluator perspective. *Legal and Criminological Psychology, 12*(1), 41–54.
Wells, G. L. (1978). Applied eyewitness-testimony research: System variables and estimator variables. *Journal of Personality and Social Psychology, 36*(12), 1546–1557.
Wells, G. L., Lindsay, R. C., & Ferguson, T. J. (1979). Accuracy, confidence, and juror perceptions in eyewitness identification. *Journal of Applied Psychology, 64*(4), 440–448.
Wells, G. L., Small, M., Penrod, S., Malpass, R. S., Fulero, S. M., & Brimacombe, C. E. (1998). Eyewitness identification procedures: Recommendations for lineups and photospreads. *Law and Human Behavior, 22*(6), 603–647.

Wells, G. L., Kovera, M. B., Douglass, A. B., Brewer, N., Meissner, C. A., & Wixted, J. T. (2020). Policy and procedure recommendations for the collection and preservation of eyewitness identification evidence. *Law and Human Behavior, 44*(1), 3–36.

Wilford, M. M., & Redlich, A. D. (2018). Deciphering the guilty plea: Where research can inform policy. *Psychology, Public Policy, and Law, 24*(2), 145–146.

Appendix: Future Research Topics

Much of this list was taken from the chapters in this text and represent areas ripe for future research. We hope this compilation will serve as a catalyst for continuing and expanding the field of research on alibis and corroborators.

Alibi Taxonomy

- Can researchers better solidify and demonstrate the non-motivated familiar other category?
- Is the person evidence corroboration in the taxonomy more complicated than just motivated v. non-motivated and stranger v. non-stranger? How is the taxonomy affected by age or race?
  - Does the taxonomy change depending on the characteristics of the suspect (e.g., is an older person's spouse more believable than a young adult's spouse; does a suspect with a prior criminal record have a more difficult time obtaining a corroboration compared to someone without a prior criminal record; etc.)?
- Does a stranger make more mistaken corroborations compared to a family member/friend?
  - Is willingness to serve as a corroborator a mediating variable affecting strangers' potential for mistaken corroborations?
- Is there an additive effect of multiple pieces of physical evidence, such that X pieces of weak physical evidence are viewed as equal to or more believable compared to Y pieces of strong physical evidence (e.g., three pieces of weak v. one strong, etc.)?

J. D. Behl, M. R. Kienzle (eds.), *Alibis and Corroborators*,
https://doi.org/10.1007/978-3-030-95663-9

  - Is this effect also seen with person evidence, such that multiple weak corroborators are viewed as equal to or more believable compared to one strong corroborator?
  - Is there a saturation point where more evidence (physical or person) does not help or reduces believability?

- How do investigators use alibis, and how might they be failing to use alibis as useful parts of a criminal investigation?
- How do stereotypes and motivation affect the ways investigators evaluate suspects or integrate information into their development of a case?
- How do defense attorneys decide whether an alibi could be brought as a formal alibi defense at a trial? When do they decide an alibi defense would be less effective strategy?
- Are jury instructions on alibis sufficient to impact alibi believability at trial?
- Is person evidence believability moderated by physical evidence (e.g., is a picture or CCTV footage of you at dinner with your spouse more believable than a non-motivated familiar other absent any physical evidence)?
- How easy is fabricating person and/or physical evidence in corroborating/disproving a suspect's alibi?
- How does time of day/day of week affect alibi believability?

Alibi Generation

- Does the type of alibi/corroborator one can generate change over the life course?
  - How does type of alibi evidence/corroborator x stage of life affect believability (e.g., is it believable for a child to corroborate a grandparent v. a grandparent corroborating for a child)?
- What is the interaction of age and alibi generation?
  - Do older adults generate less accurate alibis? Are they still believable if they change them due to a memory error?
- Under what circumstances would an innocent person richly encode the memories surrounding a routine period of time in their life?
- Are innocent suspects relying on scripts or schemas to generate their alibi?
- What factors might impact alibi generation? Should moderating and/or mediating variables be considered to assist in alibi generation understanding?
  - What effect do extralegal factors (such as gender identity, sexual orientation, age, race, ethnicity, SES, relationship status, etc.) or legal factors (such as prior criminal history, private v. public defense attorney, etc.) have on alibi generation?
- Can new, physical evidence change an original account of one's alibi statement?

  - Can physical evidence (even weak) influence a suspect's alibi statement and/or the collection of person alibi corroboration?
- What is the effect of memory altering substances on alibi generation (e.g., drugs/alcohol)?
- Do suspects with more traditional, 9–5 workdays have and/or rely on more consistent schemas compared to suspects with more flexible daily schedules (e.g., traveling workers, workers with high degrees of movement during their shifts, etc.)?

Alibi Believability

- What is the effect of the number of corroborators on alibi believability?
  - Is there a saturation point?
  - Does it matter if it is five motivated familiar others v. one non-motivated stranger?
- What is the effect of other evidence on alibi believability (e.g., DNA, surveillance, etc.)?
  - What evidentiary factors could interact with alibi statement/corroborating evidence? (e.g., A witness saw you do it v. an alibi corroborator saw you not do it, etc.)
- Does timing of alibi disclosure affect believability (e.g., investigation v. trial; after 24 hours v. after 3 weeks)?
- Does the interaction of timing and change affect believability (e.g., changing your alibi after 24 hours v. changing it after 3 weeks)?
- How does salaciousness affect juror views of the alibi statement? What degree of salaciousness is needed to detect an effect (e.g., is a petite theft more believable than an assault which is more believable than an affair)?
  - Are behaviors that do not align with one's religion viewed as more believable compared to religion-consistent behaviors?
- How much evidence of fabrication is needed for evaluators (e.g., investigators, jury, etc.) to question physical corroborating evidence? Does it matter where that potential for fabrication came from or who is responsible for the fabrication?
- How do evaluators balance both exculpatory and inculpatory evidence when considering an alibi statement?
- How does law enforcement investigate alibi claims and how does alibi evidence factor into investigator decision-making?
- Is changing an alibi, even a change that has potential to improve the quality of the alibi, always detrimental to their case?
- Does the term "alibi" elicit an assumption of guilt?

- How does an understanding of a continuum of gender identities affect alibi believability (e.g., gender non-conforming behaviors, etc.)?
  - How is an individual who is closeted with respect to their gender identity/orientation viewed by evaluators in the context of alibi believability?

Alibi Theory

- How well does the schema disconfirmation model measure alibi generation and accuracy?
  - How does this model fit with our understanding tunnel vision?
  - How much effort will investigators put in to disprove an alibi?
- Are suspects who are given time to access potential evidence more accurate in their alibi generation compared to suspects who are not given this time?
- Can the cognitive interview model be applied to alibi corroborations?
  - Does traditional police interviewing work better than a cognitive interview to increase diagnosticity of alibi?
  - How effective is the cognitive interview approach at eliciting truthful information from a suspect?
- Does allowing memory aids help innocent suspects generate an alibi?
  - Are some memory aids better than other?
  - What is the diagnosticity of memory aids?
  - Do memory aids assist generation of both true and false alibis equally?
- How good are police at detecting a false alibi? What strategies could be used to detect deception from corroborators?
- Is the cognitive load different with truth-telling v. lying alibi corroborators?
- What is the difference between an alibi statement that relies solely on the suspect v. one in which the suspect relies on the ability to confirm with potential corroborators – how does allowing a suspect a few minutes to check/call people affect alibi details? Alibi believability?

Comparative Systems with Alibis

- How does alibi evidence factor in at different stages in the legal process – e.g., early investigation v. late investigation v. early prosecution v. late prosecution?
- Are the alibi generation and evaluation processes dual process? (e.g., generation and validation; evaluation and discrimination?)

- Is there a difference in alibi believability and generation in adversarial v. inquisitorial contexts?
- Does the taxonomy work the same way in inquisitorial systems compared to adversarial?
- Is there a difference in police/prosecutor training in both systems on the handling of alibi evidence?
- How do LEOs/attorneys/judges evaluate what is strong v. weak alibi evidence?
- Do Judge view alibi believability differently compared to jurors (strong v. weak; physical v. person evidence; changed v. unchanged stories; the effect of expert testimony, etc.)?
- Are student samples substantively different than practitioners in alibi research?
- Do non-European inquisitorial countries see similar trends as European countries in how alibi evidence is handled/interpreted?
- Do all common law countries see similar trends as England/the USA in how alibi evidence is handled/interpreted?

Age and Alibi

- Are child alibi corroborators that express stereotype-consistent emotions viewed as more credible compared to those who do not?
- What is the difference between child and adult alibi corroborators?
  - Do children rely on schemas more or less than adults when developing an alibi corroboration?
  - Are children more suggestable to police pressure than adults?
- How does alibi corroborator credibility vary over the life-course (e.g., juvenile, adult, elderly)?
  - When is too old or too young to be believable?
  - Are grandparents inherently more believable?
- Does age and relationship with the suspect interact?
- Does the suspect age interact with the corroborator's age?
- What role will age play in the evaluation of an alibi statement?
  - Which age drives the evaluation of credibility: time of encoding (child) or time of retrieval (adult)?
  - If the alibi corroborator is a child at the time the event took place, but when asked to recall that event later, the corroborator is an adult, how will their testimony be evaluated? Is this effect the same for adults transitioning to older adults?

Defense Attorneys and Alibis

- Do police ask questions using a "fuzzy" time frame in order to make locating an alibi more difficult? What are the effects of a "fuzzy" timeframe (e.g., midnight v. between the hours of 12–3 am)?
  - Would a corroborator be less likely to offer an alibi if questioned using a fuzzy timeframe v. a set time?
  - Is it more difficult to obtaining evidence during a fuzzy time frame v. a set time frame?
- What are defense attorney's perceptions of alibi strength?
  - Do attorney perceptions match the taxonomy?
  - How much time do defense attorneys spend investigating an alibi statement?
  - Do defense attorneys look for physical evidence if person evidence is viewed as weak?
  - Do defense attorneys get tunnel vision when viewing evidence of alibi corroboration?
- Does law enforcement discourage people from being corroborators? What tactics might be used in this endeavor (e.g., violating parole/probation, phrasing of alibi/corroborator questions, threats of retaliation for offering a corroboration, etc.)

Erroneous Alibis

- What is the effect of the overestimation of one's ability to gather corroborating evidence on alibi believability/credibility?
- Would legal decision-makers fault suspects more for failing to provide (remember) the testimony of a motivated-familiar other (e.g., a family member) than for some difficult-to-fabricate physical evidence? What is the combined, intersectional influence of person, physical, strong, weak, changed, and unchanged alibis on believability?
- Do attorneys think enough weak evidence can bolster an alibi defense to the level of usefulness in court?
- To what extent do participants believe that providing erroneous alibi evidence could cast doubt on their claims of innocence and influence the course of an investigation?
  - Are participants that are unsure of their ability to obtain alibi evidence less likely to offer an alibi initially? Which may be why they offer one later?
- If suspects knew not to offer an alibi without evidence, would that affect their willingness to offer one before investigating it themselves?

- How often do suspects provide alibis merely to appease their interrogators' demands or to contradict the investigator's claims that they are guilty?
- How do detectives handle an alibi claim during an interrogation?
- Do mistaken alibi statements vary in the magnitude of the errors (e.g., wrong time by 1 hour v. wrong day completely v. wrong week)?
- Are legal decision-makers and law enforcement more or less sensitive to partial alibi changes when they pertain to a suspects' whereabouts versus who they were with or what they were doing during that time period?
- What is the effect of a changed alibi on perceptions of guilt – how does a changed alibi interact with other evidence?
- How does context affect alibi generation? How do frequency and timing of alibi disclosure, content being recalled, and the type of evidence impact alibi generation?
  - E.g., is it reasonable to expect a store receipt from 3 to 6 months ago?
- Does a delay between when the event occurred and when a provider is questioned matter?
- What is the effect of employment status, race, or socioeconomic status on one's ability to generate an alibi with corroborating evidence?
  - E.g., a wealthy person may have a house alarm with a camera v. someone who is less wealthy.
- What are the effects of system variables such as interview techniques (e.g., avoiding using suggestive questioning, verifying multiple pieces of evidence, emphasizing to suspects that it's okay if they can't remember/not pressuring them into generating alibis, and giving them a chance to think about/return upon independently verifying their account) on alibi generation/believability?
- How do prosecutors view erroneous alibis? How relevant are they in decision-making and might they fall back on the same bias against an erroneous or changed alibi as police and laypeople?
  - Is there a difference between prosecutor v. defense attorney v. judge v. lay person perception of a changed alibi?
- What are the effects of expert testimony v. jury instructions v. nothing on juror believability of changed alibis?
- Are there ways suspects could work with LEOs to help corroborate an alibi (e.g., the use of self-administered interviews)?

Race and Alibi Corroboration

- What is the effect of race on alibi corroboration?

  - Are members of certain racial groups more willing to serve as an alibi corroborator compared to others?
  - Do evaluators rely on racial schemas when considering alibi statements?

- Is there a cross-race effect in alibi corroboration?

  - Are cross-race alibis less accurate than same race for non-motivated strangers?
  - Are cross-race alibis believed?

- Does alibi believability change based on race of corroborators or suspect?
- Does race predict willingness to get involved in the alibi process (e.g., do historically marginalized groups who have bad experience with law enforcement hesitate to get involved with the CJ system)?
- Does type of corroborating evidence differ based on race (i.e., have we structured what we view as "strong" evidence based only on the white experience)?

Public Policy Analysis

- Should we legislate that alibi investigations must be done in every criminal investigation?

  - Should the results of that investigation be turned over the defense? Should a failure to disclose alibi evidence qualify as a Brady violation if withheld?

- If there is no evidence to support the alibi, should the jury be instructed that that is not evidence of guilt?

Index

J. D. Behl, M. R. Kienzle (eds.), *Alibis and Corroborators*,
https://doi.org/10.1007/978-3-030-95663-9

Printed in the USA
CPSIA information can be obtained
at www.ICGtesting.com
LVHW052105021224
798139LV00003B/74
* 9 7 8 3 0 3 0 9 5 6 6 2 2 *